The Foo

The Food of Love

Reflections on Music and Faith

Christopher R. Campling

SCM PRESS LTD

0 334 02691 1

First published 1997 by
SCM Press Ltd
9–17 St Albans Place London N1 0NX

Typeset by Regent Typesetting, London
Printed in Great Britain by
Biddles Ltd, Guildford and King's Lynn

To Juliet

If music be the food of love, play on;
Give me excess of it, that, surfeiting,
The appetite may sicken and so die.
That strain again! It had a dying fall:
O! it came o'er my ear like the sweet sound
That breathes upon a bank of violets,
Stealing and giving odour!

(William Shakespeare, *Twelfth Night*)

Contents

Foreword by Richard Baker OBE RD

During the year 1996 I presented the weekly Classic FM 'chart show', a survey of the top-selling classical CDs, and it was interesting to see how often discs of devotional music were in demand in the record stores. Recordings by the choir of New College, Oxford, by the monks and choirboys of Downside Abbey, and Gregorian chant from the Monastery of Santo Domingo de Silos in Spain all became best-sellers. I suppose a large number of those who bought such discs had no particular religious affiliation, but the music obviously did something for them. I think it induced a sense of timeless peace, providing a welcome experience of tranquillity amid the conflicting demands and uncertainties of modern life.

Wise old Confucius said that 'music provides a kind of pleasure which human nature cannot do without'. Because it appeals to the instinctive side of our natures (though of course it often has an intellectual dimension too), its effect can be orgiastic as well as contemplative. But that too can be beneficial. I once knew an autistic boy who found release for his imprisoned being in very loud, heavily rhythmic organ music.

Christopher Campling, whom I first met when he was Dean of Ripon Cathedral, a place alive with music, has decided in this book to explore the relationship between music and prayer. Both are concerned with the inner, true nature of human beings, and although Christopher's viewpoint is naturally Christian, he is well aware that the language of harmonious sound is universal.

The Ancients, in a theory which seems to have originated with Pythagoras, believed that the universe itself made music, a notion expressed by the young lover Lorenzo in Shakespeare's

The Merchant of Venice. Looking up at a starlit sky with his beloved Jessica, he tells her:

> There's not the smallest orb which thou beholdst
> But in his motion like an angel sings,
> Still quiring to the young-eyed cherubins;
> Such harmony is in immortal souls;
> But whilst this muddy vesture of decay
> Doth grossly close it in, we cannot hear it.

Christopher has clearly found in the music which appeals to him spiritually a point of access to the music of eternal life, and I am sure he would share the sentiment of John Milton's noble prayer:

> That we on earth with undiscording voice
> May rightly answer that melodious noise:
> As once we did, till disproportioned sin
> Jarred against Nature's chime, and with harsh din
> Broke the fair music that all creatures made
> To their great Lord, whose love their motion swayed
> In perfect diapason, whilst they stood
> In first obedience and their state of good.
> O may we soon again renew that song,
> And keep in tune with heaven, till God ere long
> To his celestial consort us unite,
> To live with him, and sing in endless morn of light

('At a Solemn Musick').

Richard Baker

Preface

This book began with a 'Musical Quiet Day' held at Spennithorne for the congregation of Ripon Cathedral in the summer of 1990. In the beauty of the place, the silence, the prayer, the thinking and the music, we set out together to find 'the peace of God'. My daughter joined us for a session of 'music therapy' in the afternoon. Here the word 'quiet' really did become inappropriate. She armed us each with an instrument, mostly but not all percussive, depending upon our skills. After a few exercises together during which we learnt to watch one another's eyes and bring people in with a nod, we 'performed' Psalm 148 with resounding joy and a lot of decibels.

From the talks I gave that day this book was born. It is a book on music and faith, faith and music; written for people who are prepared to love music and to love God and can find, as I have found, that the love of each can strengthen and illuminate the other.

The book is written in a personal way because I am writing about my own feelings and thoughts. I do not disguise this. But I hope that readers may be able to discern what it is that I am experiencing in 'my' music and 'my' faith and find it to be true in their own music and their own faith; for the truth is much deeper than any one person's experience of it. Meanwhile I affirm that I love God and I love music. My object in writing is to share the love of both – and both together – with whoever reads this book.

At this point I have been urged to write something about myself. I am loath to do this, but can appreciate the moral logic of the request. It is, after all, my love of music and my love of God that I am writing about and hoping to share; so it is probably right to begin by unpacking the word 'my'.

'My love of music' suggests my personal taste, and I will be exposing this throughout the book. It no doubt speaks of the limitations as well as the breadth of my experience, and there will be readers with different tastes and wider knowledge. But this will not affect the argument of the book: indeed it could strengthen it in ways that I do not know about. On the other hand, if some readers are introduced for the first time to some of the music I know and love, that will be a bonus.

The 'love of God' is in a different category, and is not a matter of personal taste. God is, or God is not. One may be 'inventing God', if one believes in a God who does not exist; or failing to perceive God, if God is there and we do not believe it. Personal choice makes no difference to God, whose existence or non-existence is independent of ourselves; but it makes a difference to us. We can choose to live as if God does exist or to live as if there is no God. Either way, it is a dare. If it is right to think that God exists and makes possible a relationship with human beings, then different people will experience this relationship in different ways: ways which depend upon the circumstances of race, nationality, religious denomination and upbringing. But although people can choose whether and how to respond, they do not choose the way by which God is revealed. I do not 'choose' God out of a variety to choose from. God (it seems to me) comes through the particular circumstances that have been my life. When I think I can perceive God, I can respond by saying, 'Yes' or 'No' or 'Perhaps' or 'When I have time' or 'I should but I won't' or 'I don't want to but I will'. So overwhelming is the love of God – once one finds it in the beauty of the world, the love of people, the love-bearing life of Christ, and the harmonizing peace in one's inner life, that one can only be grateful – and long to share it.

But why 'music' and God? Because I love both; and I love them together; and they are the same love. Rather, I find that music is one experience of the love of God. It 'feeds' the spirit with the 'food' of love, the love of God. And here is a feast that I would share.

My son said to me, 'You could just as well write about God and football'. This is true, except that I do not know so much about football, much as I have enjoyed playing, refereeing, watching and following the game. For all its faults (and do not musicians also have their faults?), there is the emphasis on individuality, the 'harmony' of the team, the faithfulness and discipline required, the pattern of rules, method, and method-defying inspiration. Maybe I would have to revise what I have to say in Chapter 11 about 'excitement,' and recognize its strength as well as its dangers; but a love of football can indeed be a manifestation of the God-given zest for life.

Anyone who thinks such unfashionable thoughts and is writing a book about them should say something about how he came to have these thoughts, in order to lay bare his credentials. These may speak against what I am writing; but I must take my chance on that and be as truthful as possible.

The music side comes out in the book itself. I am not a good 'practitioner'.[1] But all my life I have been an enthusiastic listener, who loves music and always wants to hear more. There is plenty about the music I love in the book.

As for the love of God, both my parents shared this with me in their different ways. My father's[2] influence was very strong. He was literally a 'great priest', six foot six inches high, a strong athlete and a scholar of Trinity College, Cambridge, where he achieved a 'first' in the Natural Science Tripos. Much to his disgust he only got a 'second' in Theology; but he used to do his daily Bible reading in Hebrew and Greek. Having served as a chaplain in the trenches in the First World War, he went to Australia to be Principal of the Anglican Theological College at Brisbane, where I was born. He came back to England to work in the Diocese of Southwark and was much in demand as a conductor of retreats and missions. He had a strong Catholic/Evangelical outlook. The secret of religion and life to him was daily attention to God in silent prayer. My mother was less intellectual, perhaps more joyful in her faith. The motto of her life could have been the opening words of Psalm 103: 'Praise the Lord, O my soul: all that is within me, praise his holy name. Praise the Lord, O my soul, and forget not all his benefits.'

In school days I accepted Christianity and consciously enjoyed the community life of my school 'house' at Lancing – particularly when the school was evacuated to Ludlow. We had daily chapel in a stable loft, much outdoor activity; and in the moments I could spare between games and music and cycling

around Shropshire, I studied classics, which I found difficult,
but rewarding.

When I joined the Navy in 1943, all this was put severely to
the test. It began on my first night at the Initial Training Station,
HMS King Arthur, situated at the holiday camp at Skegness.
Should I or should I not wear pyjamas? No one else did. But I
always had. Plucking up my courage, I decided that I would –
only to discover that no one took any notice at all. Everyone
had his odd ways. I had mine. No one minded. There were other
things to mind about, like getting on together, beating the
system (for example, always having a broom in your hand so
that you could appear to be sweeping something up when an
officer came round), and, once at sea, being able to trust in one
another's professional skill. Early in 1944 I joined HHMS³
Kanaris at Massawa in the Red Sea. This was a British Hunt
Class destroyer manned by the Greek navy, with a British
liaison officer and five communication ratings, of whom I was
one. We convoyed ships up and down the Adriatic, covered the
invasion of the South of France, and, most excitingly for the
Greek seamen on board, covered the invasion of Greece. At sea
in the Mediterranean I have never been so violently uncomfortable in my life. In calm weather the ship merely rolled and
lurched, heaved and dipped. In high winds it leapt and reared
and staggered and plunged like a drunken steeple-chaser; and
this went on for days. I remember once calling up the voice-pipe
to my friend on the bridge, 'What's the weather like up there?',
only to get a bucket of sea water down the pipe. And have you
ever gone down on your knees and scrubbed a heaving deck?
For my first few weeks I slept between watches on a mess-deck
bench, because there was no room to sling my hammock.
Then I graduated to the mess table, which was less uncomfortable, but more public; and I used to be turfed off when the
others wanted to eat. Only when two of my mess-mates had
left the ship did I have the convenience of a berth for my
hammock.

Three things dawned on me slowly, though this analysis did
not take place till later. One was the conviction, as I said my
prayers over the side of the ship in off-watch moments, that
God was indeed great: God of the sea in all its moods, serene,
restless, furious; God of the infinite expanse of the night sky

with its myriad of stars, so close and so far; God of my home and school, set in a different world, thousands of miles away; God of my new friends at Alexandria; God of the music in my head, and of everything I loved. At sea I experienced as never before (and I believe that many sailors did the same) the sense of God as Harmonizing Immensity, touching all things and holding them together.

But secondly, once I had put the days of the nubbly bench and the rolling table behind me, I began to enjoy the sacred privacy of my hammock. In this I found, as it swung gently against the roll of the ship, reducing the movement somewhat, that God was there with me in my most private life. A hammock can be made to close up over you so as to shut out the world. Certainly it was stuffy; but in one's hammock one could think and read and pray and sleep – till rudely shaken for the morning watch at 4 am. There in the hammock, God, the same God, was intimately my God.

Thirdly, there was 'God in everything in between', reminding me of the title of a book by Bishop John Taylor, *The Go-Between God*.[4] This realization came slowly, and only with hindsight. God was in the mess-deck and on the bridge and in the wireless-telegraphy office where I did my coding; in the staccato babble of the Greek language and the kind, rough teasing of the Greek sailors; in the blunt and highly intelligent leading telegraphist, Ben. He had a weakness for drink when ashore, and probably this had kept him from promotion. But he could chat to the fleet on his w/t, with his own morse 'hand-writing' (widely recognized), his mastery of signals procedure, laced, I suspect, with his scatological humour. He was tough with me, but so kind whenever things were bad. He taught me to be as good a coder as I could possibly be, and a lot of shipcraft besides; not least how to cope with sea-sickness. In the worst circumstances he never thought of himself – only the help he could give to others; and with his colourful language and the stories of the 'wives' he had in all the ports we visited, he would be astonished to know what (looking back!) an inspiration I found him to be. And they were all good: Les, leading signal-man, a born leader; Arthur, a tireless Cornishman, sweet-tempered in all conditions, but barely articulate; Jack, clever, left-wing, a 'lower-deck lawyer', but always ready to help out when someone was in difficulties. He had a burning desire to make the world a better place when the war was over (I often find myself wondering what he achieved). And there were my particular friends, Jo and Arthur, hardly more than school-boys, like myself. We were in this thing together. We talked football, boxing (it was the time of Tommy Farr), class, heated politics, sexual ethics and practice; and religion, though they could not draw me on this.

I learned to recognize the goodness of God in that company in ways I never really did when I was commissioned and on the Admiral's staff in HMS Nelson, flagship of the East Indies fleet. This was in 1945. I was much the youngest and most insignificant member of the ward-room mess. There was friendship, plenty of banter and frantically hard work when on watch; but none of the direct, uninhibited, affectionate criticism and support that I found on the lower deck. But three important things happened. One was that I was sent from Trincomalee to Colombo for my 'Selection Board' (CACTM[5]) as a candidate for ordination, under the chairmanship of the Bishop of Colombo. The chief of the admiral's staff said that I could not possibly go: we were too busy preparing for Operation Zipper, the invasion of Malaya. But the Admiral (Vice-Admiral H.C.T. Walker, known as Hooky Walker for having a hook instead of a right fore-arm) was a devout Christian and said that I was to go: I could fly in his aeroplane.

When I emerged from the Selection Board four days later, the first of the two atom bombs had been dropped and everything was changed. The Admiral's plane had been taken by a senior army officer and I was left to hitch-hike across Ceylon to Trincomalee. I was with two others in the same plight; and we lit a fire at night to keep the wild animals away. When I reached Trincomalee, the Nelson was sailing; but a boat was sent for me and I reported on board – much to the relief of my two colleagues who had been hard pressed in my absence. We sailed to Penang with the East Indies fleet and received a Japanese admiral on board for the surrender. We cyphered up the surrender terms, while the world waited. I went ashore to set up a signal station, and took over the Eastern and Oriental Hotel for this purpose.[6] When the Nelson reached Singapore, Lord Louis Mountbatten joined us to take the surrender, and (my

second important encounter, one that affected my whole life)
Bishop Leonard Wilson came aboard.

Bishop Wilson had been a prisoner of the Japanese in the
notorious Changi camp and had been brutally beaten. As I was
known to be destined for 'the church', and as there was now
little cyphering to be done, I was asked to take care of Bishop
Wilson and his chaplain, John Hayter,[7] while they lived with us
for the next three weeks in the Nelson.

Never have I known such a man as Bishop Wilson. He was
very prayerful and devout; kind, and interested in everyone and
everything, but not himself; physically as frail as could be; but
spiritually, *calm:* with no complaining, no aggression, just the
strength of serenity. God was most certainly in him, I thought.

My third significant experience from those days was a
humbling one. I thought that I ought to visit the ex-prisoners of
war who were in Changi hospital, because they were considered
too ill to make the voyage home. I nervously made my way
into the hospital ward and tried to talk to them; but they were
too shocked to respond at all. I had never seen such lifeless,
emaciated men, though it is a common enough sight these days
on television. One of them managed to say, 'Got a fag, mate?',
but as I hadn't, he turned away uninterested. These men had
physical and mental needs which required healing with much
more skill and much more patience than I had to offer.

Soon after that I joined HMS Howe as assistant to the
Captain's secretary. From Singapore we went to Colombo,
Mombasa, the Seychelles, Adu Atoll in the Maldives (then the
complete 'desert island', now a holiday camp, I believe),
Bombay, Suez, Gibraltar and home, showing the flag. At
Portsmouth we were met by Princess Elizabeth and her fiancé;
also by my mother and sister! At Portsmouth I joined HMS
Ranpura as Captain's secretary. We sailed for Singapore, but
stopped at Malta because of trouble with Egypt and the Suez
Canal. The Ranpura was a heavy repair ship. We cruised the
Mediterranean and the Aegean, being helpful to everybody
wherever we went, and ending up at Corfu to take charge of
affairs when two British destroyers, HMS Saumarez and
Volage, were mined off the Albanian coast. We then returned
home, and I was demobilized.

After nine months teaching I went up to St Edmund Hall,

Oxford, to read theology. For the first time I learnt to examine the sources and early development of the Christian religion. I was privileged to be invited to join a small class to study the Gospels in Greek under Professor R.H. Lightfoot; and my tutor was the college vice-principal (later principal), Dr J.N.D. Kelly. He gave me a zest for theological thinking for which I am eternally grateful.

I find now that I cannot write much about my ministry, its problems and joys. After Oxford I went to Cuddesdon theological college and nearly abandoned the life of a priest for that of a schoolmaster. But I stuck to ordination and became a curate at Basingstoke under the renowned curate-trainer, Archdeacon A.W.Chute. At Basingstoke I married Juliet, who was then training at Moorfields Eye Hospital as an orthoptist. We lived in a council house and started the church of St Peter's on the South Ham estate. These were pioneer days, and Juliet helped me in everything. Then we went to Ely where I was appointed minor canon of the cathedral, with responsibility for singing services, and chaplain to the King's School. From there I was appointed chaplain of my old school, Lancing College. By this time we had two daughters, Penelope and Angela; and at Lancing we had Peter. The 1960s were difficult days for any school chaplain, but I loved the work, even if I had to make controversial changes in the chapel services and the number of these that the boys had to attend. I started an A-level divinity set which grew to about eighteen, some of whom could study the Gospels in Greek without difficulty. When two boys urged me to start Hebrew with them, they soon left me behind! I became the honorary, tame manager and referee for the third eleven football team. Juliet had an endless succession of boys to tea; and she and the children and I thoroughly enjoyed every facet of school life.

Then I went to be vicar of Pershore Abbey, never having been a vicar before. We were very happy there with my five churches, one of which we converted into a parish centre. Our family grew up and Juliet became a teacher. I was appointed rural dean; and then moved to Droitwich where I was Archdeacon of Dudley, Director of Religious Education, and priest-in-charge of the delightful mediaeval church of St Augustine's, Dodderhill.

In 1984 I became dean of Ripon Cathedral. Ripon is nearly unique in that the dean is also the incumbent of the parish. Indeed I had responsibility – shared with the canons ('the chapter'), and with minor canons to help – for the services and pastoral work of seven church buildings, including the cathedral. I had been a member of the General Synod since its inception in 1970. I became the chairman of the Open Synod Group, and in 1988 was appointed by the Archbishop of Canterbury to be chairman of the Council for the Care of Churches. At Ripon there is a choir school, a cathedral state primary school, and for daily worship a fare of music of surpassing beauty, from Tudor to modern, Taverner to Tavener! The music which the cathedral offers is for the glory of God; but it also works for the spiritual strengthening and inspiration of all who attend it, including the dean. How could I not write a book on music and faith?

The book itself falls into three parts. The first part (Chapters 1 to 7) is about music and 'belief', its justification and interpretation. The second part (Chapters 8 to 14) is about music and the practice of faith: worship, behaviour, involvement. The third part is about particular composers' affirmations of faith, including, in the last two chapters, affirmations about resurrection and eternal life.

As to the argument of the book, I know that analogies never gell to one's complete satisfaction; and even if they do, they prove nothing. There are no musical proofs for religion, and there are no religious proofs for music. But there is common ground, and there are similarities. I invite readers to take a zig-zag course with me from one to the other, and on again back to the one. If you can share these with me and enjoy the mutual illumination with which music and faith can light each other up, then I shall have succeeded in my business of writing this book.

Finally, I wish to thank members of my family: Penelope Campling, Angela Magor and Peter Campling; Michael Campling (my brother), Andrew and Clare Campling (my nephew and niece) and my cousin, Francis Webb; my friends, Bob Aiton, Philip Haynes, Joanna Knight, Ronnie and Heather McFadden, and Sam Randell: all these for helping me with encouragement, criticism and suggestions: Michael and Rosalind Hore for letting me use the St Mary's, Goring, parish office; Malcolm and Joan Beer for the hospitality of their apartments in Mallorca when I was writing the second half of the book; Tony and Sally Giblett for their hospitality at Lazy Acres, near Sligo, when I was revising it; Carol Oldroyd for typing the whole of the first draft; John Bowden of SCM Press for making the book possible; and Juliet for all her help and for bearing with me and *The Food of Love*, and allowing it to dominate the first year of our retirement.

I am grateful to Michael Joseph for permission to quote from C. S. Forester, *Captain Hornblower RN: A Ship of the Line*, on p. 66 and to Carcanet Press for permission to quote from Hugh McDiarmid's 'In Memoriam James Joyce' on p. 74.

Christopher R. Campling
Worthing, November 1996

I

Music and Faith

Praise him in the sound of the trumpet: praise him upon the lute and harp.
Praise him in the cymbals and dances: praise him upon the strings and
pipe.
Praise him upon the well-tuned cymbals: praise him upon the loud
cymbals.
Let everything that hath breath; praise the Lord (*Psalm 150*).

My idea is that there is music in the air, music all around us, the world is
full of it and you simply take as much as you require (Edward Elgar).

> The music in my heart I bore,
> Long after it was heard no more
> (William Wordsworth, *The Solitary Reaper*).

Sam Weller put on his hat in a very easy and graceful manner, and thrust-
ing his hands in his waistcoat pockets, walked with great deliberation to
Queen Square, whistling as he went along, several of the most popular airs
of the day, as arranged with entirely new movements for that noble instrument the organ, either mouth or barrel (Charles Dickens, *The Pickwick
Papers*).

Of all the pastimes that people delight in, there is none so deeply
and universally enjoyed as music. If we were to play the balloon
game and debate which of these to throw overboard: moun-
taineering; sport; gardening; football; the fine arts; music, a
strong case could be made for the preservation of music. The
others might win in the judgment of their own enthusiasts; but
music is universal in its appeal, and there is scarcely a person
who is not moved by it in some form or other. Most people
enjoy it occasionally, and there are some to whom music (after
love) is the most stimulating and deeply satisfying of all human
experiences.

Music enhances pleasure at times of celebration. We have
music at weddings; we use it for worship. Football crowds
break into song when their team is doing well;[1] family anni-
versaries are celebrated with music and dance, and even when

they are not, there is likely to be music in the background, musical wallpaper, as it were. People sing patriotic songs in pubs; at least they do in Ireland and Wales. Music is played at times of nostalgia and sadness, reunions, memorials, funerals. People go to balls and discos: they step sedately in formal groups or glide in pairs round a dance floor; or they girate ecstatically to the flashing lights and raucous noise of heavy rock. Many people nowadays listen to music all the time, as they go about with a player in their pockets and headphones glued to their ears. People sit and listen to music at home or in the concert hall. There is music for all tastes and all moods. Music can express and communicate human feelings from the deepest pain to the wildest joy.

Is this just a phenomenon of the twentieth century? With music being constantly broadcast and so much made available on records, there is more music and there are more kinds of music now than ever before. To many the pop charts are an important feature of modern life; and besides pop you can buy every sort of classical music, jazz, folk songs from all over the world: music from the Australian bush and the jungles of Africa and Borneo. There is also a huge variety of religious music as sung by monks in Tibet or in the mosques of Iran or in Jewish synagogues; and Christian music, including plainsong, the deep-throated chanting of Orthodox priests, congregations singing hymns and hallelujah songs, cathedral choirs singing Byrd, Stanford and John Tavener.

In terms of variety and availability, therefore, the twentieth century has more music than ever before, largely due to modern technology. But the seventeenth, eighteenth and nineteenth centuries were also saturated with music, and saw the development of Western music in all its complexity of form and harmony, rhythm and colour. Because of the growing demands of composers, who were also performers and who learnt from one another, great advances were made in instrumental technique and also in the development of the instruments themselves. Put these together – and the orchestra evolved. Is not this multi-individual body of highly skilled people one of the most astonishing and enjoyable phenomena of life today?

If we go further back into history we find that music was always important, both for individuals and for public and religious occasions. There may not have been so much variety, and there was certainly no broadcast availability; so music was individual and local and tended to remain so. But music seems to have been important in all ages, even when by our standards the means of making it and the opportunities of hearing it were limited. It is interesting, for instance, to look at the Bible, because it covers such a large span of history.

The first reference to music in the Bible is the mention of Jubal, the 'ancestor of those who play the harp and pipe'.[2] Then there were David and Saul.[3] King Saul was a man of moods. Possibly he had been chosen to be king because of his physical size and prowess in battle. But morally and intellectually the task of leadership was too much for him, and he had periods of despondency. His courtiers recommended that David the shepherd should be called from his father's house to play the lyre and sing to him. This he did, and Saul loved him for it, finding that with David's playing his 'evil spirit would leave him'.

Robert Browning in his poem 'Saul' writes movingly about David bringing God's healing grace to the stricken king Saul through the beauty of music. It was a slow process. He started by singing:

> The tune all our sheep know, as, one by one,
> So docile they come to the pen-door till folding be done ...

Then:

> The tune, for which quails on the cornland will each leave his
> mate
> To fly after the player; then, what makes the crickets elate
> Till for boldness they fight one another; and then, what has
> weight
> To set the quick Jerboa a-musing outside his sand house –
> There was none such as he for a wonder, half bird and half
> mouse!
> God made all the creatures and gave them our love and our
> fear,
> To give sign, we and they are his children, one family here.

Then I played the help-tune of our reapers, their winesong,
    when hand
Grasps at hand, eye lights eye in good friendship, and great
    hearts expand
And grow one in the sense of this world's life. And then the
    last song
When the dead man is praised on his journey – 'bear, bear
    him along ...'

Saul stirs and David renews his singing in praise of life:

Oh, the wild joys of living! The leaping from rock to rock,
The strong rending of bows from the fir-tree, the cool silver
    shock
Of the plunge in a pool's living water ...

Then he turns to praise Saul himself:

High ambition and deeds which surpass it, fame crowning
    them, – all
Brought to blaze on one creature – King Saul!

Then he sings in praise of God, Creator and Redeemer, source
of all love; and then in a climax of inspiration he sees and sings
the truth of the incarnation:

Oh Saul, it shall be
A Face like my face that receives thee; a man like to me,
Thou shalt love and be loved by, for ever: a Hand like this
    hand
Shall throw open the gates of new life to thee! See the Christ
    stand!

Poetic licence, romantically anachronistic! Yet sound Christianity. The book of Psalms – surely amongst the finest and most
used collections of poetry in all the world's literature – is traditionally ascribed to David, even though we know that many of
the psalms come from a later date in Israel's history. They
abound in references to music and they were made to be sung.
Musical instruments of the age – including ram's horns, lyre,

harp, strings and pipe, resounding cymbals and loud clanging cymbals (Psalm 150) – are summoned to give praise to the glorious God of creation. Besides being paeans of praise the Psalms sing mournfully of human suffering and greed and spite and long-suffering and courage. They glory in the love as well as the power of God; in God's compassion as well as God's inexorable judgment. Christians use them daily in their worship because the Psalms express the height and the depth of devotion and relate to God not only as the source of justice but also as the source of love. Browning's anachronism in mentioning Christ in the context of David singing to Saul a thousand years before Christ lived on earth is the same anachronism as it is to worship Christ through reciting the Psalms. But this is good practice, for the truth of Christ transcends the time-bound story of history; and this transcending is enhanced and made real to our experience through the poetry and the music of the Psalms of David.

When he became king himself, David felt compelled to fetch the precious ark of the Lord from the Philistines, whom he had just defeated, and take it to Jerusalem. We read of the ark being mounted on a new cart and conveyed from Abinadab's house on the hill towards Jerusalem. Ahio walked in front and he and his brother Uzza[4] guided the cart. 'David and all Israel danced before the Lord with all their might to the sound of singing, of lyres, lutes, tambourines, castanets and cymbals.'[5]

It is clear from the Book of Chronicles[6] that music played an important part in the worship in the Temple. Indeed, Amos and Isaiah gave stern warnings in the eighth century BC (Amos to Israel, the northern kingdom; Isaiah, a generation later, to Judah and Jerusalem in the south) to those who liked to indulge in the excitement of music without any corresponding pattern of behaviour that would please the Lord their God.

> You thrust aside all thought of the evil day
> And hasten the reign of violence.
> You loll on beds inlaid with ivory
> And lounge on your couches;
> You feast on lambs from the flock
> And stall-fed calves;
> You improvise on the lute

and like David invent musical instruments,
You drink wine by the bowlful ...
Now, therefore, you will head the column of exiles;
Lounging and laughter will be at an end.[7]

Woe betide those who rise early in the morning
To go in pursuit of drink,
Who sit late into the night
Inflamed with wine,
At whose feasts there are harps and lutes,
Tabors and pipes and wine:
Yet for the work of the Lord they have never a thought,
No regard for what he has done.
Therefore my people shall go into captivity.[8]

Music is not exactly being blamed; but it is seen as something which can go with and may even exacerbate depraved attitudes. Both prophets were right in their prognostication, though the disasters did not happen in their own lifetime.

It is clear, however, that music was not the sole property of the Jews. The Medes and Persians also had their music, and according to the story in Daniel 3, king Nebuchadnezzar of Babylon ordered all the people to worship the golden image which he set up, as soon as they heard 'the sound of horn, pipe, zither, triangle, dulcimer, a full consort of music'.[9] Three Jewish young men, exiles from their fatherland, Shadrach, Meshach and Abednego, heard the music – no doubt with dread. But they refused to bow down to Nebuchadnezzar's image; so they were ordered to be thrown into 'the burning fiery furnace'. Nebuchadnezzar looked at what he had done, and to his astonishment saw the three men walking about in the furnace unharmed, along with a fourth figure who 'looked like a god'. So courage prevailed; they emerged unscathed and the king and his subjects learnt their lesson about the one true God, the God of Israel. This was a story told to encourage the Jews in the time of religious persecution by king Antiochus Epiphanes about 160 years before Christ. The story is told with weighty and fearsome repetition, and I have to say that it lost something of its impact when my naval captain read the lesson at the Sunday morning service on board HMS Ranpura. Coming to the description of the music for the third time he barked, 'Band as before!' There was no ship's band present on that occasion. But there might have been; and musical bands are as important on religious and national occasions today as they were in the time of the Medes and Persians.

In the New Testament it is pleasing to find that, when Jesus told the story about how God loves to forgive a repentant sinner, he said that the sinner's family celebrated his return 'with music and dancing'. No doubt there was joy in heaven – but we are not told how they celebrated it there. Here on earth it was 'music and dancing' that the disgruntled elder brother heard as he tramped home from his day's work, and found, upon inquiry, that his bad younger brother had returned and had been forgiven.[10]

Otherwise, music is not mentioned very much in the New Testament. Jesus speaks of children 'piping' when they play funerals and weddings;[11] and Jesus and his disciples sang a hymn together before they left the Upper Room to go out to the Garden of Gethsemane.[12] St Paul speaks of the power of the trumpet and requires it to play clearly when it summons soldiers to battle;[13] and the author of the book of Revelation speaks of the music as well as the silence (for half an hour) of heaven.[14]

Not everyone responds to music, but I am writing this book for those who do. It has always been one of the most constant pleasures of my own life, next only to God and my family and my work. Indeed, I have come to find a kinship between religion and music, in the theory and practice of each; in feeling, in performing, in listening, in worship. What I have discovered in one has often enhanced my appreciation for the other; both ways round. Musical experiences have strengthened my faith; Christian insights have stimulated my love for music. Music, I have found, is like a Christian sacrament. It both creates and expresses a truth. It makes things happen inside; but it also reflects and magnifies what a person is already feeling.

My earliest memory of music is from childhood days, hearing my father play the piano when I had been put to bed. He used to play Chopin Nocturnes. There was one I remember particularly, no. 12 in G major. It has two moods: a restless, impulsive mood and another of peace and serenity. These alternate,

almost vie with one another. There was a particular moment I
used to wait for. A cascade of impetuous chords ('Anything
might happen', I thought: but I knew that all would be well)
came suddenly to rest on a single note held in suspense. This
was then strengthened, undergirded, reassured as a deep bass
octave made that note the fifth of a major chord. All was now
well in a world of ultimate peace: the waltz tune went on its way
serenely – and I was soon asleep.

There is a similar moment at the end of the slow movement
of Beethoven's Choral Symphony. I find this movement beautiful beyond words; and at the end of it Beethoven seems to be
wondering what else he can say. Is there anything more beautiful to tell? The music comes to rest on a note that might lead
anywhere. Indeed, the first time round it does so; that is, it goes
on and back to a previous theme. But the second time round
the music stops, as it does in the Nocturne. Suddenly the suspended note becomes the major third of a vast and unexpected
chord. This gives the listener a feeling of profound certainty.
'All shall be well and all shall be well and all manner of thing
shall be well.'[15]

What if someone (like the late Sir Thomas Beecham) objects
that this is just fanciful? Foolish, subjective feelings, poorly
expressed, and not worth sharing; because music is music is
music. It is organized sound. It cannot express or create or
convey anything but itself.

'Badly expressed', maybe; for if words could say what the
music 'says', why have music at all? Music does not define,
limit, or accurately describe facts, events or emotions, as words
can attempt to do. Nevertheless it can convey a meaning
beyond, not less than words have power to do. The symbols of
sound are not precise in the way that words are; but they are
very powerful indeed to those with ears to hear. So any attempt
to describe the effect of a suspended note becoming the major
third or fifth of a new chord is likely to be a failure. Nevertheless, however difficult it is to re-express through words a feeling
induced by music, it remains true that those moments of music
do induce such feelings. Indeed the power of music to affect the
mind has been recognized and is widely used for therapeutic
purposes. Music therapy is becoming a strong arm of the
medical services. Autistic children find a glimmer of communi-

cation; adults with personality problems can learn to relate to one another and so find themselves in performing and listening to music;[16] and am I the only person who drives a car more considerately when listening to Haydn, and less so when listening to Stravinsky?

I find another example of the effect of music on the mind in Mozart's G Minor String Quintet. Urgent and sad throughout the first movement, it becomes fiercely determined in the first eight bars of the Minuet, and then, as you expect the restless mood to continue, touches a major chord. The sun shines through tempestuous clouds; a smile lightens the eyes of a suffering face. There is conflict, yes; but now there is light, hope, yearning, inner peace as well. The slow movement is serene; and the finale, though still wistful, is in the major key – like a person who has come to terms with suffering and whose eyes shine with an inner joy.

Music creates and expresses feelings that are too deep for words: of joy, ecstasy, serenity, anger, conflict, love, eroticism; of the grandeur and complexity of nature, and its smallest jewels; of crude sentimentality; of the stark ordinariness of day-to-day existence; and glimpses, too, I truly believe, of the eternal glory of heaven.

It is because music and religion are to such a degree all-pervasive influences in my life that I wish to write about them together. I always seem to have a tune in my head that goes round and round or on and on in unlikely development: an irritating phrase from a hymn which we sang yesterday in church, or a radio signature tune, or one of the tender-fierce bits of the Brahms violin concerto, or (as at this moment) the sweeping first theme of Dvořák's G major symphony (no. 8), or the melancholy but unhummable feeling of the Walton viola concerto; or something I am composing for the Alternative Service Book. In all moods and throughout most occupations, music is in the air; and when I have time to sit down and listen, then the music in me is reinforced by the experience of what I am listening to.

And faith? It should be like that with faith, for the religious ideal is to live life as in the presence of God; or, as I would rather put it, to find the love of God in all experiences of life. One does not do this consciously, any more than one is conscious of humming a tune. I do not believe that God requires continual, explicit attention. It is more like the under-conscious awareness of a deeply loved person, who is physically absent. One does not spend all the time thinking about her; but she tends to come into one's consciousness at scattered and important moments of the day. This is fed by specific times when we walk and talk and are together. The specific times that make life musical come about when one is listening or playing: the specific times of faith are when one is praying or worshipping. Listening times make music, worship times make faith, all-pervading factors of life.

There are many ways in which music and faith overlap and say the same thing and demand the same sort of commitment: the need for disciplined attention, practice, perseverance, openness to what is new and demanding; the unity, harmony, counterpoint as different entities combine into something that is greater than the sum of their parts; the combination of tradition and immediate inspiration; the way into the non-physical, time-less, eternal, beautiful, holy dimension of life.

But there are differences, too. Religion must be universal in its claims if it is anything at all. Music need not be so. Religion makes moral demands upon men and women. Music does not. Music entertains, or we can choose not to listen to it. Religion may please and comfort, but it also demands; and once we accept its thrall we cannot escape it or its implications. Music invades our senses and begs for the response of our ears and hearts. So does religion: but it is also concerned with the truth and it makes demands upon the will.

Religion is not music. Music is not religion, unless you commit idolatry and make (in the words of David Jenkins, former Bishop of Durham) its 'good' into a 'god'. But religion and music have many affinities. This book is about some of them.

2

Casting Doubts on God and the Second Symphony of Sir William Walton

Music demands more from the listener than simply the possession of a tape-machine or a transistor radio. It demands some preparation, some effort, a journey to a special place, saving up for a ticket, some homework on the programme perhaps, some clarification of the ears, and sharpening of the instincts. It demands as much effort on the listener's part as the other two corners of the triangle, this holy triangle of composer, performer and listener (Benjamin Britten, on receiving the first Aspen Award, 31 July 1964).

Suppose that I am wrong and that my friend who hates music and does not believe in God is right on both counts. Suppose that music is just a noisy racket (a claim to which I shall return in Chapter 7) and God does not exist at all. Suppose that it is 'all in the mind'; that the sensations induced by music and the practice of religion, based upon belief in God, are nothing more than facets of myself, saying something about how my mind reacts to certain stimulants, but nothing about what actually exists outside myself.

As I slip the CD into its slot and sit back to listen, say, to Walton's Second Symphony, a cascade of sound assaults my ear as lively and unpredictable as the wind-lashed sea in a storm. Here is very loud sound. But to me it is not noise. It is music. In the slow movement the sound shimmers mysteriously as if I have dived beneath the waves to experience the deep, colourful calm with occasional moments of sudden darkness and horror; and then the last movement drives me like the torrent of the ingoing tide inexorably towards the shore. To my listening ear the symphony is music, though my words fail to prove it or even describe it. I am not making it up in my head. It is certainly not just chaotic sound as my friend, who is not listening but hears it and will soon be asking me to 'turn it down', thinks it is. It has an objective reality on paper in the score, realized now through the vibrations of my CD player, and experienced by me because I am listening and can identify myself with it.

This is like the experience and practice of religion. There is something real there. Real things have happened. These can be overlooked, misrepresented or ignored. I can point to the fact that they are real to other people besides myself – down the generations of history and today. They are real to me because I 'attend' and identify myself with them. I cannot prove anything. But I do feel it and am prepared to share it.

This is where some people object and repeat cynically the old adage that 'man has made God in his own image', a claim that is worrying. Clearly we must consider it.

There are two forms of the argument. One is the theory known as 'the God of the Gaps'. Ever since the year nought, they say, men and women have been troubled by natural phenomena that they cannot understand. Tides flow; the moon changes its shape; storms, earthquakes, eclipses occur. Why? With no natural answer to hand people invented 'gods' who by definition can do anything they like and can therefore control nature to produce the phenomena being questioned. But now, the argument continues, scientific knowledge has come to the human race; so there is no need to invent 'God' to explain things. The human race has grown up. The 'God of the Gaps' has been ousted.

The argument is flawed, I believe, by the fact that religious belief in God or gods does not come about in this way. If you ask any intelligent believer why she or he believes in God, you will not find that that person's belief has anything to do with explaining the otherwise inexplicable mysteries of life. Religion is a relationship with God, not an explanation of the facts of existence.

The other form of the 'man made God' argument is to say that religious belief is an individual's response to a psychological need. A person needs a father- or mother-figure; or reassurance; or a purpose in life. Such a person projects 'faith' subjectively, existentially, upon a 'God' who does not actually exist but whose image nicely reflects the psychological needs of the believer.

This is challenging, because many people do indeed feel the need for God. 'Thou hast made us for thyself, and the heart of man is restless until it finds its rest in thee', said St Augustine in his *Confessions*. But the need for God may be a sign that God does exist, not that God does not exist. There are many things that a person needs: food, drink, clothing, protection; the love of other people; a sense of personal fulfilment. These needs relate to things that do exist. The fact that people need them does not make them less real; it makes them more real. Furthermore, people have minds and a set of emotions that can be subjected to psychological analysis. But the psychological aspect of life does not force us to discount those things on which it feeds. Indeed, the opposite. If God does exist and does stoop to relate to human beings, then what is more natural than that God should relate and be made known through human, psychological instincts? Put the other way round, if it is true that psychologically people do need God, could that not be because God wants them to? In which case it is not surprising to find that 'our hearts are restless until we find our rest in God'.

I do not know how I can prove to my friend that Walton's Second Symphony is scintillating music, not disorganized cacophony. I can tell him that I find it to be so. I can argue further that it is so, independent of myself and my listening, because I can point to the fact that many other people agree with me. I also believe that God 'is so'. I understand the position of those who do not discern God in life and do not feel the need to and would say to me, 'Turn it off'. It is impossible to prove – even more so than it is to prove to a reluctant friend that Walton's symphony is music. I can say of the music, 'Listen'; and of God, 'Attend'.

But it is not as simple as that. If it were as easy to believe that God is God as it is to believe that music is music, then many more people would be bound to practise religion. The fact is that by its nature music must entertain; and allowing for differences in taste, it does so. What must religion do? It must give people a credible philosophy of life which makes sense of the world they live in. If religion is 'relationship with God', this must be a relationship which affirms an individual's value together with the value of everything else. It must bring with it a sense of harmony, purpose, forgiveness, strength, love – if, as they say, 'God is love'. Does it do these things? In patches, yes: but in vast areas of the human race, apparently, no. It was Jesus who said, 'By their fruits you shall know them'; and by that test much religious practice fails to qualify. So why not just keep to music, at least, that part of it which entertains oneself?

A Christian believer must be humbled by these considerations and in the name of the church beg forgiveness of the world for its betrayal of the truth and neglect of the ideals it professes to live by. Nevertheless, if anyone wishes to make a sober judgment about the 'fruits' of religion, then that person should look at the best and not only the worst; for the best is that which fulfils the fundamental claims of faith, and it is these claims, not the erosion or the monstrous denial of them, that one should consider. There is the claim, for instance, that God creates: and that therefore everything is created and has a purpose. God makes *homo sapiens* aware of itself and its surroundings and therefore able to rejoice and give thanks. God limits divine power by creating the human race in the divine image: therefore people have the choice of acting in unity with or in defiance of God's will. God re-creates (forgives): therefore a new beginning and a new way forward is always possible. God loves: therefore people can find unity with God and unity with one another in that love.

There is positive evidence of the fulfilment of these 'therefores' in countless millions of lives: enough, surely, to tempt the enquirer to put it all to the test in her own, his own life.

Perhaps it is like the demand of a strange piece of music by an unknown composer written in strange tonality. Should one listen? Most people do not. But people one respects say that they like it and want to share it. One can ignore it (too busy); or scoff ('not my musical scene'); or a tenth listen whilst reading the newspaper; or give it one's full attention and see if it gives the satisfaction that is claimed for it. So with faith. By its own terms and stipulations one is allowed to ignore it; therefore it is no surprise to find that others do so: indeed in their personal experience they may have good reason to. By its own conditions one is also allowed to open oneself to it and, as it were, 'listen', one's confidence fortified by the example of people one trusts. In 'listening' people may find that what is claimed makes sense in their own experience. One thing leads to another, one level of commitment to a deeper level still, until a person may experience an all-pervading faith, an all-pervading love, the love of life and God, God and life. Despite failures, downs with the ups, periods of going backwards instead of forwards, blatant transgressions, implied denials, nevertheless, with honest perseverance the strange music of faith (like Walton's Second Symphony) can appear to make sense, to work, to be true.

Robert Browning wrote a poem, 'An Epistle Containing the Strange Medical Experience of Karshish, the Arab Physician'. Karshish is a worldly-wise physician who comes across Lazarus, Mary's and Martha's brother, whom Jesus is alleged to have raised from the tomb.[1] Karshish cannot believe it, but he is so deeply impressed with Lazarus' serene certainty that he begins to wonder. At the end of the letter to his friend Abib, Karshish shows profound understanding of the Christian belief that Lazarus has tried to share with him. He dismisses it, of course, but there is a hint that he will go on thinking about it, and perhaps one day try to listen to the Christian tune.

> The very God! think, Abib; dost thou think?
> So the All-Great, were the All-Loving too –
> So, through the thunder comes a human voice
> Saying, 'O heart I made, a heart beats here!
> Face, my hands fashioned, see it in myself!
> Thou hast no power nor mayst conceive of mine,
> But love I gave thee, with myself to love,
> And thou must love me who have died for thee!'
> The madman saith He said so: it is strange.

3

Time and Eternity: The Big Bang, Oratorio, and *The Marriage of Figaro*

During the last three centuries, in the Western world at least, a dangerous division has come into being in the way we perceive the world around us. Science has tried to assume a monopoly – even a tyranny – over our understanding ... It has attempted to take over the natural world from God, with the result that it has fragmented the cosmos and relegated the sacred to a separate, and secondary, compartment of our understanding, divorced from practical day to day existence (The Prince of Wales, addressing a private meeting at Wilton Park, Sussex; as reported in *The Times*, 14 December 1996).

Music is a moral law. It gives a soul to the universe, wings to the mind, flight to the imagination, a charm to sadness, gaiety and life to everything. It is the essence of order, and leads to all that is good, just and beautiful, of which it is the invisible, but nevertheless dazzling, passionate and eternal form. (Plato 428–348 BC).

Music is a strange thing. I would almost say it is a miracle. For it stands halfway between thought and phenomenon, between spirit and matter, a sort of nebulous mediator, like and unlike each of the things it mediates – spirit that requires manifestation in time, and matter that can do without space (Heinrich Heine, quoted by Tchaikovsky in a letter to Nabezhda von Meck, 1878).

Please, Sir, what you are telling us is that in the beginning there was nothing. Then it exploded. And that is why we are here (A schoolboy).

Science requires faith in the inner harmony of the Universe (Albert Einstein).

As I write, the Big Bang theory has come back into the news, and according to the media, science and religion are once more locked in furious battle. Dr John Habgood, Archbishop of York, has wrestled publicly with Dr Richard Dawkins, the Oxford geneticist, in a public debate at Edinburgh – trounced by him according to *The Observer*, but profoundly persuasive according to another witness. People are very excited, as if the

Big Bang theory were some new idea which cannot be reconciled with religious belief.

But the Big Bang theory is not new. In 1965 I wrote in a book intended for sixth-formers:[1]

> The lessons that can be learnt from the Creation Myths[2] are not the sort of lessons that science can prove or disprove. For science is concerned with the physical state of affairs; how things are what they are, how they have been and how they will be. It is not concerned with the ultimate purpose of things, nor the value of things – that is to say whether certain physical states are good or bad. Thus religious convictions, such as the conviction that the world is essentially good or that man has the freedom to choose between good and evil, are outside its scope.
>
> On the other hand Christians must remember that the physical facts about the origin of the Universe are the special concern of the scientist. Questions such as, 'What was the Universe like in the first half-hour?' or, 'What is the relationship of our earth to the rest of the Universe?' or, 'What has been the order and process of evolution?' are questions for the scientist to answer.
>
> What do scientists say about these matters?
>
> As regards the first half-hour there is fundamental disagreement. Professor Hoyle believes that there never was a 'beginning of time' of the Universe, and the process of 'creation' is going on all the time as new matter comes into being. Professor Ryle, on the other hand, believes that once upon a time there was an explosion of the 'primordial atom'; and ever since then the galaxies of stars with their planets have been receding away from each other at an ever-increasing speed. Our earth is a planet of the sun, which is a star in a galaxy we call the Milky Way. Professor Ryle claims that he has demonstrated the truth of his theory by observations he has made of the receding galaxies through his radio-telescope at Cambridge. Professor Hoyle says that he can explain these observations in terms of his own theories.
>
> As for evolution ...

Recently there have been new observations which seem to

confirm the Big Bang theory. But why should these affect one's belief in God?

Every intelligent child asks the question, 'Who made God?' There is no satisfactory 'answer' to this because it is not a satisfactory question. What the question does is to point to a more profound question: 'Is everything to be explained as existing only on the "line of time"?' 'Line of time' is, of course, a metaphor. But it is a good metaphor. As by definition a line has length but no depth or breadth, so 'time' has 'length', which you can trace backwards to the Big Bang and forwards into the unknown future, but no 'breadth' or 'depth'. It never does 'stand still'. Like the line in space, the time-line does not actually exist. It is a concept which enables us to keep yesterday, today and tomorrow apart from one another in our minds. The concept of time, like the concept of space (in which there is more than one dimension), helps us to define objects and see them in their true limitations. My body (limited in space) is here, on a spot which can be indicated, now, at this moment on the line of time: a moment that can also be indicated by our system of chronology. The space definition limits me in a way that keeps me separate from my wife who is sitting on the other side of the room; the time definition separates me from my son who was sitting in this chair, occupying my present bit of space, this morning.

Physical objects cannot be defined within the dimension of a line alone, for in defining them we need to use the terms of three dimensions: length, breadth and height. These terms of course are only relative; but it is easy enough to relate them to something that is understood as a constant (but is not so in fact), such as the earth's surface. Thus a fix in space can be described. I am here on this chair, in this house, at a known height above sea-level, at a known longitude and a known latitude.

So we use three dimensions of space as we describe physical objects. But we generally confine ourselves to one dimension of time, seeing time only as a line. If this is the only dimension of time; or, putting it differently, if apart from spatial terms the time-line is the only way we have of describing what is real, then 'Who made God?' is a fair question and is unanswerable. If you go back in time to the Big Bang, you can ask yourself what there was before the explosion that exploded. If scientists give an answer, you can then go on to ask, 'What was there before that?'; or, if you prefer a different form of the question, you can ask, 'Who or what made it so?' If the answer is, 'God', then the child (still mentally on the line of time) will naturally tease by asking, 'Who made God?'; that is, 'Who or what was there – on the line of time – "before" God?' You can define God as you like, but unless you abandon the line-of-time concept you have no answer that will satisfy your intelligent and most aggravating questioner.

If there is an answer, it must be that God exists outside, not confined by, the limitation of the time-line. So we say that God exists in 'eternity'. 'Eternity' does not mean the time-line extended indefinitely backwards or forwards; it means another dimension of existence, which is to the 'line of time' what breadth and height are to the line in space. By this understanding God the Creator is not confined to the limiting dimension of time any more than to the limiting dimension of space.

This is the most serious 'leap of faith' that a religious believer is called to make. It is a simple choice. If one believes that reality is confined to the dimensions of space and the single dimension of time, then one cannot sensibly believe in God. If one can believe, however, that there is reality outside the dimension of the time-line and space, then it is possible to believe in God; and the Big Bang holds no terrors. It is seen as happening at one very important moment, perhaps the first moment, on the line of time, just as it must have happened in a spot (undefinable) in space. God is not 'alongside' the spot in space; nor is God 'before' the moment in time. God is in that other dimension of time and space which we call 'eternity'. So we say that God is 'eternal'.

Music helps to make this leap of faith because music is 'within time' and yet is beyond its limitations. Every piece of music occupies time and lies somewhere along the 'length' dimension of it. A tune is a string of notes which begins, develops, rises, falls and ends. The first and the last notes are separated by several seconds of time. Composers take tunes and develop them, take others and combine them together, modulate, recapitulate, bring them to a close – twenty minutes, half an hour, an hour, later. So the piece is 'in time'. It is true that some music today goes round and round on purpose with no

apparent beginning or end; but it still takes time to play. I think
of a Sinhalese boy playing a drum outside my room in Kandy
where I had been delivering confidential mail to Lord Louis
Mountbatten's headquarters: 'tum-tumma-tum tum-tumma-
tum tum-tumma-tum tum-tumma-tum ...' *ad infinitum*. He
went on all night and was still going on when I woke in the
morning. He was certainly playing for a very long time – or so
it seemed to me. But to him it may have seemed time-less. That
is why he could spend the whole night doing it. For despite its
time dimension, music has the ability to hold a player or a
listener in a mode that is beyond time and space. Music has
within itself the quality of eternity, giving each present moment
a 'depth' even while it has its place along the 'length' of time.

We all know instances of music that seem to make time 'stand
still'. Here are some of mine. The Cavatina in Beethoven's
String Quartet in B Flat Major, op.130; or the shout of joy in
the middle of the scherzo of the Choral Symphony which to
Beethoven himself said something of the joy of heaven; the
gentle ruminating of the piano after the 'cello solo in the Brahms
Second Piano Concerto; the measured pedal bass in the opening
bars of the *St Matthew Passion* which ascends the scale of B
Minor with terrible foreboding, and the final chorus which
rings with resurrection joy – assured but not excited; the slow
movement of Mahler's Fifth Symphony; the 'blues' movement
in Ravel's sonata for violin and piano; the pleading of the piano
in the slow movement of Mozart's last piano concerto, no. 27,
K 595, which I call the 'Big B Flat'. These are moments of depth,
irrespective of any length they may happen to occupy along the
line of time. There is also the music of Messiaen, which I took
a long time to come to terms with but which now speaks to me
more than any music I know about the depth rather than the
length of time. The organ piece *Livre du Saint Sacrement* lasts
for two hours, so it does have a beginning and an end: it must
have been 'constructed' in 'time'. But it sounds like a series of
vastly deep, immensely rich moments which stretch up and
down into all eternity. Surely this is the music of heaven, where,
by definition, it lasts for ever!

Different kinds of music have the same effect on different
people. The Sinhalese boy seemed to be in a time-less world of
his own as he banged his drum rhythmically throughout the

night. People who go to popular music festivals find the same. They dance and jive and twist and rock and roll and have the same feeling of being transported 'out of time'. It used to be called 'being sent'. Similarly people are moved to timelessness in the course of worship. At the Christian community at Taizé people worship God through the endless repetition of words set to musical phrases, sometimes in canon, with the worshippers taking up the parts in succession to one another as they go on singing for as long as they like. Here again the very repetition gives the feeling of timelessness – which is of course exactly what worshippers are trying to find in every act of liturgy.

Perhaps that is what John Donne was reaching after in his prayer about eternity in which he wrote of 'one equal music':

> Bring us, O Lord God, at our last awakening into the house and gate of heaven to enter into that gate and dwell in that house, where there shall be no darkness nor dazzling, but one equal light; no noise nor silence, but one equal music; ; no fears nor hopes, but one equal possession; no ends nor beginnings, but one equal eternity; in the habitations of thy glory and dominion, world without end.

It could perhaps be said that these moments of timeless sublimity are not timeless in themselves; it is only that the music has a strong emotional content. I would then argue that emotions are part of our apparatus for being aware of the 'depth dimension' of time. Nevertheless, for a stronger illustration of what I am saying I turn to music that is set to words in the telling of a story. A story begins at the beginning ('Once upon a time') and proceeds through a series of events till it reaches its conclusion ('and they all lived happily ever after'). So a story in its narration alone is an 'along the line of time' exercise. But if the story is worth telling, then on the way emotions are engaged, human characterisitics displayed; good and evil contend with each other; there is passion, conflict, drama. All this can be sketched by the words of narration. But when the words are set to music, or music is played alongside the words to accompany and illustrate them, the music is able to express in depth all that is happening at any moment, including what is being felt by the different characters. This is the purpose of film music; it is also the speciality of opera.

A playwright has recently spoken out against opera, saying that the music holds up the pace of the action. Indeed it does, and if pace of narrative is all you want, avoid opera. But in exchange for pace of action opera can give you a depth of feeling in every moment superimposed upon the forward movement of the plot. This makes time appear to stand still while conflicting emotions are expressed and explored.

Think of the finale at the end of the second act of *The Marriage of Figaro*. Cherubino, the seductive page boy, has mysteriously disappeared; Figaro, the villainous hero, is busy trying to extricate himself from the implications of every new turn of events which point to his guilt; Susanna, his betrothed, and the Countess, in convenient but unlikely alliance, are trying to help him out with fresh invention to meet every situation; the Count is in a rage, certain that he is being tricked by everyone, but unable quite to see how; the gardener turns up with damning evidence, but can only think about his trampled geraniums; and Marcellino comes in, accompanied by learned witnesses, to claim revenge for breach of promise. All this seems to be happening at once, as singers and orchestra pack every second with drama. But the music also grabs you and marches you forward inexorably, like a log of wood hurtling towards a waterfall, to 'curtains' at the end of the act.

An opera has scenery and period costume and acting and much else besides music to deepen the content of each moment. But oratorio only has the words and the music. 'Tell well the story' is advice sometimes given to evangelists who seek to spread the Christian gospel. This admonition has a sound theological basis. 'The story of our salvation' is a mixture of history, saga, myth, parable, with much that is factual laced with much that is fanciful and exaggerated. It is a healthy exercise to attempt to sort it all into categories, but for the purposes of religious edification this can be a distraction. It is the depth of truth expressed in the story in its whole and its parts that matters: for it is the depth that helps people to relate to the profound truths of God.

Consider the oratorio *Belshazzar's Feast* by Sir William Walton. The story is only on the periphery of the 'story of salvation', but it is important for purposes of encouragement. It comes to us from the fifth chapter of the Book of Daniel, which was written at the time of the persecution of the Jews by Antiochus Epiphanes, in the middle of the second century BC. Antiochus was guilty in the eyes of the Jews of appalling blasphemy against God. He had sacked the sacred temple in Jerusalem (the wonder of its age), stolen its treasures and – to make things a hundred times worse – had erected a statue to Zeus, carved to look like himself, in the innermost sanctuary, the Holy of Holies. The Book of Daniel was written to encourage the faithful to resist the Greek tyrant who was trying to destroy their religion, by appealing to stories from the past and visions of the future.

One of the stories was that of King Belshazzar, son of the Nebuchadnezzar who had sacked the city of Jerusalem and the temple in 597 and 586. The words for the oratorio were picked from various parts of the Bible by Osbert Sitwell. They start, after a blare from the trombones, with a prophecy of Isaiah,[3] sung in recitative by the whole chorus, concerning the dreadful fate that was in store for the Jewish nation. The people would be taken into exile to Babylon. 'Howl ye, howl ye, therefore: for the day of the Lord is at hand!' And oh! the sadness, made terrible by the wailing of the music, as the prophecy came true and (in the words of Psalm 137), 'By the waters of Babylon ... there we sat down: yea, we wept. And hanged our harps upon the willows.' The captors jeered and called for songs from their captives; but 'How shall we sing the Lord's song in a strange land?' Walton's music sobs and cries painfully as these stark words tell the story of the nation's humiliation and shame. But then the mood changes as the story is told from the point of view of the Babylonians with their 'great city' and all its multitudinous and (we are made to think) nefarious merchandise – a list of which ends with 'slaves – And the souls of men'. There, in Babylon, 'Belshazzar the king made a great feast, made a feast to a thousand of his lords, and drank wine before the thousand'. The blasphemous scene is decribed: wine is drunk from the holy vessels looted from the temple by Nebuchadnezzar; and the false gods – of gold, silver, iron, wood, stone and brass – each represented by a rattle or a sneer or a snarl from the orchestra – are extravagantly praised. The princes and the wives and the concubines join in with timbrels and harp, and pledge themselves to the glory of the king, crying, after some thunderous discords, 'Thou, O King, art King of Kings: O King, live for ever.' The music brays in an orgy of sound which rasps and screams and snaps. Everything is there in the sound: crude sexuality, drunkenness, fierce abandon – everything but joy.

Then the baritone, in mysterious, twisting recitative, describes the coming forth of the fingers of a man's hand which wrote (to the sound of cymbals and timpani and the clanging of gongs) the dreadful words that announced the doom of King Belshazzar: '*Mene, Mene, Tekel Upharsin*'. In the Book of Daniel these words need the inspired skill of Daniel to interpret them; but in the oratorio Belshazzar knows immediately that he is 'weighed in the balance and found wanting'. That night he was 'slain' (shouted by the whole chorus) and his kingdom divided. In a moment of stunned realization the orchestra cries out sharply, and then plunges into music of joyful ecstasy. With brazen, vengeful triumph, the chorus, without drawing breath for the rest of the piece, calls on the kings of the earth to wail and lament, and everyone else to 'sing aloud to God our strength and make a joyful noise unto God, the God of Jacob: for Babylon the Great is fallen. Alleluia.'

Here is an example of very powerful music taking a story that is economically told and giving every moment of it a new dimension: a dimension that cannot be measured in time-and-space terms but is experienced in the non-physical modes of justice, sadness, courage, wickedness, punishment, redemption, joy.

Now it may be that these 'non-physical modes' have symptons in the human body that are emotional and quasi-physical. But it would seem that their source is non-physical because they are connected with the phenomenon of 'choice'. If human behaviour is simply determined by previous states and the physical laws which govern impulse and change 'along the line of time', then there is no such thing as choice in the generally accepted meaning of that term. If what I am writing now is simply flowing from the past through my pen, guided by my fingers, and governed by impulses in my brain over which I have no willing control, then there is no good reason for me to claim personal responsibility for it. On the other hand, if as a self-conscious human being I am able to stand (metaphorically) outside the process of physical change and be in the truest sense 'creative', then I can choose for myself what I write and what I will do when I finish writing. In other words, whilst at one level of my being I live within the limitations of time and space and am subject to the physical laws of change, there is another level at which I can stand outside these limitations and relate to eternity. This validates such words as incompetence, carefulness, kindness, wickedness, honesty, courage, virtue. These words are connected with time through the actions they describe; but they are also independent of it, because they imply an 'out-of-time' act of choice. When there is no element of choice, they are inapplicable. Whoever heard of a 'virtuous' atom, or a 'kind' electric current or an 'honest' explosion? The nouns in that question refer to time-and-space events. But the adjectives refer to timeless, eternal values. If there is no such thing as eternity, these and many other adjectives become meaningless.

Once more the analogy of music is helpful. To analyse music in purely physical terms is to miss the music. The physicist can analyse the sound of the symphony and demonstrate it metaphorically, as you can demonstrate the regularity of a beating heart on a screen. But the line on the screen is not the heart; nor is the physicist's analysis the music. Furthermore, a musician can write the music down on manuscript paper and a musicologist can analyse it in the jargon of music theory, but neither of these is the music. No amount of analysis and description confined to time-and-space, physical terms can stand adequately for the music itself, which invades the ear and caresses the mind of you and me the listeners. What we hear inwardly, as our ears decipher the physical impulses, is beyond time-and-space analysis. It is music. It touches eternity.

As meaning, mood and emotion are lacking from the physical analysis of music, so meaning, purpose, aesthetic and moral qualities are missing from any merely physical description of the Universe. Sounds are only sounds; but the music is real. The Big Bang may have banged, but goodness, beauty – and God – are none the less real.

4

Individuality and Harmony

Be not afeard: the isle is full of noises,
Sounds and sweet airs, that give delight, and hurt not.
Sometimes a thousand twangling instruments
Will hum about mine ears, and sometimes voices ...
(Shakespeare, *The Tempest*).

A work which in a sense is private, and therefore written for four instruments which should converse together in an intimate circle about the things which so deeply trouble me. Nothing more (Smetana writing about his Quartet).

I once watched a performance of Mozart's C Major Piano Concerto (K 467) on television. It was performed by an Austrian chamber orchestra with a woman soloist and no conductor. While the performance was going on, the camera showed the players separately, in groups, and sometimes all of them together. Thus we could see the individuality of each player, various combinations of players, and the orchestra as a whole. Using both my imagination and my memory I recall an elderly man with a moustache playing the bassoon; some very intense violin players, young and old; a young woman with beautiful long hair playing the flute; a man with a grumpy face playing the oboe; a young bearded 'cellist; and a lithe bouncy person playing the drum. The pianist, who seemed to control the performance with her eyes, was very beautiful. Her face showed that she understood suffering and had learned to accept it and resolve it; indeed, was strengthened by it for her tender, flawless performance.

I came to think of this performance as a parable for one of the mysteries of life: the relationship between fulfilled individuality and overall harmony.

I think of this at two levels, the musical and the human.

First, there is the level of the music itself: the music that Mozart had in his mind as he composed a piece which he saw as a whole even while he was writing down its component parts. This is partly a matter of the 'horizontal' shape of the music, the balance of the movements: with themes that are stated and developed, that come and go and intermingle, are matched and contrasted, and eventually come to a close – all within a space of time. This horizontal wholeness can, of course, be spoiled in performance by false dynamics, over-emphases, or tempos that meander or hurry inappropriately. There is also the 'vertical' wholeness of the sound at any given moment when the instruments are playing together, each its own part, distinct, yet incomplete without the others who are playing at the same time. So each instrument articulates and phrases its notes into a tune that is good in itself but needs the different notes that the other instruments are making simultaneously. This unity too can be broken by wrong notes or wayward rhythms or playing that is too loud or too soft in any instrument or group of instruments. So we have musical 'diversity in unity', the 'individuality and harmony' which the composer conceives, the players realize and the listeners enjoy.

Then there is the *human* individuality and harmony – which is also important if the performance is to be a good one. The pictures on the screen made it clear that the performers were human beings in their own right, no doubt with different interests, skills, personal problems, personalities. Individually they had to work hard to learn to play their instruments as well as possible. One can only guess at the disciplined practice that each had to do as part of his or her professional life, indeed, livelihood; with spouses and children depending upon it; a background, perhaps, of difficulties in marriage or with children or neighbours or the law; financial, temperamental, personal, human. Besides the differing characters and individual circumstances of the players, there must have been the usual problems that occur when people work together as a group. They do not start united. There are likely to be conflicting opinions amongst them about how the music should be inter-preted as a whole and how each part should sound within it: technically, different feelings about the tempo; humanly, jealousies and clashes of personality, and an individual's desire that his part should have prominence, or at least not be overlaid by the others. To achieve the given, created unity of the music, the very human musicians have to work hard and selflessly, listening to and respecting one another.

Self-fulfilling yet self-effacing unity with other people is the key to all ensemble performance of music. As a strange example I think of monks singing plainsong together. They sing in unison, perhaps unaccompanied; but the irregularity of the words of the psalms, canticles and antiphons that they are singing makes it more difficult than you would think for them to sing perfectly together. Humanly there may be one singer who is inclined to dominate, another whose timidity makes him likely to drag; another may sing lazily under the note, or anxiously above it, for monks are not necessarily endowed with musical gifts, nor are they always alert. What two people will read a line of prose with identical emphasis on words and syllables? Unity comes through a common aim, co-operation and constant practice. Physical circumstances may hinder, if it's very cold; or help, if there is a flattering degree of echo. The 'performance' is offered in worship to God, and the selfless unity achieved can draw into itself the prayers and aspirations of other worshippers who are present.

Then I think of chamber music, supremely the music of friendship. A posse of friends gathers together in the intimacy of someone's home. There is a piano in the sitting-room for one of them and the others bring their own instruments. They tune up and begin to play; and through their playing they converse with one another. The violin makes a statement. The others consider it, embellish it, change it a bit. Then one of them comes up with a new idea – contradictory? complementary? Together they consider it and try to find agreement, but get nowhere, going round and round – until the piano finishes off the argument with something firm and authoritative. Then they start again and go over the whole conversation as before so as to be quite clear what it is that they are talking about. When that is done they are in a position to restate some of the propositions and develop them in detail, finding new points of interest and some logical implications of what was said before. There may be stress now and disagreement. One is insisting, another vehemently contradicting; but new light is thrown that clinches the argument. The statements are repeated in ways they have collectively agreed; and that is the end of that discussion, because there is no more to be said. But now they turn to something quite different, something tender, sad, too beautiful for words. It is stated, pondered, adorned; contrasted with something rougher and less favourable; then stated again and accepted. Then they enjoy a joke together, told, embellished, retold. Then they tell one another stories that go on and on and round and round with many interruptions and anecdotes and irrelevant asides. On they go, chattering away; for why should they ever stop? But at last they do – for a drink and refeshments and departure after a most satisfactory evening.

Perhaps chamber music – like madrigals – is written in the first place for the satisfaction of the performers, though listeners may be welcome to come and eavesdrop on their conversation. They can then associate themselves with the discussion, be moved by the tenderness, share the fun. Sometimes they may notice a little self-indulgence as one of the players wrings the utmost from a contribution that he has been asked to make. The others allow him to, slowing up a little to accommodate him and to give him some space in which to make his point. They are listening as well as playing and they understand their friend's feelings; and, anyway, they will soon be wanting to say the same sort of thing themselves. I am thinking of three men, all master musicians, sharing the joy and the bathos of Schubert's B Flat Trio: Casals, Cortot and Thibaud; all giving themselves and one another more space than would be usual in a professional performance. But this is understood, allowed for, forgiven, because they are doing this thing together. Individually they agree to indulge one another, as only true friends – and the finest musicians – can do. Who will say that the unity has been impaired by such moments of heart-pulling enjoyment? It would be, but for the fact that the unity is not just the subjective unity of individuals who agree to agree. It is the *given* unity which comes from the unifying power of the music itself. The players find unity together through the music that is given them, which they come to feel part of, and so to share.

It is not always as satisfactory as that. Sometimes players do not play together. I have in mind an episode in one of the BBC's Young Musician of the Year programmes. A violinist of outstanding technical facility was playing Mendelssohn's Violin

Concerto. All went well until the last movement, when he allowed himself to gallop ahead of the orchestra regardless of the despairing gestures of the conductor. Something eventually pulled him up and they all came together again and ended as one – to thunderous applause from the audience, a pleased but slightly guilty blush on the face of the player, and looks of tut-tutting forbearance by the conductor and the professional players in the orchestra. Everyone seemed pleased – but he did not win!

Sometimes it is a player who mars the unity of a performance. But there is some music which makes the listener wonder whether there is in fact any discernible pattern, if considered horizontally; or any kind of harmony, if considered vertically;[1] indeed, any sense of cohesion at all. Sometimes we expect to be baffled even before we have heard the music. Arthur Wills' Concerto for Guitar, Organ and Orchestra would seem to be beset with problems of balance, though according to the review it comes off well. What about Fanshawe's *African Sanctus*, in which music from the African jungle has been recorded and inserted by tape-recorder into the performance? In this music disparate styles and cultures are combined with joyful success. At the Three Choirs' Festival in Worcester Cathedral in 1981 the men and women of the chorus wore coloured shirts, and after the performance there were roses and champagne all round – deservedly so. Could not this mixture of cultures be a way forward for composers of the future? There is so much music in the world that is not in the Western, classical tradition. Why not explore it and bring it together and find ways in which differing styles and cultures are valued for their own sake and brought together for mutual enrichment? This has already happened when composers like Ravel and Walton bring jazz idioms into their music. What was found to be true for individuals in the sitting-room could also be found to be true of cultures in the world. With whole musical traditions being considered as 'individuals', it can be said again that 'individuals' can find greater fulfilment as they come together and fulfil one another.

But I note. In the *African Sanctus* it was music composed by a composer that brought the strange elements together. They did not blend themselves. They came together in a 'sym-phony' of musical sounds devised and written down by a man who had travelled far to hear and record what he wanted in order to incorporate it into the Western-style music that he wrote for his *Sanctus*.

'Does music, just because it has been composed, necessarily have a "unity"?,' one sometimes wonders. There can be unity in dissonance, as in Walton's First Symphony with its immense power and drive. In listening to it you have to hang on tight and let yourself be whirled away by its tempestuous sounds. The instruments of the orchestra seem to tear each other apart; but there is harmony – like the harmony of a high wind in a forest. You feel like one of Shelley's leaves driven by the 'wild, west wind': 'yellow and black and pale and hectic red, pestilent-stricken multitudes'. Harmony in music does not mean bland concordance. Clashing dissonance has its place as long as the composer knows what he is saying and says it with integrity and conviction. Who judges? A composer may feel that he has an overall purpose and unity in his composition; but if listeners cannot discern this, can it be said to be there? This is a question about the ear of the listener as well as the skill of the composer, and the intriguing question of the unmusical – and the irreligious – is one I am keeping for Chapter 7. Meanwhile I have to say that whereas I enjoy both Walton's symphonies and feel lifted and stimulated by them, I have difficulties with the twelve-tone music of Schoenberg. I cannot 'get it'. I am sure that I could never sing it. However, rather than conclude that there is no purpose and no unity in this music, I would rather agree to the possibility that there is a failure of discernment in myself!

It may be a similar failure of discernment that makes one think that some music fails to give a sense of unity, because it sprawls. I remember a performance of one of Vierne's organ symphonies which seemed to sprawl most drearily whilst I waited impatiently for the familiar last movement. A first and only hearing in a cold chapel is not a good time to judge; and I could hardly believe it when someone made a similar charge with regard to the Mahler Eighth Symphony which he recently heard (standing!) at a Promenade Concert. He should try again, (sitting down!) and play it over and over until he knows it well enough to appreciate how all the parts do come gloriously together.

These thoughts on the 'unity' of music need to be gathered together.

First, the unity of the performers, and the unity of the performers with the audience, examples of which I have been describing with some relish, arise from the music itself. When the music which is outside a person sings inside him so that he identifies himself and plays his part in it, then he is 'at one' with the other people who, similarly immersed, are playing their parts in it.

Secondly, the music has to have been *composed*. The composer had his own purpose for it, which he could not have expressed otherwise. The unity which performers and listeners find in it is inseparable from the purpose of the composer. 'Purpose' and 'unity' go together. There may be 'purpose' in the intention of the composer but no consequent 'unity'; in which case the composer has failed in his purpose. But there cannot be 'unity' unless there is or has been a composer first, with a 'purpose'.

Thirdly, there are two modes of unity. There is the 'vertical' by which notes and tunes fit together at any one moment; and the 'horizontal' as different parts of the music, different themes and episodes played out along the 'line of time' 'add up' to something that is complete. The truth is, however, that the two modes are inseparable – and, indeed, come to the aid of each other. One finds oneself saying, 'That sounds very ugly; and if that discord were to stay there, coming out of nothing and going to nowhere, it would be intolerable. But in fact it is the logical result of what has gone before; and it will surely become resolved as it leads on to something else.' So by seeing the ugly vertical moment in terms of the general, horizontal progress of the piece, the ugliness is redeemed and is heard as part of the process of the music. Furthermore a passage that seems to be irrelevant to the whole may be found to have meaning because it contains some new harmony or a new accompanying rhythm or some new tone of orchestral colour or an unexpected modulation of key that gives it its purpose. This means that no single moment of the music can be judged by itself: it has to be heard as part of the whole.

Fourthly, as a listener one may find it difficult to appreciate the unity and purpose of a piece; in which case one has to ask the question, 'Is it me? Or is it the music that is at fault?'

Finally, when one does sense the unity and purpose of a vast multitude of sounds that ring together deep in the present moment and change and develop over a period of time, then one may be experiencing something that is beautiful beyond words.

5

Harmony and the Love of God

We in the Western world seem to have lost a sense of the *wholeness* of our environment, and of our immense and inalienable responsibility to the whole of creation ... In my view, a more holistic approach is now needed. Science has done the inestimable service of showing us a world much more complex than we ever imagined. But in its modern, materialist, one-dimensional form, it cannot explain everything (The Prince of Wales, addressing a private meeting at Wilton Park, Sussex; as reported in *The Times*, 14 December 1996).

For there is a music wherever there is harmony, order or proportion; and thus far we may maintain the music of the spheres; for those well ordered motions, and regular paces, though they give no sound unto the ear, yet to the understanding they strike a note most full of harmony (Sir Thomas Browne, *On Dreams*).

> Dust as we are, the immortal spirit grows
> Like harmony in music; there is a dark
> Inscrutable workmanship that reconciles
> Discordant elements, makes them cling together
> In our society
> (William Wordsworth, *The Prelude*).

> The soul's nobility consisteth not
> in riches of imagination or intellect
> but in harmony of Essences ...
> like as in music, when true voices blend in song,
> the perfect intonation of the major triad
> is sweetest of all sounds; its inviting embrace
> resolveth all discords; and all ambitious flights
> of turbulent harmony come in the end to rest
> with the fulfilment of its liquidating close
> (Robert Bridges, *Testament of Beauty*).

Ascension Day at my school was a whole holiday – a day of blissful freedom. In 1938 I spent the day walking to Chanctonbury Ring. After a picnic lunch sprawling on the grass, my friend Philip went off with his camera to take photographs, and I just sat and looked at the view. The Sussex Weald stretched before me for thirty or forty miles to the Surrey Downs beyond. In between everything was tiny, but the details were clear. I cannot now describe the view accurately. What I remember is the question I asked myself as I chewed a bit of grass and pondered. Was the beauty in the details that were so lovely in themselves, or in the scene as a whole? Was it the hare-bell at my knees bending in the breeze, or the curling smoke from a distant steam engine, the still clouds on the horizon, the irregular fields, sheep grazing, a skylark chirrupping, the hills sloping towards one another and then falling away into patches of wood, copses, single trees, cluster of cottages? Or was the beauty in the 'whole' that they added up to, the supremely satisfying unity of the 'one view'? Do you start with the 'many' and see them as 'one'? Or do you start with the 'ones', add them up and see them together?

Perhaps it does not matter; and I hope that I was not being too solemn about it. For the answer must be 'both': because the whole and the parts are inseparable. When I thought about it further I realized that the very small objects that I had been con-sidering, for instance, my friendly harebell, were themselves very complex organizations of much smaller parts – too small to be seen. These exist together and make my harebell (for instance) into the enormous object which relatively it is. At the other end of the scale, the huge view of the Sussex Weald was an insignificant nothing in the scale of England, the world, the universe. Yet it was part of them: a part which, however small in the scale, is significant in itself as a part within the whole. As for myself, I was inclined to feel detached, an observer. But I was no such thing. I was part of it all, with my own small but unique significance; and I too was a complex pattern of tiny 'parts', each with its substrata of still smaller parts, all in the harmony of my being. As I contemplated the vastness of the uni-verse on the one hand and its microscopic pieces on the other, I felt myself to be somewhere nicely in the middle; and with this comforting thought I joined Philip and his camera and we tore back to school only just in time to avoid the dire consequences of being late.

The mysterious sense of the unity of things remained with me and has often recurred. The overall beauty of nature – in stars and planets, oceans and mountains, the harebell and the bumble-bee – makes it difficult to believe that there is not an ultimate unity, in the pattern of which all the parts fit. And the existence of amazing pieces – this million-year-old rock, that splash of water thrown up on the sand, my own body – make it hard to believe that there is no order but that of change and chance, and no creative purpose but that of the survival of the fittest. If chaos is the ultimate, how is it that things fit – in the physical patterns that we have learnt to expect, in the beauty we experience and the love that we live by? If a willed and continued act of creation is the ultimate, then things would be expected to fit, and the individual things we have noticed would be expected each to have its place. It would then be possible and sensible to speak, as we have in the context of music, of 'fulfilled individuality' and 'overall harmony'.

But do things fit? Certainly not in easy concordance. To find a 'fitting' pattern we have to accept a great deal of dissonance. Sir David Attenborough has shown us grotesque examples of harmony and dissonance in his television programmes about nature. These show that nature is very red indeed and extremely cunning and sometimes very caring and beautifully ugly 'in tooth and claw'. Some of its reproductive arrangements, for instance, and the ability of individual creatures to adapt themselves to harsh circumstances, appear to be distinctly gruesome. The concept of 'overall harmony' is denied nearly as often as it is vindicated, if the convenience of the individual is the only criterion. The parts do not live happily ever after. Furthermore, 'overall harmony' can only be perceived if the parts are understood in relationship to a dynamic, ever-changing, ever-developing 'whole', in which decay and death are essential to new life, growth and evolution. Remember the discords that were considered intolerable unless they were heard in the context of the development of the music as a whole. Any state of affairs has to be seen in terms of that from which it comes and that which emerges from it. Whatever pattern there is in the universe, it is dynamic like the development of a symphony, not static like a jig-saw puzzle.

(An ethical principle of great importance emerges here. 'Goodness' is not a state: it is a direction. Never mind what people are; it is what they are becoming that matters ultimately. This maxim can be very encouraging – but also a warning.)

What of human beings? In the first place they are not detached observers of the universal scene. They are part of it. It is tempting for them to think that some of the dynamic changes within the universe are inimical to themselves and therefore evil. Indeed when human beings are caught within the discords of creation, the consequences to themselves can be appalling. Logically there is nothing surprising in this and one has to say – as part of a detached explanation – that an earthquake here and a volcano there take place in the process of dynamic change which the physical universe is always undergoing. The difficulty then is to believe in the value of the 'parts' in themselves. If the parts are not self-aware, then there may be no problem: their demise happens within the redistribution of energy that is always going on. Human beings, however, are self-aware and therefore have an individual value that is greater than the role they play in the physical process of change. Many of us believe that human beings have an eternal value beyond their physical existence. If that is true, then the scale of judgment cannot be confined to time-and-space life alone; and what is certainly tragic in these terms may make more sense when seen in terms of the eternal. It takes a great deal of faith to accept this view when the tragedy concerns oneself or a person one loves; and no one can write or read about this in a mode of easy acceptance.

The more difficult problem to understand, however, is that of the unity and disunity of human beings amongst themselves. When a group of people is working together for some collective cause they can be united in that cause, each person making an individual contribution, all using one another's strengths, in a way which serves the cause and gives them unity together: until one is jealous or another is lazy or another is dishonest and self-seeking; in which case the cause is harmed and the unity broken. There is also the unity brought about by mutual affection which binds together those who know one another intimately. They may be friends with shared experiences, or members of a family with parental and filial instincts, ties of blood and a shared upbringing. Is there anything so deeply satisfying as a happy home in which the parents love one another and the children grow up in a pattern of life which gives them scope to be themselves in mutual affection?

Sadly we all know of frequent failures; of homes where one

man's cruelty or lust or drunkenness or a woman's fecklessness
or a child's wanton behaviour tyrannizes the family and creates
bitter, life-long unhappiness. It does not take two to make a
quarrel, and the disloyalty of one partner can break up a
marriage even after years of apparent happiness. In the best of
families there are tensions and tempers. Family harmony can
never be assumed, and members have to work at it to resolve
the discords. Most do so; but much criminal behaviour springs
from cruelty and abuse suffered in the home; and the break-
down of love where love should be most intimate is the cause of
much lasting unhappiness.

There are many happy families in the world, and I find myself
asking, 'Which is the norm, a united or a broken family?'
Leading on from that: 'When a family is united, is it because the
individual members, through the circumstances of a shared
home, create in themselves an affection for one another? Or is
love in the home, springing from the love of husband and wife,
a power that naturally welds the members together, except in as
far as it is broken by individual selfishness?'

On a larger scale there is unity and disunity at every level of
human life: racial, international, tribal, social, class. There is
unity where, despite the babel of languages, men and women
meet across the frontiers for holiday and sport, commerce
and exploration, in scholarship and art, in the international
language of music, in travel and hospitality. People help one
another in the sharing of knowledge and technology and in
times of disaster. Above all in our own day there are the means
of communication which enable us to watch cricket matches
while they are being played the other side of the world, talk to
people we know three thousand miles away as if they were in
the next room; chat, as radio hams, to fellow but foreign radio
hams: a student in Nigeria, a housewife in Nyasaland, a
freedom-fighter in Nicaragua. Furthermore, through the Inter-
net, we can seek and obtain knowledge – from gross prurience
to the profoundest scholarship – from anywhere in the world.
Distance and culture are no longer barriers. At its worst the
'global village' syndrome of twentieth-century life is destroying
local languages and cultures and producing a world stew of
such glutinous thickness that the identity of its ingredients
is being lost. At its best – what a stew! rich in diversity of

substance and taste. The ingredients need not be lost. If they can be made to blend, they and the stew are all the tastier for it.

Yet some of the stew is horribly burnt and some of the ingredients would rather destroy one another than blend. So we have our twentieth-century '-isms': racism, for instance, seen where there is still apartheid, exercised flagrantly in football stadia, practised violently on the streets, sometimes affecting the administration of justice. Then there is the narrow nationalism which shouts jingoistic slogans and would keep a nation locked up within its own resources in order to keep the world out. There is the brutal tribalism which sucks its strength from ill-remembered historical incidents, sceptical prejudices and the bullying rantings of power-crazy men. The world suffers this, as a human body suffers from a boil or a poisoned tooth, in Ireland, Bosnia, Palestine, Rwanda ... Sexism, ageism, elitism are all attitudes which keep people apart. Then there are political and economic '-isms' which are terribly divisive. Capitalism is about creating wealth; but because of the difficulty of distributing the wealth that has been created, it spreads poverty in its wake. Socialism affirms the corporate nature of humankind, but sometimes stresses it so lop-sidedly that individuals seem not to matter.

Rather than continuing with this catalogue of well known '-isms', it is important to remind ourselves that human disunity is not an abstract about society as a whole: it is a fact about ourselves. The Christian church has always tended to make too much of 'sin' as if it is simply a collective term for private faults. Our 'general confessions' in church services are worded as if we go about dripping with iniquitous actions, which in fact – speaking generally – is not the case. The bad truth is that by birth, upbringing, circumstances, prejudices, ignorance, failures of imagination and sensibility, we continue to allow ourselves to be divided from one another. Sometimes this is through the committing of sins. Much more often it is through the acceptance of some of the '-isms' just mentioned that we find ourselves (if we care to notice it) living in disunity with other people. Furthermore, if we believe in the God of uniting love, then we have to say that to that extent we are at disunity with God as well.

The worst thing about human disunity for a person of faith

to have to come to terms with is the fact that religious feelings often exacerbate rather than heal the wounds. When Protestant Christians inveigh against the Pope, and Catholic communities persecute the Orthodox, Muslims wage 'holy war' against Christians and Christians persecute Jews, one can only be desperately ashamed and confess that in these and other examples religion as a healing force has not worked.

The truth is that human beings are free to hate, this being complementary to their being free to love. Love would not be love but for that freedom. When people hate in a way that is directly contrary to their most profound beliefs, there is good reason for condemning their hatred; but this does not invalidate the beliefs, nor does it excuse the rest of us from continuing to try to put the beliefs into practice. On the whole people do so successfully. Most men and women of faith do love one another.

So we come back to the same question. Which is the norm? Are human beings essentially 'separate', so that co-operation and affection and mutual concern only come about through individual taste and effort? Or is the human race essentially a 'family' created in harmony for mutual satisfaction and service, though torn assunder by the exploitation of selfish interests? In terms of individual behaviour, do people love one another for their own convenience as a kind of truce based on the maxim 'live and let live'? Or are people born into love? If the world is without purpose and created unity, then binding love is no more than an individual's private impulse, with no significance beyond the person who activates it. But if there is purpose and an ultimate created harmony, then this binding love is the norm; and we need to get back to work to restore it as a universal force.

There is no doubt at all about what Christians believe in this matter, because this is the central 'credo' of the Christian faith. Until you get to the part played by Jesus Christ himself, it is also the basis of other monotheistic religions. It is that God is love – not just subjectively as in the sentence 'God loves', but essentially in God's own internal being. Through this dynamic, creative, harmonizing love, the universe is created in diversity and harmony. God's loving self creates the parts and unites the whole. In so far as the parts are limited physical beings and states, their harmony is a physical harmony which can be analysed and described as 'the laws of nature'. How consistent and predictable they are seems to be uncertain; but inanimate things cannot wilfully change themselves. In as far as the parts are human, created (in the Jewish/Christian phrase) 'in the image of God', then the harmony is such as can be accepted and rejected and restored as people exercise their God-given freedom. Where harmony is broken, Christians say, the love of God can restore. The instrument and the sign of this restoration is the human life of God's Incarnate Word, Jesus Christ. Christ's life and teaching and work and death and resurrection encapsulate, exemplify and make effective through the limited terms of human living the unifying love of God. Jesus himself found words for this (according to the Fourth Gospel) when he prayed to the Father 'that they may be one, as we are one; I in them and thou in me, may they be perfectly one'.[1] St Paul claims that the fullness of God is in Christ: that, in order to unite it, Christ's love fills the universe and that Christ renews his Spirit in those who accept it, with the effect that they become 'one' together in the great spirit-filled 'body', which he calls the church, the 'body of Christ'. With this in mind he prays for his fellow Christians at Ephesus:

May you, in company with all God's people, be strong to grasp what is the breadth and length and height and depth of Christ's love, and to know it, though it is beyond knowledge. So may you be filled with the very fullness of God.[2]

A few verses later he exhorts them to live up to this belief:

We are to maintain the truth in a spirit of love; so shall we fully grow up into Christ. He is the head, and on him the whole body depends. Bonded and held together by every constituent joint, the whole frame grows through the proper functioning of each part, and builds itself up in love.[3]

Unless a belief can be proved or disproved, one has to choose, positively or negatively. Having chosen, one tries to live by one's belief. Experience then tends to cast doubt or to vindicate it. If one's belief is negative, perhaps it does not matter if one does not live by it. If a person says, 'love is no more than an individual's personal foible: therefore loyalty to the loved one is not ultimately important', no one minds if that person belies this statement by showing loyalty when put to the test. But if one believes that love is the essential law of living, a law that sometimes requires unselfish-action, and then one behaves selfishly, it does matter. It affects not only the person being hurt but the person who is hurting and the integrity of his belief. It is the person, not the belief who is being tested; and the truth is that many people 'lose their faith' because they have stopped being faithful.

Choosing one's belief and living by it is not a snap judgment but a lifelong struggle requiring intellectual assessment, a series of moral choices and the ability to adjust and re-adjust and go on trying again and again. In this respect it is wise to look not only at oneself but also at other people to learn from the best of what they are and what they do. This can be a long search, but the discovery of purpose and love can be the most important experience of life. If one assumes that the music of Stravinsky and Bartok and Britten and Walton and Tippett and Schoenberg is senseless, cacophanous chaos, because that is what it seems at first hearing, and dismisses it as such, one loses out. If one believes that there is no order, therefore no Orderer; no unity, therefore no Love; nothing ultimate, therefore no ultimate morality, one may be right, however much one's behaviour belies one's belief. But one may be wrong, and missing a lot. To me an affirmative belief in God, purpose, order, ultimate love, is the affirmation of life and all that I find good in it.

In considering whether or not it is sensible to believe in 'fulfilled individuality and overall harmony' I have found the analogy from music to be helpful. I have thought of the 'music of the composer' as akin to the 'love of God'. The satisfaction of the players and their unity together is inseparable from their unity with the music; similarly, the fulfilment of people within the love of God is inseparable from their unity with God and with one another in his whole creation.

These things follow.

First, the unity of Christians together is not an optional extra to the practice of Christianity; it is essential to it. Those who wish to keep their faith private, and those who are not ashamed at the disunity within the church, are missing out on it altogether.

Secondly, however, 'unity with other people' does not necessarily include the obligatory enjoyment of 'coffee after the service' or enthusiastic participation in the parish social. It may rather mean the care of someone who is sick, or an attempt to mend some broken relationship, or to create community and friendship in the neighbourhood, or to do one's best with others to prevent an enviromental outrage. As the flautist plays in duet with the oboe at this gentle moment of the music's development, they are not immediately concerned with the climactic surge of strings and brass and tympani which this present sweet episode will lead to. The unity of these two instruments with the whole orchestra is important over a period of time, but it is only being realized now at this moment by their immediate unity with one another. So too men and women are called through the circumstances of their own lives to modes of unity which are particular and limited. In these particular and limited ways they are taking their part in the universal love of God in the harmony of creation.

Thirdly, this emphasis on the immediate as part of the ultimate leads us to consider the complications posed by the word 'loyalty'. People tend to think of a hierarchy of loyalties and expect the bigger and more embracing to be the 'higher'. In this way they think of exercising loyalty to the family, through that to society, and through society to their country, the continent and the world; with other objects of loyalty, such as their firm, football club, church and individual friends fitting in. All these find themselves in a hierarchical order of loyalties which take their place in the ultimate loyalty owed to God himself. But this is misleading; for the music of God's love is in the immediate moment and not just the ultimate whole. It calls through those who are close to us in our lives, as well as the more remote objects such as the state or continent or a political cause. Indeed over-zealous loyalty to club or cause or nation can lead to cruel and bigoted attitudes which, being impersonal, can do more harm than good. Sometimes it is difficult to sort out the right priority of loyalties. One has to try to find a way by which the immediate and the far-off ultimately go together. God is certainly in both, but comes more directly through the immediate. This consideration may justify someone in putting his children before a political principle, friendship before the firm's profit, his wife before some social obligation.

Finally, I find in the analogy from music a strong measure of encouragement, as I discover that for all my effort it is the music itself, the music of God's love, that takes over and makes things come right. I remember singing with The Three Choirs Festival Chorus in a performance of Mahler's Eighth Symphony in Worcester Cathedral under Dr Donald Hunt. It was difficult music to learn, the difficulty exacerbated by the fact that we were singing it from single parts without the whole or even the choral score in front of us. I confess that within a week of the performance I was only giving myself seven out of ten with the notes I had to sing, despite the time spent at home playing over my part on the piano – which often made little sense by itself even if I did get it right. But in the performance, with soloists and huge orchestra and brass band and chorus, it all seemed to come together, and the climax that this symphony builds up to with agonizing slowness, with stops and starts and hesitations and seeming irrelevances which somehow get drawn in as necessary and inevitable, this climax was certainly one of the music moments of my life. I lost myself and found myself, singing with precision but abandon, utterly overwhelmed, finding myself lifted up by a wave of sound that held everything and everyone together – conductor, soloists, orchestra, band, chorus (including my daughter amongst the sopranos and me with the basses) and audience in a moment of vibrant affirmation.

No description of heaven in the Book of Revelation or anywhere else comes near to this moment of musical truth. Yet I believe that heaven is like this. Heaven on earth should be like this. We are called to work to make it so, for all God's creation.

6

Interpretation

We are no longer to be children, tossed about by the waves and whirled around by every fresh gust of teaching, dupes of cunning rogues and their deceitful schemes. Rather we are to maintain the truth in a spirit of love; so shall we grow fully up into Christ (Ephesians 4.14 15).

'What is it that you are saying, Fitzwilliam? What are you talking of? What are you telling Miss Bennett? Let me hear what it is.' 'We are speaking of music, madam,' he said, when no longer able to avoid a reply. 'Of music! Then pray speak aloud. It is of all subjects my delight. I must have my share in the conversation, if you are speaking of music. There are few people in England, I suppose, who have more true enjoyment of music than myself, or a better natural taste. If ever I had learned, I should have been a great proficient ...' (Jane Austen, Lady Catherine de Burgh in *Pride and Prejudice*).

One of my favourite television programmes is *Masterclass*. In this a renowned musician takes on a group of students and shares with them what he can communicate of his insights into a particular piece of music, and the technique by which he attempts to realize the music in performance. In one such programme, Paul Tortelier was sharing his ideas on one of Bach's Sonatas for 'Cello with some 'cellists. It is a musical experience even to look at Tortelier; and when he is explaining a fine point by a combination of husky singing, excited gesticulation, a bending of himself, a contortion of his india-rubber face, half a smile round the corner of his mouth and a fiery flashing of his eyes, one hardly needs to hear the music itself. But when he relaxes and lets the 'cello tell all, his soaring bow woos love from the instrument and one is drawn into the music as if one were the bow oneself. The students were enthralled. Adjusting their bowing and their fingering they began not only to feel the music as he was feeling it, but also to express it in their performance.

By contrast, there was another programme in which the human voice was the instrument and in which the 'master' failed to communicate with the singers he was trying to instruct. As a viewer one could see a degree of arrogance on both sides acting like barbed wire between them. The master knew it all and had no patience for other peoples' feelings. The students resented his attitude and could see no reason to prefer his interpretation to their own. Here was a clash of personalities. There was also a difference of musical presuppositions. These fed on each other with the result that, however fascinating the programme was as a study of disparate styles and clashing personalities, the music itself was lost.

There are plenty of legitimate differences in the understanding and interpretation of music. They tend to go in fashions, and one is sometimes amazed at the certainty with which some people write what they think as if it is the last word on the subject. Composers, conductors, soloists and critics rubbish one another with fine abandon; and it must be hard for aspiring musicians to read some of the caustic things that critics write about them. There is no excuse for slovenly technique in a professional player, but there is lots of room for different interpretations in performance, and who is to say who is right? Musical purism springs from a legitimate historical study of what composers intended and how things used to be played. But do these considerations have to govern what we feel and how we perform today? Do Mozart's String Quintets have to be played on instruments of his day? Would not Bach have enjoyed the Forty-Eight Preludes and Fugues played on a Steinway grand piano? Would not Beethoven and Schubert have rejoiced to hear the Eroica and the Great C Major symphonies performed by The City of Birmingham Orchestra conducted by Sir Simon Rattle in Symphony Hall? And just because they used to be sung so slowly and heavily, is there any reason why the choruses in *Messiah* should nowadays be sung so racily fast?

It was at this point in my thinking that I came upon a book by Frances Young, Professor of Theology at Birmingham University, called *The Art of Performance*.[1] Professor Young's concern is not musical but biblical interpretation; but in her search for a way of interpreting the Bible that is true both to a critical analysis of the text and also to the nature of the Bible as the Word of God, she goes to the problems of musical interpretation and sees in them an analogy which is helpful in the understanding and use of the Bible. She speaks of theologians and preachers 'performing' the Bible, and Christians in their pews and in their homes sharing the performance as musicians perform music and others share it by listening.

The differences in the interpretation of the Bible are much greater and more complicated and even more vehemently felt than are the differences in musical interpretation, and in the next few pages I am going to give a short account of the different styles of interpretation, for such readers as are interested. Some who read this book will have more exact knowledge than I have; others may not be interested in what they regard as theological technicalities. But there may be those who would like to have a sketch of the different kinds of biblical interpretation, before we go on to explore the parallels with the interpretation of music.

Many people interpret the Bible without any critical sense at all. They read it simply for the comfort and inspiration that they get from it. They find strength through the scriptures rather as one finds strength in a letter from home or from a son abroad. Never mind accuracy of places and names and dates – though they are certainly interesting: it is the mood that matters, and through the mood (sometimes betrayed by scrambled thoughts or stilted sentences or rushed, untidy handwriting) the character and the feelings – indeed, the very presence – of the writer are conveyed. In the same way it is possible by reading the Bible to find a comforting sense of the presence of God. But people who do so are inclined to confine their reading to their favourite bits, and they do not appear to be puzzled by the difficulties they would find if they were to compare passages or interpret what they read in the light of human knowledge in the world today.

Indeed there are some students of the Bible who would have us interpret everything literally as it stands, making light of the inconsistencies and overlooking the fact that much of the writing is poetic and not meant to be literal. One difficulty they have is that if all texts are equally 'true' as the 'Word of God', then they are all of equal authority and importance. Thus an obscure law from the Book of Leviticus or an imprecation from the prophet Nahum or a saying of Jesus from the Sermon on the Mount have to be given the same consideration – for are they not all the immutable 'Word of God'?

There are others who point out that nowhere in the Bible is there a claim that the Bible as a whole is the 'Word of God'. In the Bible it is Jesus who is 'The Word of God': the Word of God 'made flesh' and dwelling among us, so that we can see his glory.[2] The Bible is a library of books that relate to the incarnate life of Jesus; and the value of any part of the Bible lies in the light it throws upon his life, work, teaching and significance. They also say that it is a mistake to confine one's understanding of Christianity to what one reads in the Bible alone. For one thing the different books of the Bible were written within the limitations of the authors' understanding in their particular historical age; for another thing the Spirit of God has not been at rest since the canon of Scripture was closed, and much has been written since then which helps people to understand the central truths of God, Christ and the Christian life.[3]

Some have treated the Bible allegorically, finding different layers of interpretation. 'Allegory' is taking one thing to mean another. St Augustine (Bishop of Hippo, 354–430), for instance, interpreted the parable of the Good Samaritan as an allegory in which the man who walked from Jerusalem to Jericho was a Christian soul; the thieves were the evil of the world, into whose clutches he fell; the callous passers-by were the ineffective 'Law and the Prophets' of the Old Testament; the Good Samaritan was Jesus Christ; the inn into whose charge he put the restored man was the church; the innkeeper the priest; and the two pence the sacraments vital to his continued salvation. One does have to admit that the parable with its usual interpretation does not fit into its context very easily as an answer to the lawyer's question.[4] But it is hard to see why St Augustine's particular interpretation should be more authoritative than any other you could make up. On the whole, scholars are against allegorical interpretation even of Jesus' parables, although sometimes it does seem as if he intended it.[5] The allegorical method was frequently used with the Old Testament – even by writers of the New Testament. St Paul, for instance, in Galatians 4.24 writes, 'This is an allegory', referring to the strange story of Abraham's two sons, one born of a slave woman and the other of a free woman. This is to teach us (reasons St Paul) that Christians are 'free' from the shackles of the Jewish Law.

The point is that much of the Old Testament is very odd indeed if it is taken at its literal face value. Thus some of the Fathers of the early church (Origen, for instance – an Alexandrian theologian, 185–254), without disputing that things actually happened, nevertheless interpreted the happenings as God's way of saying deep truths which would be seen in their fullness in Jesus Christ. Origen said that there were three levels of interpretation, the literal, the moral and the allegorical; these to suit Christians according to their different intellectual and spiritual states.

In this century theological fashion has tended to be for 'historical criticism', which comes from the labour of putting passages into their historical context. This can be merely negative, drawing the sting (or the glory?) of a passage by showing the circumstances in which it was written. But it can also be positive and inspiring. Take, for instance, the famous prophecy of Isaiah in the passage heard every Christmas and sung every time we listen to *Messiah*. 'Behold, a virgin shall conceive, and bear a son: and shall call his name Immanuel.' 'Immanuel' means 'God with us'. Out of its historical context this is a straightforward prophecy: 'This will happen'. And we nod with satisfaction when we read St Matthew's account of the birth of Jesus, and say, with him, because he points it out, 'There in Jesus, the prophecy has come true.'[6]

But Isaiah was not consciously speaking about the distant future. He was speaking about the immediate future: the fate of Jerusalem. Jerusalem was being besieged by Kings Rezin of Aram and Pekah of Israel.[7] As Isaiah was speaking, the enemy was camping round the city walls. Humanly speaking there seemed to be no hope. But Isaiah the prophet had hope. 'Consider,' he said, 'this young woman. By the time she has her baby she will want to call him "Immanuel", "God is with us"'; yes, because the enemy will have fled; Jerusalem will be saved; the Lord God who loves and saves his people will be vindicated; and the truth of this will be rightly marked by the name given to the baby'. If it were left at that, this could indeed be a glory-emptying interpretation. But it is possible to say, 'This is the truth of God and his world. God was with his people at that moment of history. God is seen to be with us ("Immanuel") for all time through the birth of his Son, Jesus Christ, our

Immanuel. What was true to the people of Jerusalem in 602 BC was made for ever true in Jesus and is true today.'

A development of historical criticism is that which examines the life and time and circumstances of the writers themselves. Thus the characteristics of St Luke are deduced from the text of his Gospel and the Acts of the Apostles (which he also wrote) – especially as these are compared with the other Gospels and the known history of the times; and the text is interpreted and applied accordingly. St Paul's letters are seen in the light of his Jewish and Greek education and his privileged status as a Roman citizen; also in the light of the conditions and the customs and the state of Christian understanding in the churches he was addressing.

Alongside the study of authorship, attention is drawn to the very obvious differences in genre of the different books of the Bible. Some books are letters, some are stories; there are books of law and custom and 'wise sayings'. There are books which were written to be historical; and some which are frankly history interpreted in the light of religious understanding. If you compare the books of Chronicles with those of Kings, you will see how Chronicles gives an idealistic version of the same events. The Book of Deuteronomy, also, is clearly history interpreted with a strong nationalistic bias. Does this destroy its credibility and usability? Not if you make allowances and let it tell you about the way people thought of God in those early days of religious development when the book was being written.[8] (They are not so very different from the primitive ways in which some people continue to think of God today!)

Much scholarship has been concerned with comparing the texts within the Bible. Thus the Pentateuch (the first five books) has been analysed in terms of its literary sources, and the sources roughly dated. A progression can then be seen in the religious understanding of the Jewish people. The first three Gospels too have been shown to be textually related, the usual theory being that Matthew and Luke both used Mark's Gospel as well as another source which we do not have – but we call it 'Q'. Besides these, each used material peculiar to itself. To study the Gospels in this way, far from diminishing them, greatly enhances their meaning. We begin to see a threefold, and then, adding in the Fourth Gospel, a fourfold gospel of Christ, very much richer in its information and understanding and inspiration than the Gospels seem to be when each is read simply at its own face value.

Then there are the 'form critics' who have attempted to trace the development of the Gospel material through its various stages between the event that originally occurred and the accounts we have of it in the books. Such scholarship does not belittle the meaning: rather, it gives us important insights into the developing faith and understanding of the early church.

There are also the 'textual critics' who are concerned with reconstructing the text itself, because, of course, we do not have the originals. They use the great many versions and quotations and variations that survive, and then try from various principles of procedure to decide what it was that the writers originally wrote.

Professor Young asks:

How can we treat the Bible as Holy Scripture if it is to be subjected to literary or historical criticism like any other book?

How can we submit to the Bible's judgment on us if we insist on submitting it to our critical judgment?

How can we respect and appropriate beliefs and injunctions which we know were the result of past cultural conditioning?

How can we regard the Bible as having sacred authority if it is found to be story and fable, not history?

How can we live in and worship with the Bible – how can we 'perform' the Bible – in a modern world so different from the past which produced and used it?[9]

These questions are not put in order to cast doubt on the validity of biblical scholarship. Nor are they meant to suggest that the Bible is anything less than essential to Christian understanding and practice. They are meant to lead us forward into an understanding of the Bible which is both analytical and inspirational. We want to have it both ways! This is right, for the two ways are complementary. The more we study with our intelligence, the more profoundly we begin to glimpse the truth of God revealed by Christ. The more we love God through

Christ, the more we want to go back to the Bible, which is the literary source of our faith. Whatever truth is revealed cannot by-pass intellectual discipline; yet the intellectual discipline must lead not only to knowledge but to deeper love and commitment. This is the way for an individual disciple; and it has also been the way of the church as a whole. In the early centuries of Christendom, when the church was struggling to formulate its beliefs, there were always the two forces at work: that which came to be known as the *lex credendi* – 'the law of believing', with reference to the intellectual work of learning and thinking things through; and the *lex orandi*, the 'law of praying' – with reference to the day-to-day life of the praying, worshipping church. These were like two horses in harness together, supporting, strengthening, sometimes correcting one another. So it is for ourselves as individuals. The more of the Bible we know, the more we want to love; and the more we love, the more we want to know.

It is like that in the appreciation of art, drama and music. The notion that the disciplined study of a play by Shakespeare, such as students are called upon to make for GCSE, spoils the enjoyment of the play seems to me to be much mistaken. Of course it depends upon the infectious enthusiasm with which the play is taught; but when the conditions are right, knowledge and enjoyment enhance one another. This is certainly true of music. I continue to have a special affection for the pieces I studied at school; and I find now that there are many ways in which studying, performing and listening to music are akin to the study, exposition and inspiration found in the Bible.

In the first place the player tries to be technically efficient in the mastery of the music, able not only to play the notes accurately but also to understand the kind of music being played, whether it is baroque, classical, romantic or modern, so that the interpretation can be true to the composer's intention. The performer would want to know what the composer would have heard in his head or in his own performance, even if there is no certainty in these matters, only a variety of strongly held opinions.

Similarly, the person who expounds the Bible must have an intimate knowledge of the text itself and the world of religious experience from which it comes. He must know if what he is studying was written as myth or idealized history or as a manual of instruction or a pastoral letter or indeed (because they fit no other literary genre) a Gospel. He may need to go into such questions as, 'What is a Gospel? For what and for whom was it written? What are its presuppositions?' He will find himself with no certainties, but he will consider the difficulties and share these and his own insights with his readers. Dogmatic certainty may be attractive to some, but it obstructs the path to truth and it makes the faith of those who depend upon it brittle and unsatisfactory.

A second condition common to musical performers and biblical exponents is that they enter as fully as possible into the experience of the music, the text. The disciplined study just mentioned may inform the performance, but it is not enough by itself. The performer, knowing the music and inspired by it, experiences it for himself and makes it his own as he shares it with his audience. He cannot stay detached and say, 'This is what Beethoven wrote'. He has to be involved in what Beethoven wrote and feel it and even go beyond it, if he is to communicate it to others.

What of the teacher of the Bible and the preacher? It was Jesus himself who quoted the text, 'Physician heal thyself', at the beginning of his address to his townsfolk at Nazareth,[10] and a preacher knows that he comes under the judgment of what he is saying to others and that he must himself experience the impact of the passage he has studied and is expounding. Then he can perform the music of the text and communicate it to other people.

There is another condition that is common to the performance of music and the exposition of scripture: that is the positive participation of those who attend as listeners. Performance makes for a dynamic relationship between composer (author), performer and audience. If this is lacking, and the performer feels himself to be performing to a blank wall or to an audience as inert as a herd of cattle, then the performance, falling on deaf ears, falls flat. The same is obviously true in the theatre, and true again of the sermon. Attentive listening stimulates the performer. Indeed, performance can only be a sharing of experience when there are people there who are sufficiently familiar with the subject matter and who want to hear it. A sermon, like a musical performance, is a shared experience, or it is nothing.

Tortelier was able to share the music of Bach and instruct his pupils to realize it themselves because of his own understanding, love and mastery, but also because of their willing response. It is the same with the exegesis of the Bible. Ignorance or superficiality on the part of the exegete, or prejudice, flippancy or a too easy sentimentality on the part of the listeners, can distort the message. With intelligent and faithful sensitivity on both sides the music of God's love can be wooed from the pages of the Bible like the music of Bach from Tortelier's bow.

7

The Unmusical and the Non-Believer

> Some cry up Haydn, some Mozart,
> Just as the whim bites. For my part,
> I do not care a farthing candle
> For either of them nor for Handel.
> Cannot a man live free and easy,
> Without admiring Pergolesi?
> Or thro' the world with comfort go,
> That never heard of Doctor Blow?
> (Charles Lamb, *Free Thoughts on Several Eminent Composers*).

> *All*:   The music, ho!
> *Cleopatra*:   Let it alone; let's to billiards
> (Shakespeare, *Antony and Cleopatra*).

> The man that hath no music in himself
> Nor is not moved with concord of sweet sounds,
> is fit for treasons, strategems and spoils ...
> The motions of his spirit are as dull as night
> (Shakespeare, *The Merchant of Venice*).

Delius was ferociously and fanatically anti-Christian. His anti-Christianity was suspect, it was that of a rabidly and injudicially prejudiced person who is fiercely opposed to something in which he subconsciously fears there may be a good deal more after all than he is willing to admit (Kaikhosru Shapurji Sorabji, *Mi Contra Fa*).

Captain Horatio Hornblower glowered at the men as he settled down, and began to read. As the thing had to be done, it might as well be done well ... Bush read the lessons in a tuneless bellow as if he were hailing the foretop. Then Hornblower read the opening lines of the hymn, and Sullivan the fiddler played the first bars of the tune. Bush gave the signal for the singing to start ... and the crew opened their throats and roared it out.

But even hymn singing had its advantages. A Captain could often discover a great deal about the spirits of his crew by the way they sang their hymns. This morning either the hymn chosen was specially popular or the crew were happy in the new sunshine, for they were singing lustily, with Sullivan sawing away at an ecstatic obbligato on his fiddle. The Cornishmen among the crew apparently knew the hymn well, and fell upon it with a will, singing in parts to add a leavening of harmony to the tuneless bellowings of the others. It all meant nothing to Hornblower – one tune was the same as another to his tone-deaf ear, and the most beautiful music was to him no more than comparable with the noise of a cart along a gravel road. As he listened to the unmeaning din, and gazed at the hundreds of gaping mouths, he found himself wondering as usual whether or not there was any basis of fact in this legend of music – whether other people actually heard something more than mere noise, or whether he was the only person on board not guilty of wilful self-deception.

Then he saw the ship's boy in the front row. The hymn meant something to him, at least. He was weeping broken-heartedly, even while he tried to keep his back straight and to conceal his emotions, with the big tears running down his cheeks and his nose all beslobbered. The poor little devil had been touched in one way or another – some chord of memory had been struck. Perhaps the last time he heard that hymn was in the little church at home, beside his mother and brothers. He was homesick and heartbroken now. Hornblower was glad for his sake as well as for his own when the hymn came to an end; the next ceremony would steady the boy again.

He took up the Articles of War, and began to read them ...

(C.S. Forester, *Captain Hornblower RN: A Ship of the Line*).

Captain T. W. Marsh, DSO, RN, Commanding Officer of His Majesty's Ship Ranpura (in which I was Captain's Secretary in 1946), did not like music, any music. In fact he thought that all music was a 'racket' which musicians impose upon the gullible public. He would have likened musicians to 'artists' who throw paint at canvas, or poets who write rhyme-less, rhythm-less, meaning-less verse, or sculptors who make grotesque shapes for the fun of it, persuading people that their creations are genuine art. In the same way (he thought) musicians make noises that are disorganized and raucous; and people for appearance's sake pretend to like them. Captain Marsh was a fine seaman – known to be one of the best in the Navy – and a man of clear-eyed integrity. He had the ability to see to the heart of things in matters of judgment and justice: he was a brilliant judge in court-martial cases. Nevertheless I suspect that in the matter of music he was partly imitating his fictional hero, Captain Horatio Hornblower, and partly pulling my leg. However, the honesty of his judgment was demonstrated on a particular occasion when he changed his mind and decided that it was something lacking in himself rather than the knavery of musicians that made him dislike music. The occasion was a concert in Malta which he was obliged to attend because HMS Ranpura (a heavy repair ship which could do anything for anyone – and did so, to the enhancement of British popularity throughout the Greek islands in the Aegean) was providing the electrical equipment needed for this gala occasion. A piano concerto was played (if I remember rightly it was the Emperor), and Captain Marsh noticed that the pianist, playing without music, and the orchestra and its conductor, played in accord with one another all through the forty minutes of its duration. The sheer athleticism of the pianist also delighted him and convinced him that there must be something in music after all, and people like his secretary were not necessarily pretending when they affected to like it.

This brings me to the question of why it is that some people appear to be tone deaf and incapable of enjoying music of any kind; and why there are others too who seem to have no sensibility whatever to religion and to get on very well without it. In both categories there are those whom I number amongst my best friends.

I find no philosophical difficulty with the first category, those who do not like music. Presumably there is something in their brain that prevents them from distinguishing musical notes from cacophonous noise, just as there is something in the brain of other people that makes them colour-blind; or something in the mind which makes some people unexcited by games and others indifferent to the taste of good wine. Thank God that in response to these and many other sources of enthusiasm people are different. The fault comes when a person despises another person's enthusiasm and states arrogantly that 'there is nothing in it', just because he cannot appreciate it himself. If there is enthusiasm, there must be something positive to be enthusiastic about. The difference between the enthusiast and the non-enthusiast is in themselves, not in the object of the enthusiasm. 'Beauty' is said to be 'in the eye of the beholder'. But this saying is only half the truth. Beauty is in the thing that is beautiful, even if it needs the responsive eye of the beholder to be appreciated as beauty. But whereas it is impossible for a sincere person to interpret noise as music if there is no music, only noise, it is nevertheless possible for a tone-deaf person to hear the same sounds and not be able to interpret them as music. So music is music; and it is the difference between the ears of Captain Marsh and his secretary that makes one hear 'just a noise' and the other 'the food of love'.

But there may be more in this than just the physical composition of the brain or a difference in genes. For instance there is the matter of influence, environment and education. Such experiences as being sung to sleep as a baby, joining in family singing as a child, singing in church, singing and playing and listening in school: all these can have a profound effect upon a person's musicality. Some families learn to sing rounds on long car journeys; some primary schools have suitable pieces of classical music played every morning at assembly while the children come into the hall and settle down. After a week of hearing one piece (from the *Water Music*, for instance, or the 'Harvest Song' in the Pastoral Symphony), they find themselves listening to the tune at the time and humming it later without anyone having told them what it is or giving them a lecture on it. One of the great advances in education in the last fifty years has been in music. More children can play more instruments at a higher level of attainment than ever before, though sadly with financial cuts this state of affairs is now on the decline. The cream of it all is seen publicly in the BBC Young Musician of the Year competition, and this shows not only the high standards achieved but also the large number that are achieving them. And what exciting programmes the finalists choose when they perform! It is clear that they have ears for the best music of the twentieth century as well as for the nineteenth-century classics and romantics. But they would not choose this music, and they would not be able to play it, if they had been left alone with no music in their upbringing.

But this is not all. Inborn genes and outside influences cannot alone make a person want to hear music and perform it well. Besides the inner desire, there has to be the steeling of the will to accept and exert the necessary discipline, and the readiness to be open at every stage of development to what is new and challenging. It is easy for someone who likes music to get stuck in the groove of today's opinions; but it is more rewarding to listen, learn and be prepared to enjoy new experiences. With young musicians at competition level, youth orchestras, and countless school concerts, the absorption in the music itself, as well as the technical ability to perform it, is most impressive. One senses the enjoyment – but knows that the preparation for these occasions has not been painless. The ultimate reward comes from internal, continuing *choice* – leading to a high degree of perseverance. But choice can only be exercised within the limits of inborn talent and musical experience.

Can the same be said of the capacity to appreciate religion? If so, is it not very odd that God has made some people instinctively susceptible to religious experience, and others not?

The truth is that individual people do not live their lives separately, uniquely, apart from all others. Every person comes from a combination of two other persons, and through them, many more. The lines, with their accumulated influences, go back to the origins of the human race. Through these lines people inherit particular characteristics and propensities. This is as true of religious responsiveness and moral inclinations as it is of anything else; for in so far as a particular characteristic has been affected by choice, this choice (or series of choices) becomes part of the human scene, casting an influence upon contemporary people and situations as well as affecting people in the future and their situations. In so far as such spreading influences are detrimental, they are part of what in theological jargon is known as 'The Fall'. This doctrine is often misrepresented to mean that people are born into a state of guilt. This must be wrong, because 'guilt' implies a degree of choice which a newborn baby cannot possibly have exercised. The truth is that all people are born into a state that is impaired because of the faults of previous generations of humankind. Some are born into squalor, economic impoverishment, or moral, spiritual or physical depravity as they inherit the flaws of physique and temperament and circumstances from those who have preceded them. People are born into a state of tribal hatred; or radiation; or a tendency to asthma or alcoholism. She has her father's irascibility, he his mother's untidiness. This person was born tone deaf. These children live in a home that is depraved; there is a boy being taught to steal. That man has inbred moral rectitude and an apparent inability to be aware of the presence of God. But there is no 'guilt' until people choose to do what they know to be wrong.

There is disagreement, amongst those who assess individual capacities and tendencies, between those who attribute the differences to heredity and those who attribute them to the influence of environment. There are people, however, whose genius or saintliness or depravity seems to confound either theory held by itself. Furthermore there is a third factor, individual choice, which is affected by both the others, yet can to a certain extent overcome them. What is true of a person's physical strength, intellectual ability and moral attitudes is also true of religious attitudes. These are partly inborn, inherited; partly influenced by education and peer-group attitudes; partly chosen by oneself. But none of these influences is necessarily dominant. Whatever difficulties one inherits, one may still encounter the love of people and learn to recognize the love of God. Similarly, whatever good you inherit, as a child you may be subject to influences which make you fearful of people and God. When I was Chaplain of Lancing I sometimes gave boys who were struggling with religious faith Bertrand Russell's book *Why I am not a Christian*.[1] They were surprised, but generally saw the point that with Russell's upbringing it was almost certain that he would reject Christianity, just as Freud's experience of his own father may have influenced his 'father figure' theories – and his rejection of the 'Father God'. Outside influences upon ourselves of which we are not aware may make us 'tone deaf' to religion: intellectually, emotionally or morally. Choice is then difficult – but not impossible.

This argument, of course, can go either way, and it may be that it is religious people who are believers because of heredity and childhood experience and perverse choice rather than because of any objective truth in what they believe. In that case, the argument is equal: fifteen all. But, as with music, it is the positive rather than the negative that is likely to be true. If someone hears beauty in a string quartet by Bartok it is likely to be beautiful, even if others cannot hear it. If this person believes that religious experience is something real that relates her to God, then it is better evidence for God's existence than someone else's negative experience is evidence against God's existence. Of course the claim to 'religious experience' may well be bogus and merely self-induced. 'False prophets' were a problem in Old

Testament times and in Jesus' day; but Jesus had a clear answer when asked how to distinguish true religious claims from false ones. 'By their fruit you shall know them.'[2] This test of 'true religion' is reiterated throughout the New Testament, particularly by St Paul and in the Epistles of St John, where it is made clear that 'love of God' and 'love of neighbour' are inseparable, and that anyone who claims to love God without loving his neighbour is a liar.[3] More positively, the latter author says, 'My dear friends, let us love one another, because the source of love is God. Everyone who loves is a child of God and knows God, but the unloving know nothing of God, for God is love.'[4] As I write today, the news is about the churches in London that are making costly efforts to help destitute refugees. Those involved are not being self-righteous about it; but I would claim that their practical love for these unfortunate people is the logical outcome of their awareness of God's love for all, volunteers and refugees alike. Any claim to love God by a person who is aware of receiving God's love is very convincing when it is seen that the love of God goes with his or her increasing love of life in all its forms, an increasing love of other people, and a deeper understanding of oneself, one's blessings and faults. I have seen this in men and women, boys and girls, old and young, past and present, famous and unknown. Many people believe in, love and dedicate their lives to God in a way and to a degree that I find positive and reassuring.

What about people of other faiths and denominations who feel equally that through their faith they have a relationship with God? I want to listen to what they have to say, respect it and be open to it. If God exists, then God is one; but until all human beings know all about God it is unlikely that they will have the same insights and understanding. People can deepen their own understanding by sharing and comparing it with other peoples'. But there are certain important *caveats*. It is right to be suspicious of aggressive certainty because this generally goes with ignorance. The experience of a growing faith is like that of inflating a balloon. The more it is blown up through the breath of the Spirit ('spirit' and 'breath' are the same word in the New Testament), the greater it becomes; but the greater, too, the surface area of mystery and uncertainty. It is also right to be suspicious of any creed that makes God so small that only a few human beings come within the orbit of divine favour. God's love is universal, or nothing.

This leaves us with the problem of the differences in circumstance that human beings are born into. Where these are seen in the gaps between rich and poor or the inherited hatred between nations and tribes or anything else by which some people are born at a disadvantage, then the differences are a problem of humanity which it should be everyone's aim to destroy. We should weep for those who are born at a disadvantage and strive at the personal and political level to help them. But people in deprived circumstances do not necessarily find that these circumstances constitute a barrier in the relationship between themselves and God – either now in this world or in eternity. It needs to be remembered that according to Christian belief God through the Spirit of Christ is close to all humanity whatever its circumstances; and that ultimate judgment is in God's hands and may have little to do with the kind of judgments that human beings are inclined to make. We are like golfers with a built-in handicap; and we are judged not by 'par for the course', but by 'par appropriately adjusted by our handicap'. So what matters is what we are born with, what we encounter; and how we cope with these. As human beings we are forbidden to judge other people.[5] The truth is that the poorest and most hurt can respond to God and find love to be real; just as the richest and most splendidly endowed can reject God, fail to find the love, and lose out – certainly in this life, perhaps eternally. If God does exist, then in all circumstances of life people are better living with the realization of God's love than in ignorance of it. That is why the Christian instinct is to want to share the realization of the love of God with other people; not because God is not with them already, but because it is better for people to realize God's existence than not to do so.

It is my personal belief that many people have been blocked intellectually from a realization of God's presence by the arrogance and pious stupidity of ignorant Christians – our fault, in fact, as much as theirs. In this case it is surely right to enter into open discussion as profound and well-informed as we are capable of making it. But such arguments are morally neutral. No one should judge anyone else, for no one knows all the truth, and no one knows another person's way to the truth.

Sometimes, however, there are reasons for not believing which would appear to be influenced by a particular moral stance. I think of the student whose rejection of God – in whom he believed most faithfully two years ago – coincides with his rejection of all authority, particularly that of his parents and teachers; and the person who obviously does not find it convenient to believe in God when he is out committing adultery with his neighbour's wife, or is systematically cheating his firm. One does not know what influences and what precise choices have led to this sort of behaviour, so one does not judge. Ultimately – with understanding that we do not have and consequences that we do not know – God judges. What is certain is that God does not judge people by their intellectual beliefs but by what they are and how they have lived. Maybe a rejecter or a non-believer has responded more sensitively and with greater integrity to the goodness and truth which he perceives, and has produced a better harvest of the 'fruits of the Spirit' than many a so-called believer. Judgment is the consequence of how a person responds to the goodness that is within and the moral challenges that come from without. By that test we all start equal. Indeed those of us born into religious faith may have reason to tremble for the little good that we have done with it. Ultimately, God is just. There may be an interesting mix of people in heaven!

8

Faithful Listening

Serinthia: Your Lordship, I suppose, is fond of music?
Lord Foppington: Oh, passionately on Tuesdays and Saturdays, for then
there is always the best company, and one is not expected to undergo the
fatigue of listening (R.B. Sheridan, *A Trip to Scarborough*).

Come, follow me into the realm of music.
Here is the gate
Which separates the earthly from the eternal.
It is not like stepping into a strange country
As once we did. We soon learn to know everything there
And nothing surprises us any more. Here
Our wonderment will have no end, and yet
From the beginning we feel at home.

At first you hear nothing, because everything sounds.
But now you begin to distinguish between them. Listen.
Each star has its rhythm and each world its beat.
The heart of each separate living thing
Beats differently, according to its needs,
And all beats are in harmony.

– Your inner ear grows sharper. Do you hear
the deep notes and the high notes?
They are immeasurable in space and infinite as to number.
Like ribbons, undreampt-of scales lead from one world to
another,
steadfastly and eternally moved
(Hugh MacDiarmid, *In Memoriam James Joyce*).

A musical experience needs three human beings at least. It requires a
composer, a performer, and a listener; and unless these three take part
together there is no musical experience (Benjamin Britten, on receiving the
first Aspen Award).

Accordingly he always used to shut his eyes while hearing music; thereby
to concentrate his whole being on the single pure enjoyment of the ear
(J.W. von Goethe, *Wihelm Meister*).

A concert in the Leeds Town Hall given by the Warsaw Symphony Orchestra was nearly spoilt for me by a man in the audience who was sitting in the seats behind the orchestra. He was conducting the music to himself. Clearly he was enjoying it so much that he could not keep his hands still as he identified himself with the unfolding drama of Brahms' First Symphony. But the fact that he had to express his feelings physically, together with the fact that I could not look at the orchestra without seeing him, made his behaviour very irritating to me and, I suspect, other people also.

In contrast I have a friend who does not like to see or do anything while he is listening to music. He will never, for instance, watch a performance on television, as I enjoy doing. He says that he does not want to go to live concerts when he can hear the music just as well performed in the comfort of his sitting-room, through the amazing reproduction of his music system. In this way he does not have to be distracted by the sight of the conductor or the performers or people in the audience coughing – or conducting.

Not being such a purist in my listening, I disagree with him. How the *St Matthew Passion* would be reduced if the two choirs were not there facing, questioning, challenging one another! The critical moment in *Fidelio* is when the trumpet sounds off-stage to herald the approach of salvation. The Monteverdi *Vespers* have a golden moment when an echo-choir sings from a remote part of the auditorium; and cathedral music would not be the same if it were not for the two sides, Decani and Cantoris, who sing, as it were, against one another across the aisle. I like to see where the music is coming from, for music has an element of direction in it. I also like to see *who* the music is coming from and, if possible, the instrument that is being played. Jennifer Bate, the organist famous for her playing of Messiaen, likes to have her performance in the organ-loft seen by the audience through a television monitor; and I have no doubt at all that this enhances the audience's enjoyment of her recitals. The personality of a singer and the mood of the music being sung comes through the physical presence of the singer as well as the sound of her voice. This is all part of the musical experience.

The truth is that a listener's perception of music is more than the reception of sound alone. Music comes through space. The sight of its source and a sense of direction do matter. Does one not *feel* music? Some deaf people certainly do. Listening to music is the response of one's whole self. Any kind of distraction hurts because it interrupts the listener's identification with the music, the performer, the composer and the other people present who are equally absorbed. The purist in his sitting-room by himself loses a lot.

Listening is not a passive state, as if one merely absorbs the sound and resonates within oneself. Listening is an *activity* by which one's attention goes out to the music so that the music comes into one's mind. By this two-way process the listener becomes identified with it. No wonder the man in the audience wanted to conduct. Only self-restraint and conventional good manners prevented me from leaping up and conducting myself – as the pizzicato passage ended and it was nearly time for the horn to prepare us for the big tune in the finale of the Brahms First Symphony.

As listening is a two-way process, so is performing. The performer listens with his inward ear to the music and then expresses what he hears on his instrument. This is even true of the beginner learning his first pieces. If he does not listen and listen again to what he is playing, he will never play well. To play is to receive as well as to give, and to listen again to what is being played. Furthermore, do not performers need an audience to perform to? I do not know how performers manage in recording and broadcasting studios. Perhaps they treat the microphone as if it were a person; for multiplied by thousands that is what it in effect is. A professional pianist once came to my deanery to give a recital, and he wanted me to arrange the furniture so that he could enter the house and proceed to the drawing-room and sit at the piano without seeing any human faces at all. He certainly played very well; but I believe that he was glad to know that there were people present when he finished the performance and they applauded. The truth is that a full musical experience requires an openness of mind and an effort of concentration and a readiness to share it with other people. That is why in an audience with others – but never alone in the sitting-room – we clap to show and share our appreciation.

All this is echoed in the exercise of faith.

One Sunday morning after a service in Ripon Cathedral, I was distressed to hear a couple saying to one another, 'We'll never come here again. They don't even let you join in the Lord's Prayer.' There was truth and untruth in their charge. We have many services at which the congregation does join in saying the Lord's Prayer and much else; and even when the choir is supposed to be singing by itself, no one complains if someone joins in aloud, though the lay clerks may look a bit cross. But we do invite everyone present to 'join in' every moment of the service through their listening and the offering of their listening in the worship of God.

'Prayerful listening' is hard work. So is singing hard work. When they perform, singers find that the music takes most of their attention. We listeners attend to God; and by our prayers we do something for the singers which complements what they by their singing are doing for us. So the whole becomes a corporate act of worship in which all participate. In this way the congregation does join in. Indeed, whether a performance is a genuine act of worship depends on the congregation as much as it depends on the singers. The music and words that the choir sings become worship through the prayers and devotion of the other people present.

Music listened to can be offered in worship: but what is the effect of it upon the worshippers themselves? As long as people think that to listen is to be passive they may well think that it has no effect and that by listening alone they are not 'joining in'. But the music is there to help them to join in. This can be done at two levels: first, as they *hear*; secondly, as they *listen*.

To worship hearing is to let the words and music go on and to pray without giving them particular attention. So a person's prayer can be supported by the general effect of the music, its peacefulness, its sonority, its excitement. In this way, without actually following the music a person can adore God helped by its beauty. As prayer does not have to be precise and word-bound, neither does worship through music have to be tune-bound. Nevertheless, the hearing of suitable music during worship can help to make music and the worship spirit-bound and God-ward.

However, there is much to be said – both in the context of

worship and at other times – for the practice of listening to
music with attention; following with the mind and identifying
with what is being played; taking part inwardly in the development, the ebb and flow, the tensions, the yearning, the contrasting moods and colours and emotions that the music can
evoke. The difference between merely hearing and listening to
music is like the difference between being present at a cricket
match and reading a book throughout, on the one hand, and
watching the game with its unfolding drama and so feeling part
of it, on the other. There is no law against reading books at
cricket matches, but you miss the cricket. You can read a book
throughout a concert but in doing so you miss most of the
music. However, listening can be difficult. It requires concentration and an openness of mind that welcomes new sounds and
new combinations of sound, and the perseverance to discern
what it is that the music is saying. If the idiom is new, the
harmonies strange, the music apparently tuneless ('But it's all
tune,' I once said angrily to a friend who complained that he
could not hear a tune in Walton's Viola Concerto) and shape-
less, it is difficult, and several hearings may be necessary to sort
it out. But the reward can be great. Faithful listening opens a
person to musical experiences that enhance the whole of life.

I had a friend whose hobby was listening to music. She loved
Handel and Bach and Mozart and Beethoven and Brahms and
Tchaikovsky and Gilbert and Sullivan. 'But I can't stand
Britten,' she said. 'Modern, discordant stuff.' She came to
Noyes Fludde in Pershore Abbey and 'quite liked it', but could
not begin to like *Curlew River*, which simply reinforced her feel-
ings. 'But,' I wanted to say to her, 'You do not listen. In this
respect you are closed, faithless'.

I could have added, 'Ephphatha: be opened', which was
what Jesus said to the deaf and partially dumb man in the story
in Mark 7.31–37. Perhaps that word was remembered and
recorded by Mark in the Aramaic which Jesus spoke because it
continued to be used just like that when the Christian gospel
was told. Christianity was proclaimed as the gospel that 'opens'
people in ears and mind: to hear and so to speak; to receive and
so to give. One kind of 'opening' and 'closing' goes with
another. Faith is being opened so that one can say 'Yes, please'
to new music and much else. It involves trusting in the honest

intentions of composer and performer and speaker; and then listening to what they have to say.

Faith is saying 'Yes please': to the beauty of the world; to the insights and good sense and enthusiasms and the needs and longings of other people; to God, ever-present, ever-loving. Exercising faith in God is like listening to music. It is the difficult matter of attention. Both consist of a positive action by which one makes oneself receptive: in listening, to whatever one is listening to; in faith, to God.

This is what is meant by 'faith' in the Gospel stories. When Jesus commends a person's faith, he is not referring to a blind belief in the impossible. He is referring to some trustful action by which a person makes himself or herself or someone else receptive to God's healing love. So the woman with the haemorrhage pressed through the crowd and 'touched' Jesus in faith when everyone else was also touching him, so thick was the crowd. Her faithful touch was noticed over and above all the pushing and shoving; and she was healed.[1] When another woman came in off the streets and in penitence and love anointed Jesus' feet with very expensive ointment, Jesus showed up the difference between her loving generosity and the inhospitality of his host and said that because of her faith she was forgiven.[2] It is a good exercise to take the Gospel stories where faith is mentioned and analyse what it is in the action of the people being healed that constitutes their or someone else's faith: approach, obedience, penitence, bringing, touching, listening, persistence. Always the people concerned *do* something by which they make themselves able to *receive* the gift of Christ.

So faith is exercised through a threefold process. The person of faith is 1. active, 2. receptive (and so 'actively receptive'), and then, as a result, 3. active again.

I have used the phrase 'actively receptive', putting the first two parts of the process of faith together, because it is difficult to separate them. As the listener actively sets himself to listen and so, through his ears and mind, receives the music, so in faith a person prays to God through a positive act of will and thus opens his mind to receive some sense of God's presence. This exercise can be performed through everyday experiences as the person of faith learns to find God coming through all that is beautiful and all that is painful in life. The beauty of God is

received through the awareness of beautiful things; the love of
God through the love of people; the suffering of God-in-Christ
through all that hurts. This is the faith that gives the God-
dimension to all living experiences, as all that is received is
accepted as coming from God, and all that is done is offered to
God. The result is a growing sense of 'God out there and God
within', taking charge of one's motivation, so that one wants to
do the will of God in one's daily living.

There is another complementary way of exercising faith
known as 'contemplation'. This is done at a suitable time and in
a suitable place and is the conscious mode of 'actively receiving'
knowledge of the presence of God. It is a difficult exercise
because of the many distractions of sight and sound that keep
coming into the mind, and one's thoughts that keep wandering
away. The way to proceed is not to try to drive the distractions
away but to gather them in and to hold them up, as they occur,
to God. Here there is an important difference between listening
to music and praying. The only thing you can do with distractions in music is to try to ignore them and concentrate harder
on the music. But in prayer the distractions are part of the God-
given world and the God-given self that one is offering. They are
part of God's gifts to us, as they are part of what we give back
to God. This is true of the bad as well as the good. If the cause
of the distraction is bad, all the more does it need to be taken,
accepted and offered. But when one gives oneself time, and
when one can find a place in which there is as little distraction
as possible, and when there is something to aid one's concentration, such as a lighted candle or a mental image of Jesus or a
physical object – then, gradually, a sense of the presence of God
takes over. As one holds oneself up to God, one finds oneself
held by God. The self one holds up is the whole self of body,
mind and spirit, with all feelings, sensations and those things
that were being considered distractions. That which holds is all-
embracing love. For a second, ten seconds, half, three-quarters
of an hour (one hardly knows the difference: time is not important) the worshipper is filled with the love which is God – and
nothing else matters. For most people this is a rare experience,
though it can be striven for often. The effect of it lasts – as
music, wholly or partly heard, goes on singing in the mind.

In music the third part of the process is to try to perform –

which only some can do. In the practice of faith, whether this is
done by finding the God-dimension in the everyday experiences
of life, or in time specifically set aside for prayer (both are
necessary, though some will find one, some the other, harder to
do), the third part of the process is what one is called to do
in the gritty world of everyday life. This involves all work,
behaviour and relationships. It is essential. In this respect men
and women who pray in faith are called upon to be performers
of their faith in their daily lives.

The 'activity of reception' was described in terms of an
individual person at prayer. But 'individual' does not mean
'private'. Just as people are called to perform their faith in daily
living, so are they called to share it with other people in the
corporate act of worship. Their presence will be an occasion for
their God-given love to overflow to others and strengthen the
whole act of worship. It makes all the difference to a church
service if some worshippers have been trying to pray faithfully
and receptively to God in the course of the week.

This is important because there are many people whose
awareness of God comes not so much from times of personal
prayer and contemplation as by acts of worship in church. It is
true that there can be much to distract in the course of a service.
Any self-centredness on the part of clergy, choir, servers or
members of the congregation causes distraction. Cold, stuffy
heat, discomfort, distract; so does bad music, sloppy ritual and
poor reading. Wandering thoughts and the cares of life distract.
But all these can be gathered and offered penitently or thank-
fully to God. Meanwhile there is much in a service of worship
to direct the worshipper's attention to God: the words of the
liturgy; the reading of scripture; the beauty of the building, the
music, the flowers; the love of people around; the solemn words
of forgiveness and blessing; the bread and wine of the sacrament. Worshippers are called to 'listen', to attend to God
through all this; to find one another in the love of God; to find
God through the love of one another. It is not always possible
to measure success by feelings at the time of the service itself;
it can be the after-effect that matters. But sometimes – as an
unsolicited bonus – a worshipper who comes to give and not
just to receive can feel uplifted and strengthened in spirit.

As in individual devotion, the worshipper in church finds the two-way process of giving and receiving in the course of a service. The third part (the 'activity') is what people do together as 'the church' – which St Paul dares to describe as the 'body of Christ' – in the neighbourhood. There may be events which express the affection people have for one another as a result of God's love for them. More important, there may be activities by which people – individually and corporately – 'perform' their faith in the neighbourhood and the world beyond. Archbishop Michael Ramsey once said, 'A parish that lives for itself will die by itself.' This is true of all individual Christians and of all groups of Christians of all churches and denominations in that complex, global association of men and women which we call 'the church'. All are called together through their individual instruments, their individual voices, in their various groupings, to perform the symphony of the kingdom of heaven, God's will to be done on earth. We fall short of this; but are still being commanded to try to succeed.

In the liturgy of the eucharist there is a moment that particularly expresses and creates the sense of 'community together in the love of God' which is one of the objects of Christian worship. That is 'the peace' at which worshippers symbolically declare the 'peace of the Lord' to one another. Not everyone likes it; and some people like it so much that they go over the top about it, like the Australian bishop in the congregation at a eucharist in the chapel of Brisbane Theological College who at the peace hugged my wife and told her a long Irish joke, thus creating a nice example of distraction for her to 'offer up'. The truth is that some people by their God-given nature are inclined to be personal and private in their devotions, whilst others are inclined to be outgoing and socially orientated in theirs. There is no singular virtue in either, and most people are a mixture. All people need to know themselves, the positive as well as the negative aspects, and to discipline and balance what they are in the service of God and the love of other people. Worship must be both personal and shared, for the fullest experience of the music of God's love.

As for the couple who wanted to join in the singing of the choir services in Ripon Cathedral, I will simply say that in most churches it is right to join in the singing because this is part of the 'performance' of faith. But in cathedral worship they could find that 'faithful listening' will not only open their hearts and minds to very beautiful music; it will also create a 'Jacob's ladder' of music which brings angels of God from heaven to earth and from earth to heaven.

9

Music for Worship

But if someone has been introduced from earliest childhood, as I have been, into the mystical sanctuary of our religion; if there, if you did not yet know how to cope with your dark but urgent feelings, you waited for worship with an utterly fervent heart, without really knowing what you wanted, and went away with a lighter and uplifted heart without really knowing what you had had; if you thought how lucky were those who had knelt down at the moving *Agnus Dei* and received the eucharist, and at the communion the music spoke in quiet joy from the hearts of those kneeling there, *Benedictus Qui Venit*, then it is all quite different (Mozart in a conversation reported in Hans Küng, *Mozart. Traces of Transcendence*).

Henchard did not take the trouble to reply for a few moments, and his eyes rested on his stretched-out legs and boots. 'Yes,' he said at length; 'that's true. I've been down in spirit for weeks; some of ye know the cause. I am better now; but not quite serene. I want you fellows of the choir to strike up a tune; and what with that and this brew of Standidge's, I am in hopes of getting altogether out of my minor key.'

'With all my heart,' said the first fiddle. 'We've let back our strings, that's true; but we can soon pull 'em up again. Sound A, neighbours, and give the man a stave.'

'I don't care a curse what the words be,' said Henchard. 'Hymns, ballets, or rantipole; the Rogue's March or the cherubim's warble – 'tis all the same to me if 'tis good harmony, and well put out.'

'Well – hey, hey – it may be we can do that, and not a man among us that have sat in the gallery less than twenty year,' said the leader of the band. 'As 'tis Sunday, neighbours, suppose we raise the Fourth Psa'am, to Samuel Wakely's tune, as improved by me?'

'Hang Samuel Wakely's tune, as improved by thee!' said Henchard. 'Chuck across one of your psalters – old Wiltshire is the only tune worth singing – the psalm-tune that would make my blood ebb and flow like the sea when I was a steady chap. I'll find some words to fit en.' He took one of the psalters and began turning over the leaves ...

'Now then,' he said, 'Psalm the Hundred-and-Ninth, to the tune of Wiltshire: verses ten to fifteen. I gi'e ye the words.'

'I know the Psa'am – I know the Psa'am!' said the leader hastily; 'but I would as lief not sing it. 'Twasn't made for singing. We chose it once when the gipsy stole the pa'son's mare, thinking to please him, but Pa'son was quite upset. Whatever Servant David were thinking about when he made a Psalm that nobody can sing without disgracing himself, I can't fathom! Now then the Fourth Psalm, to Samuel Wakely's tune, as improved by me.'

"Od seize your sauce – I tell ye to sing the Hundred-and-Ninth to Wiltshire, and sing it ye shall!' roared Henchard. 'Not a single one of all the droning crew of ye goes out of this room till that Psalm be sung!' He slipped off the table, seized the poker, and going to the door placed his back against it. 'Now then, go ahead, if you don't wish to have your pates broke!'

'Don't 'ee, don't 'ee take on so! – as 'tis Sabbath-day, and 'tis Servant David's words and not ours, perhaps we don't mind for once, hey?' said one of the terrified choir, looking round upon the rest. So the instruments were tuned, and the comminatory verses sung (Thomas Hardy, *The Life and Death of the Mayor of Casterbridge*).

Last week a row blew up between a church choir and a vicar. The choir did not like a hymn the vicar had chosen, so it resigned *en bloc*. The extraordinary thing about this row was not that it happened, but that it became national news, splurged abroad by the media, both press and radio. The local importance of such an unfortunate dispute is obvious. People feel strongly about musical taste and worship. If you put the two together and fail to agree, then you are in trouble. But why should this local affair be considered to be of importance to the nation? Is it that the nation likes to gloat over a family row in a village church? Or is it because the media recognizes a residual feeling in all of us about taste and tradition, about making faith 'relevant', about village churches – and what goes on in them (even if we ourselves are never likely to enter their doors), about old-fashioned choirs in cassocks and ruffs, about vicars: about the worship of God. It must be newsworthy that people still worship God and feel so strongly about something that most of us gave up in childhood. Certainly, the story is still rumbling on. People are writing to the press, and ringing up phone-in programmes on the radio. Perhaps the media pundits – in the absence of a good piece of political sleaze – are on to something.

Those of us who are seriously involved in the worship of God have to give a lot of thought to it. As we make our choices, there are different pressures upon us, resulting in much tension. For on the one hand we are thinking about people; and on the other hand we are thinking about God. We want to have music that people can relate to and enjoy, but people vary. Different people come from different cultures, in music and language. Some are bound by traditions; others are unaware of them. People are influenced by their age, their peer group, their education. Some think of the music as something put on to draw more people into church; so they want it to be as appealing as possible. Others think of it as something that those who come to church do together in the course of their response to God; so their chief aim is to make it worthy of God.

But who can judge what is 'worthy'? Is it a matter of musical taste? Or sincerity of heart? If the latter, what sort of music is 'sincerity' best expressed by? Is it more or less sincere to 'listen positively' (as described in Chapter 8)? Or to sing loudly? Or to do just what one 'feels'? Or to shake one's body and clap one's hands? If these questions could be about private choice, then they would be easy for us to answer, each according to taste. But as worship is something we do together, we are bound to be affected by other peoples' choice. It can be disquieting if you are a 'faithful listener' to find yourself worshipping God amidst a congregation of 'shakers and clappers'. And if you like to express the exuberance of worship by singing loudly and/or with physical actions, then cathedral-like 'listening' can seem very empty.

In 1993 the General Synod of the Church of England produced an excellent and comprehensive report on the subject of music in worship, called *In Tune with Heaven*.[1] This has been widely studied at diocesan and parish level, and some dioceses (such as Ripon) have set up working parties to help implement its practical suggestions. Saturday morning workshops, a pooling of ideas and resources, advice for amateur organists and choir-trainers, the encouragement of instrumental groups and soloists to complement the organ: all these can be made available; and with this report to help and with new enthusiasm for good and lively music in church, things are very much better today than they were ten years ago. In general the quality of worship has been much enhanced.

It is not my intention in this chapter to re-examine the practical issues; nor do I want to give lists of what is available. I wish, however, to examine the fundamental question, 'What kind of music is best for worship?' – even if I know that there is no simple answer. There are three points I have to make: first, that there is a wide spread of cultural differences amongst worshippers of all religions, denominations and nationalities. These must be allowed for. Secondly, different pieces of music express different moods. These moods must be the right ones for the purposes of worship. Thirdly, music does not only express moods; it reinforces, even creates them. Thus it affects the feelings and attitudes of the worshippers.

1. In the matter of culture, we find bewildering differences in type and taste which represent the pluralism within human society, making barriers that are hard to cross. The music of India, Africa, South America, China, Japan; the folk music of Ireland or Eastern Europe; classical music that has developed in the West; the jazz of New Orleans; today's many kinds of 'pop': these are the product of their own culture. Whether you like any one of them or not depends upon your cultural upbringing and your readiness to go beyond it. In this respect we all start from a different position due to our heredity and upbringing. Sometimes a composer in one tradition ventures forth into another and achieves a rich syncretism. Thus Bartok and Vaughan Williams, reared in the classical tradition, were able to use the folk traditions of their native countries with great effect. Many composers – Dvořák, Gershwin, Ravel, Walton – used jazz idioms; and in *African Sanctus* Fanshawe actually lifted African music into the piece by recording it in the jungle and then having it played in the course of performance. These differences of cultural tradition and their occasional combination are matters of fact, not of judgment. It is not sensible to say that one culture is 'better' than another; they are just different. But it is still necessary to remember that individual people and congregations are all to a certain extent 'culture bound'; and this affects the question of the music they can respond to in their worship.

2. A more difficult problem is posed by the different moods of music: that is, what the music is 'saying'. To speak of the 'mood' is not to imply that a piece of music literally 'represents' some object, scene or person. Debussy does not make us see the light of the moon, nor Holst the planets, nor Elgar his friends in the Enigma Variations. Beethoven does pause to give us some birds in the middle of the Pastoral Symphony (surely, with a smile); but there is no need to go along with the ludicrous professor in E.M. Forster's *Howard's End* when he gives a

lecture on music and meaning and describes the goblins he sees prancing around during Beethoven's Fifth Symphony.

Nevertheless, the music of *Clair de Lune* does conjure up something of the cold and peaceful luminosity of a moonlit night; Elgar does say something about the character of his friends: one a rumbustious fellow, one rather melancholy, and another all perfume, frills and lace. It is possible to feel the mood of music and to find oneself transported to other categories of experience, such as love, happiness, the seaside, or 'a night on a bare mountain'.

I think of the effect upon me of: Stanford's *Magnificat* in G Major with the youthful ecstasy of the solo boy; the sprightly happiness of Ronald Perrin's *Magnificat* in A Flat; the measured certainty of Purcell's *Magnificat* in G Minor which over-spills into a long, rapturous Amen at the end of the *Nunc Dimittis*; the tentative joy of Howells' *Gloucester Service* which soars to conviction at the beginning of the *Gloria*; the confidence of Poulenc's *Gloria* in the Mass in G Major, written shortly after his conversion to Christianity.

And I think of Britten's *Michelangelo Sonnets*, which speak of love in all its moods: passionate, surprised, impulsive, deeply hurt, resigned, fulfilled, in peace.

I think too, of the 'happiness together' effect of music that gets people dancing, mixes them up, unites them as they step to tune and rhythm and go through a prescribed routine of moving patterns into which individuals and couples fit, whether they glide, prance, hobble or strut; and the overwhelming effect of passion, fidelity, infidelity, jealousy, the climax of love, the hurt and the tragedy in the six hours or so it takes to be transported into the world of larger-than-life characters who fight their puny fights against fate and circumstance. I am thinking of *Tristan and Isolde*.

Those who heard them will never forget the effect of the bagpipes at Winston Churchill's funeral, as the procession wound its way through the streets of London. The martial notes wailed over the drone bass in triumphant sadness. The nation wept but was proud.

Indeed the martial playing of bugles, pipes and drums, as St Paul himself affirms,[2] can urge soldiers to battle and keep them going forward together to fight.

There is also the music of protest – which is the secret of Elvis Presley's deifying popularity. Clearly he played and sang for his generation music which challenged the conventions then – and is still very powerful today.

3. Music also *creates* moods. This is true of much that has been said above and it leaves one wondering whether the mood was there first and the music nicely fitted it (as in Churchill's funeral procession), or whether there was no mood at all until the music 'created' it. The word 'reinforce' fits both possibilities.

Last week I received with my *BBC Music Magazine*[3] a CD of music celebrating the October Revolution in Russia: Shostakovich's Second Symphony and Prokofiev's *Cantata for the 20th Anniversary of the October Revolution.* Each may have been written with the composer's political tongue uneasily in his cheek, and the cantata was forbidden to be performed in Stalin's day despite the jingoism of the words. I wish that I had heard the music before I had read about it, because if I had not known the circumstances and the meaning of the words in both works, I might not have felt the force of them and the power of the music that contained them so strongly. I found myself repelled. But who knows? If a different explanation had been given to me first, I might have liked these works. Certainly they are immensely effective. I am grateful to the *Music Magazine* for introducing them to me.

With slightly diminished confidence I turn to some music whose effect I dare to say is bad, evil: not because it is incompetent and fails to speak, but because it expresses feelings that are degrading. This is stormy water, but I am judging by the effect that I know the music has on me and the effect I can see that it has on other people. Whether one happens to like it or dislike it is beside the point. The point is, what this music does to people.

As an example I cite some music and a dance that were very evil in their effect. They are from *A Tale of Two Cities* by Charles Dickens, a description of the murderous hordes in Paris who were dancing out their blood-lust as they scoured the streets screaming for victims to be sent to the guillotine.

Presently she heard a troubled movement and a shouting coming along which filled her with fear. A moment after-

wards, and a throng of people came pouring round the
corner by the prison wall, in the midst of whom was the
wood-sawyer hand in hand with The Vengeance. There could
not be fewer than five hundred people, and they were
dancing like five thousand demons. There was no other music
than their own singing. They danced to the popular
Revolution song, keeping a ferocious time that was like
a gnashing of teeth in unison. Men and women danced
together, women danced together, men danced together, as
hazard had brought them together ... Suddenly they stopped
..., paused, struck out the time afresh, formed into lines the
width of the public way, and, with their heads low down and
their hands high up swooped screaming off. No fight could
have been half so terrible as this dance ... This was
the Carmagnole. As it passed, leaving Lucie frightened and
bewildered in the doorway of the wood-sawyer's house, the
feathery snow fell as quietly and lay as white and soft, as if it
had never been.[4]

Was it the music that had that evil effect? Or was it the blood-
lust of the crowd that made the music and dancing so evil
on this occasion? It was both. Music is like a sacrament. It
expresses and creates a mood. This particular music and dance
expressed the evil of the situation. But it also reinforced that evil
in those who were already bent on it and, maybe, drew into it
those who otherwise would have been no more than bystanders.

I once saw a drummer on television improvising brilliantly in
a way that spoke to me of depraved depths of ultimate nega-
tivity. The effect on me was evil. Sometimes rock music is
played so hideously loudly that all thought and all possibility of
human communication are shattered. Aggressive, unbridled
rhythm takes over, and those who hear it and dance to it
are reduced to a world of sheer, beating noise. Is this just
exuberance, a happy release of high spirits? Or is it the expression of natural and justifiable aggression? Or is it actually
depraving, as it seems to me? I remember a mother writing to a
newspaper a year ago complaining that her son had been drawn
into the drug scene by music like this.

There is also music which you could call 'background'
because it goes on while you are doing other things. You are

aware of it, but for reasons to do with yourself and your occu-
pation, or for reasons to do with the music itself, you do not
attend to it. Such music used to be played for the radio programme *Music While You Work* to encourage people in
factories and on the land in their war effort. Tuneful, easy on
the ear, it makes no demands but eases part of your consciousness. Nowadays this is musak, played in superstores and in lifts:
sweet-smelling musical wallpaper. But there is also music that
has been written with serious intent to 'fill the space'. This is
'ambient', 'new-age' music, which puts the emphasis on the
sensation of sound (enhanced by electronic skills) rather than
movement and form. Why have background, ambient music at
all? Because it engages and soothes part of one's mind and
induces helpful relaxation. But could it not also be to keep away
the dreaded silence, reminding one of the town-child who was
taken into the depths of the countryside and did not like it.
What didn't he like? 'The 'orrible 'ush.' Yet, 'There was silence
in heaven.'[5] Can our souls grow without it?

There is also 'minimalist' music which engages yet frees the
mind through repetition, development and subtle variation. In a
religious context one thinks of Tibetan monks chanting end-
lessly with their prayer-wheels revolving; and the Christian
chants at Taizé with their musical 'canon' and Latin words
repeated again and again like the passing waters of a slowly
moving river.

The effect of music also depends upon the responsiveness and
mood of the listener and the purpose she or he has for listening.
Some music can be good in one context and intolerable in
another: good to this group who have come to dance, inappropriate for those who are waiting for a performance of *King
Lear*; good for doing the ironing to, distracting if you are
writing a letter; fun for the barn dance after your daughter's
wedding but not what you want when you go to a recital at the
Wigmore Hall; hot stuff for a charity concert in Wembley
Stadium, as it is being broadcast to a million potential givers in
their sitting-rooms but not necessarily right for a service of
worship.

At a meeting of diocesan liturgical officers in the 1970s, Michael
Ramsey, the Archbishop of Canterbury, was asked what he

considered to be the best way of introducing the new forms of
worship to parish congregations. 'Do not ask people what they
like,' he said, 'because what a person likes is nothing more than
a subjective judgment acquired at mother's knee. What matters
is what serves best to fulfil the particular function for which it
is being designed.' 'For instance,' he added (eyes flashing, eye-
brows wagging), 'if I am asked which form of confession I
prefer, I would undoubtedly say "Series Two", because it makes
much less of my sinfulness than does the General Confession in
the Book of Common Prayer. But that does not make it the
better prayer! So,' he went on, 'we should ask them which form
of the confession is the best expression of their penitence; which
form of intercession most helps the congregation to pray for the
needs of the world; which form of service best emphasizes the
meaning of the word "eucharist" ("Thanksgiving"); which form
of service helps us best to express our corporate life together as
we gather at the Lord's table ...'

In choosing music for worship, we should ask the same sort
of questions. Not 'What do I like best?' (Beethoven Late
Quartets) or 'What does she like best?' (Heavy Rock), but
'What helps the congregation most in the many facets of
worship? What helps us to know God better?'

Some may also ask, 'What sort of music will bring more
people to church?'. But there is a *caveat* here. There is music
which will draw people to itself, but if it cannot also draw
people to God, then it may not be right for worship. People
would be better off looking for it in a concert hall or at a rock
festival. But there is the other side of this, expressed in the
question, 'Does some music actually deter people from going to
church?' If people come to hear their banns read, for instance,
or if they are brought by a friend, or if they come because of
some personal or national occasion, the music they encounter
may help them, or deter them utterly from ever coming again.

What sort of music does which of these things? I have already
said that it depends upon the cultural presuppositions of the
people concerned; also upon the mood – and therefore the effect
– of the music being played and sung. But it will also depend
upon the performance, and one has to say that some of the
music performed in church is very poor indeed. Badly performed music – whether it be by choir or congregation –

expresses an attitude of not really caring about the quality of what is being offered to God. Of course there is a limit to peoples' competence, and some people sing badly but with genuine sincerity. But is not sincerity best expressed by people who are trying in choir and congregation to make the music as good as it can be? Some people may not be aware that they are singing out of tune, like a curate of mine (now a provost) who was indignant when it was suggested that singing in tune was not necessarily part of the gift conferred at his ordination. But the effect of a congregation singing well generally comes from the fact that its members are singing *together;* and this is something everyone can do.

The quality of performance is important in every facet of liturgical worship: reading, music, ritual, the physical arrangements and decoration of the church, and much else. Sincerity, spiritual alertness, the desire to find and worship God, the rapt listening to God through silence, word, music and sacrament: all this is hindered when people play their parts in a way that is slovenly or self-centred. It is all helped when people do what they have to do as well as they can do it. When people join a worshipping congregation from outside, unused to liturgical forms, they may be confused or mystified or drawn into fellowship, drawn indeed towards God. But they will be deterred if they find that what is being done is being done badly.

What sort of music draws people only to itself? What sort of music repels? What sort of music draws people together? What sort of music lifts people up to God? An answer to these questions can only be subjective, and what will help some may hinder others. The list I am about to write is my own: other people can have their thoughts and make their lists, and share them and compare them with other members of their congregation. It is the sort of exercise best done by parish music and worship groups.

I want music that will draw me with others into that dimension of timelessness in which one can find God, but which is not a substitute for God.

I want music that says something of God's presence in the everyday affairs of human life, yet is not so blatant that it makes God-filled life seem banal instead of glorious.

Put another way, I want music that sings the truth that God

is with us and in us in all things great and small; yet that God is holy, unearthly, sublime. I remember that pile of stones which Jacob used as a pillow; and when he woke up after a very strange dream he exclaimed, 'How awful is this place: this is none other than the house of God, this is the gateway of heaven.'[6]

I want music which gives me and other members of the congregation a sense of 'being together': not in a mere, human 'chumminess', but in that interlocking of spirit which is the particular gift of the Spirit of God.[7]

I want music which helps me to find something of that inner peace described as 'the peace of God that passes all understanding': but this is not the same thing as complacency and self-satisfaction; nor does it necessarily go with a trouble-free life.

I want music that stimulates, drives, fills me with zest and fervour, but does not merely titillate or excite. (The test is that true Christian zest leads to the love and service of other people.)

I want music that speaks of the suffering of Christ and the suffering of the world, but not sentimentally or morbidly. If it makes me feel penitent and sorrowful, all the better. But self-conscious wallowing (individual or collective) in the sins of oneself or other people is not good.

I want music that demands the attention of the mind, but is not beyond my capacity to grasp.

I want music that makes emotional demands; but this must be to lift me out of myself, not to allow me to be self-absorbed or self-indulgent.

I want music that sounds a note of joy, yes; but this is much more than happiness. Happiness can be complacent and self-centred. Joy makes one yearn for what is even more beautiful and joyful. It makes one reach up and long to be filled with God's love.

Music must lift me out of myself and yet give me back to myself. I want its harmony to harmonize me: within myself, with other people, with all God's creation, with God.

Maybe there is no such music on earth, only in heaven. But in worship, are we not aspiring to heaven? We should expect a lot from music in worship. Other peoples' lists will be different from mine, just as their estimate of the effect of different kinds of music will be different from mine. But one principle is common to all who love music and love God. Music is the means. The object is God.

10

Playing and Living

Algernon: Did you hear what I was playing, Lane?
Lane: I didn't think it polite to listen, Sir.
Algernon: I'm sorry for that for your sake. I don't play accurately – any-
one can play accurately – but I play with wonderful expression. As far as
the piano is concerned, sentiment is my forte. I keep science for Life (Oscar
Wilde, *The Importance of Being Earnest*).

The notes I handle no better than many pianists. But the pauses between
the notes – ah, that is where the art resides (Arthur Schnabel, reported in
Chicago Daily News, 1958).

> Music do I hear.
> Ha, ha; keep time! How sour sweet music is
> When time is broken and no proportion kept.
> So it is in the music of men's lives
> (Shakespeare, *Richard the Second*).

The metronome has no value ... for myself I have never believed that my
blood and a mechanical instrument go well together (Brahms, *Letter to
George Henschel*).

In this chapter I wish to consider the playing of music and the
living of Christianity, recognizing that the music of God's love
is not just to be basked in; it is something to do. How do we do
it well? There is plenty of advice around: there are books to
read, teachers to be taught by, precepts and rules and codes of
discipline to follow, scales and strengthening exercises to
practise, periods of sustained effort, prayer, fasting and self-
denial to undergo. What is the object of these? Do they become
ends in themselves? Do they really help? Are the human guides
people who are ahead of us on the way towards excellence? Do
their methods give us the particular guidance that we need? Or
are they experts who would have us all be the same? Are they
trying to make up in us what they lack in themselves, like
sergeant-majors who scream at their squads to get from them an

unattainable perfection? (I have been reading about Terry Waite's experience in the Guards.)

Arthur Schnabel was once asked by an admirer whether he played 'in time' or 'as he felt'. He answered, 'I feel in time'. The question is a real one. There is a school of thought according to which the tempo in baroque and classical music should not be changed within a piece, except at obvious points such as the *rallentando* at the end. On the other hand there are those who are happy to 'borrow' time here over some lovely phrase, hasten it there at a *crescendo*, and slow down somewhere else so as to give the notes more space. I have a recording of an Italian clarinetist playing Mozart's Clarinet Quintet doing just that, infuriatingly, to my ear. I can remember, too, listening to recordings of Beethoven Piano Concertos on the old 78s with my friends at school and pouring collective scorn on those pianists who committed the sin of 'pc', 'pace-change'. Only Walter Gieseking won our full approval. His performances were crisp and clear and unrelenting – with no sentimental pcs. Romantic music, which we affected to despise, has built-in pcs. That includes Elgar; but he always gives precise instructions about these. The performer is not expected to play just 'by feeling'. So what was Arthur Schnabel's view?

He might have said: 'There is no question. I feel in time. I feel either the strict tempo as set, or the tempo with its in-built flexibility as intended by the composer. It is not a matter of personal whim. The music itself dictates. I feel the music. I go along with it. There are no "rules" except in the nature of the music itself. I do not dogmatize about never changing the tempo. Nor do I allow my feelings at the moment to dictate, except in as far as these feelings are true to the music itself.'

Easily said, until someone like the Italian clarinetist with the luscious tone disagrees about what 'the music' does in fact demand. Who is to say that he is not right? That the ebb and flow of tempo may be just what Mozart had in mind? And that it is only modern dogmatism that demands a strict, perhaps restricting beat?

There is a Prelude by Bach, No. VIII in E flat minor, in Book I of the Forty-Eight Preludes and Fugues. In terms of technique it is not difficult to play, as long as you can get your fingers round the decorations, and once you are used to playing in all those flats. But the piece is full of temptations to the over-indulgent. The simple, pleading tune is undergirded by massive, luxuriant chords that spread upwards from the bass like deep pools of water. It is tempting to linger by these pools, gaze into their depths and feel their stillness and the faintly rippling reflections on their surface. But the pools are not the music separately, by themselves. They join one another as the very slow three-minims-in-the-bar stream takes the music gently onwards from pool to pool to the three-part fugue beyond. If the forward impetus is lost, the prelude just wallows in lazy sensuality. 'Keep it moving' I say to myself as the tune continues to plead and the chords get deeper and stronger. Towards the end, the tune allows itself to slow down and close so that the fugue subject can arise, clear, calm and emphatic, taking us out into the breadth and depth of the sea beyond. So I feel it; but I have heard performances that, far from lingering over the spread chords, splash through them in a perfuctory way like a busy spaniel, disturbing any thoughts of peace and beauty that may be around. 'Wait,' I want to say. But there is no time for waiting. Here comes the fugue.

People sometimes treat religious ceremonies in a similarly perfunctory manner, behaving as if the only thing that matters is to get them over quickly. Others are tempted to indulge in religious practices, making them into a kind of opiate, not, indeed, to 'feed the people', but to lull themselves away from the urgency of God's will. One's particular religious indulgence may be the glory of cathedral music, or the glamour of high-church ritual, or the sleepy quiet of the eight o'clock service, or exuberant singing and arm-waving, or the stifling atmosphere of a religious in-group, or the giving or receiving of counsel; each to his need. But the purpose of these is missed if people do not go on and through them and obey Christ's terse command to the lawyer, after telling him the story of the Good Samaritan, 'Go and do likewise'; and to his followers, 'Love one another: proclaim the kingdom: follow me.'[1]

The practices just mentioned may all be good in themselves, but they need to be thought out and disciplined and balanced with other, complementary and equally important observances. There is indeed a place for 'rules of life', and there is the need to learn by instruction how to worship and pray and live as a

Christian. Many people have an instinctive desire to pray but stop doing it because they have never advanced beyond childish methods which reflect childish attitudes to prayer. The performance of prayer, like the performance of music, needs to be taught.

Arthur Schnabel was no doubt able to feel 'in time' and play 'as he felt', but most of us cannot do so because we have not acquired the technique. Having played the piano all my life, I am sadly surprised to find how difficult it is to play even the simplest piece well; and I am astonished at how formidably well other people do play. When he was at Gresham's School Benjamin Britten played Rachmaninoff's *Polichinelle* at a school concert. The chaplain wrote in the school magazine:

> The interpretation of Raff's *Fileuse* alone was enough to establish him as a past-master of delicate workmanship, but the *Polichinelle* of Rachmaninoff held one bewildered, spellbound. Two thoughts arose: 1. How on earth could anyone have written it? 2. How on earth could anyone play it? The effect was devastating. The more the fire and fury, or the leaping and plunging increased, the more rapturously I could have shouted for joy.[2]

This is how I always feel at a piano recital. How is it possible to move one's hands and fingers so swiftly and unerringly? Virtuoso violin playing looks even more difficult, with the two arms doing different things in co-ordination and the instrument tucked uncomfortably under the chin. Anyone, of course, can sing, but in fact good singers take years to develop their technique. James Bowman taught himself to sing all over again when, after a long career as one of the world's leading counter-tenors, he found, at the age of forty, that his voice was deteriorating. By technical application he got his voice back to its best; and he is still extremely good.

With Bowman a master's technique is allied to sensuous musicianship. His performance of *Evening Hymn* at a Purcell concert broadcast from Westminster Abbey at the end of 1995 displayed, through the golden sonority of his voice and the intimate way in which he phrased the words, a melancholy joy which made a fitting finale to the year in which the nation celebrated Purcell's tercentenary. Nor is this alliance of technical ability and musical sensitivity rare in performances today. Could it be that there is more and better playing today than ever before? Youth orchestras at national and county level give astonishing performances of major works; and the world continues to produce youthful prodigies in all instruments.

One reason for this abundance of talent must be the good teaching that is now available. This can be seen in schools. Although in recent years the number of music teachers has been reduced through cuts in educational resources, the standard of music in schools is much higher than it used to be – making me feel quite let down by those who taught me when I compare them with those who taught my children and who now teach my grandchildren. To give an example I know from personal experience, the school orchestra of Ripon Cathedral Choir School, which includes girls and boys aged between seven and thirteen, plays – with a complete range of instruments – every week at the school assembly and sometimes in the cathedral with accuracy and fine sonority.

Good technique does not come without a great deal of personal discipline, however good the teacher; and it is sometimes suggested that, as with tennis prodigies in the United States, too much too young breaks rather than makes the musician. At the choir-school level we have not found this to be so; rather, we have found that the discipline practised in the pursuit of music serves choristers well for the rest of their lives in other activities: intellectual, artistic and athletic. The danger comes when technique is considered the end rather than the means to the end. If technical facility is all a person is trained to have, performances become deadly and mechanical. Certainly the education of musicians should be as broad as possible. Musical performance is not a physical activity, such as the muscles can be trained for, alone; it needs a trained intelligence and some understanding of life to support it. Above all it needs a love of music itself, the desire to enter into it and share it with others. Can this be taught? Technique can be instilled to the limit of a person's natural ability; the mind can be trained and fed and stimulated; the ABC of musicianship can be taught to an assiduous-learner. But the DEF stretches ahead – and then the Greek and Hebrew alphabets before the learner knows it all.

The necessary zest and technique can be partly caught from other people, by rules and by infectious enthusiasm; those who succeed are the ones who open their hearts and their minds not only to the grammar and the love of music but also to the wonders of the world around them. Physical, intellectual, technical and personal demands upon a musician are very great indeed. The reward is in the music: heard, felt, shared.

Back to Christianity. The music of God's love is found in the symphony of living that all human beings are born to share. Christians are called to practise this 'music' with the example of Christ to follow, and the responsibility of living through the restored goodness that Christ's spirit brings. All can enjoy the music they hear and try to play with it and not against it. To some people (of all cultures and religions) this comes instinctively. One often meets people with or without religious leanings who live unselfish, fulfilled lives in happy relationships with other people. But to many there is a pull away from the music, a resentment against those with whom they should live and work in the world's counterpoint, and a need to find the meaning of life, its beauty, its direction, its tunes, before they can play their own part in it. When we accept the music, do we have the understanding, the technique, the moral agility and perseverance to play the part we would like to play? Sometimes it is possible to feel what St Paul felt when he wrote to the Christians in Rome:

> I discover this principle, then: that when I want to do right, only wrong is within my reach. In my inmost self I delight in the law of God, but I perceive in my outward actions a different law, fighting against the law that my mind approves, and making me a prisoner under the law of sin which controls my conduct. Wretched creature that I am, who is there to rescue me from this state of death? Who but God? Thanks be to him through Jesus Christ our Lord! To sum up then: left to myself I serve God's law with my mind, but with my unspiritual nature I serve the law of sin.[3]

There are some who, contrary to what St Paul is arguing for in the context in which this passage occurs, turn simplistically to 'rules', as if they have all the answers. They want to see, in bold type, what to do and what not to do. Let everything be laid down so that people do not have to think but obey – as the young Terry Waite, along with his fellow squaddies, was expected to do to the satisfaction of his sergeant-major, but not, one suspects, to his own sense of fulfilment. Now, if the rules of living can be laid out in a code of plain 'dos' and 'don'ts' (they argue), what could be a better source of authority than the Bible? And what better code than the Ten Commandments? These should be posted up in every church and repeated at every service. Children should be made to learn them by heart. Never mind musicianship and what people feel, the rules of the music of life should be drummed into the young so that they play in tune even if they do not feel it. There are people who think this way about the Bible and others who think in the same way about their own particular religious-moral code: funda-mentalists of all religions. The Bible says ... The Qur'an says ... The Book says ...

But people who think that the Bible gives us a code of morals written in tablets of stone about how to behave in all circum-stances are bound to be asked whether they are prepared to follow the code with regard, say, to the treatment of slaves (pierce their ears to show they belong)[4] or those found guilty of adultery (stone them to death).[5] Homosexual practice is wrong, says the Bible.[6] But what about usury? That too is wrong if the money is lent to a 'poor fellow-countryman'.[7] And what about the laws regarding the Sabbath? Should a man be put to death if he breaks them?[8] We know that Jesus' attitude (for instance about the Sabbath) was not fundamentalist: indeed, he rebuked those who thought it should be, for the hardness of their hearts and their failure to understand the law and the prophets.[9] Without going to extremes, there are still many who believe that the Ten Commandments are the bedrock of Christianity; and that all human behaviour is subject to rules that are found in the Bible.

The truth is that the Bible contains many sets of moral codes and axioms for human behaviour. These differ from one another in detail and emphasis because they were written at different stages, nomadic, agricultural, urban, in the history of the Jews. Throughout these stages the Jews advanced in their understanding of the nature of God. Christians believe that

Christ is the love of God and the wisdom of God incarnate in a human life. Indeed, the Christian interpretation of any single passage in the Bible, be it to do with human behaviour or anything else, is to be seen in the light of the words and the example of Jesus Christ. Therefore, instead of drawing a line from any single passage ('stone the adulteress') straight to one's behaviour today, one draws it from the passage to oneself through the example and words of Jesus. 'Neither do I condemn you. Go; do not sin again.'[10]

So what are we left with to guide us as we set about trying to play the music of God's love in our lives? The Ten Commandments,[11] interpreted through the life of Christ, are an excellent guide, astonishing in their embrace, in their scope and their universal relevance. They show that morality begins with a proper worshipping of God himself. They go on about human living: how there should be the right balance between work and recreation. They insist that human life and truth and property should be respected, family relationships revered, greed eschewed. The motivation for all this is shown to be the realization that the Jewish people owed all to the Lord God who had saved them from slavery in Egypt. This remained the springboard of Jewish religion for many centuries whilst they thought of themselves as 'the Lord's people'. But when through more experiences, particularly the Exile in Babylon, they came to believe that 'their' God was in truth the One God, Creator of the Universe, their motivation became loyalty to God who created as well as redeemed them. Christians inherit this loyalty with an enhanced understanding of 'redemption'. Christian loyalty is not to 'our' God, who has rescued us from captivity in an alien land, but to 'God the Creator', who through the life of Jesus has shown his love, living and dying for the restoration (St Paul calls it 'the new creation'[12]) of all the world.

In this context we see the Ten Commandments, not as rules given from outside to be obeyed in all circumstances, but as a description through imperatives of the best way of living, that is, a description which shows in simple 'do this' form what sort of people God creates us to be. If we live together in this way we fulfil our humanity; if we do not, we go against our created nature, individually and corporately. It is like the instruction manual of a motor car. The nature of the engine is not described in technical terms, it is indicated through dos and don'ts. 'Do put oil in the engine when the light goes on on the dashboard.' No one will come and punish you if you fail to do so. But the fact is that engines are made to go on oil. If you deprive them of oil, you are violating their created nature and they will seize up. In this way the Ten Commandments indicate that human life is made to be God-centred, life and truth and family-affirming, and the rest. Of course there is a great deal of 'imperative description' in the Old Testament besides the Ten Commandments: for instance in the 'Holiness Code'[13] from which Jesus took his 'second commandment', 'you must love your neighbour as yourself', and linked it with the 'first commandment', 'you must love the Lord your God with all your heart, with all your soul, with all your mind, and with all your strength'.[14]

Jesus himself – according to St Matthew, who may have been consciously remembering Moses in the Old Testament – gave us the stern, Heavenly-Father-conscious, life-affirming Sermon on the Mount, beginning with Beatitudes.[15] 'Blessed' ('favoured by God') are those who are gentle, peaceable, merciful, determined on God's righteousness, prepared to suffer for God ... and the rest. If we study all Christ's words about human behaviour and see how they are exemplified by his own behaviour, then we have a Heaven-on-earth pattern of living to go by; but not a set of rules. It is true that people have made their own codes of rules in order to help themselves and others to attain the Christian ideal. Some of these (such as the Benedictine Rule) have been helpful to generations of Christians. But they are disastrous if they are made into 'absolutes', and particularly disastrous if they are enforced as absolutes on other people.

Christ-like living with its joyful dependence upon God, its integrity, its humble readiness to serve, its self-giving love, even unto death, is not a code of law. It is the music. It is that which we listen to, feed on, feel within ourselves, aim to emulate, as we translate it into the terms of our own playing, the living of our own lives.

What happens when we fail? If we are limited to the anthropomorphic ideas prevalent in the primitive stages of Old Testament history (and recurring ever since) we may talk of God 'punishing' us. Indeed the Old Testament writers often spoke of

God's 'jealousy', describing him as a jealous husband punishing an adulterous wife. This was understandable in an age when the Lord God was thought of as one among many gods, and therefore liable to be jealous if his people went like a whore after other gods. Idolatry was seen as religious adultery.[16] But it is better to put aside anthropomorphisms and speak of God creating a world which runs according to certain principles. When human beings defy these, they are not vindictively 'punished'; but they bring upon themselves the inevitable consequences of what they have done wrong, just as the engine seizing up is a consequence, which you would not normally call 'punishment', of failing to feed it with oil.

But this is not all there is to be said; for although on one level we have to take responsibility for our actions and accept the consequences that flow from them, yet God does not let the consequences roll on to our ultimate destruction. Through Christ God gives us the love to mend broken relationships and the power of his goodness (which we call 'grace') to put things right that have gone wrong. It is difficult to find a parallel for this in music; but the truth is that God renews the music within us and makes us want to get it right in performance, the performance of everyday living.

In music, correction does not come from the bullying clicks of the metronome, though we may resort to using this in our desire to get a passage right. It comes from feeling the music all the more strongly within ourselves, and therefore pushing ourselves (with no self-satisfaction: only the feeling of never succeeding) to make it come right. Rules may help to discipline the fingers, but 'grace' is the strength of the music itself. Good advice will help to give us new insights and a better technique: but rules and advice are merely mechanical unless the music itself makes us 'feel' 'in time'. As 'love' makes us 'fulfil' the 'law'.

Over the Top

Back in the living room Nutbeem said, 'Wait until you hear this,' and switched on a tower of sound components. Red and green running lights, flashing digital displays, pulsing contour bands, orange readouts sprang to life. From the speakers a sound as of a giant's lung. Nutbeem slipped a silver disc into a tray and the trailer vibrated with thunder. The music was so loud that Quoyle could not discern any identifiable instrument, nothing but a pulsating sound that rearranged his atoms and quashed thought (E. Annie Proulx *The Shipping News*).

During the war my school was evacuated to Ludlow. Each house occupied its own country mansion and we went daily to a central one, Moor Park, for school work. In the afternoons we withdrew to our own residence (my house occupied Overton Lodge) where real life took place: games, fishing, forestry work, 'digging for victory' (unpopular because it was inclined to be used as a punishment), worship (we converted a stable loft into a chapel), the Gramophone Society (definitely classical), the Jazz Society (Nat Gonella was a favourite with a hot number called 'Shadrach, Meshach and Abednego'), play-reading and everything else: all presided over by a housemaster who combined a naughty sense of fun with a strong sense of principle in things that mattered. In the summer of 1942 we had two guests: Benjamin Britten and Peter Pears.

Peter Pears was an old boy and he clearly relished the day-to-day crises of school life. He was easy and kind with all of us and told us delicious stories of his own school days and the present world of music. Benjamin Britten was more reserved but also enjoyed being with us. He could beat us all at tennis; and he and Pears performed the Michelangelo Sonnets and some of the Folk Song arrangements one Sunday evening at a house concert.

Britten, it must be said, had an acerbic manner of speech – especially when matters of music were concerned. One thing he said has remained in my memory ever since. It was that in his Late Quartets, Beethoven (I think he may have said 'poor

Beethoven') 'exceeded his art'. We did not challenge him, I regret to say, on what he meant precisely by 'exceeded his art', but we argued about it furiously amongst ourselves. I did not in those days know the Beethoven Late Quartets, but, loving Beethoven's music in general, I questioned his stricture with some vigour. I now know the Late Quartets well (though I often muddle them up) and find them searingly beautiful. I cannot accept B.B.'s judgement; yet I think I know what he meant. In today's language he meant 'going over the top'.

The story of religion has been most unfortunately punctuated by movements within it that 'go over the top'. This is not necessarily due to any particular moral fault, though a craving for power, or excitement for its own sake, can be part of the cause. With the very broad expanse of religious faith and experience (broader than the breadth of human differences: as broad as the comprehensive breadth of God's love) there are many truths that need to be emphasized individually and then balanced together. It can easily happen that one facet of the whole gets forgotten. Then it is rediscovered, emphasized and over-emphasized. Then it has to be corrected; and the correction can be the beginning of a new falseness, a new imbalance. For all the parts to balance there must be tension between them and a shared purpose, that of glorifying God. In the performance of music the conductor keeps the tension and tries to ensure the right balance in the performance of the piece. In the orchestra of Christendom the Pope could perhaps be the human conductor; but experience has never validated this. By this suggestion, the players would be Christian souls and the different sections of the orchestra would be different countries and cultures at different stages of their development. This would be too much for the baton of one person or a succession of persons, however wisely advised by close counsellors and however well supported by world-wide affection. The fact is that no group can experience the whole truth, because truth is particular to circumstances as well as being a summary of the universal whole. So the balance has to be found not on earth but in heaven. Here on earth we have to be true, in our own circumstances, to the truth as we see it. Others, back in the past, forward in the future, elsewhere in the world, heirs to different traditions, may see things differently. This is to be expected in the totality of mankind. 'Going over the top' occurs when an individual or group lives to itself and behaves in the false certainty that it alone is right in every respect.

Thus the second-century Marcionites, flushed with freedom from the minutiae of the Jewish Law (a freedom which St Paul had fought for), decided that the Old Testament should be jettisoned altogether and that Christianity should continue without deference to its Jewish past. So too the Desert Fathers, following the example of St Antony of Egypt (c.251–356), thought that the church of their day was too effete in its way of life and too remote from the cross of Christ; so they went off into the deserts to live harsh and lonely lives in their pursuit of perfection. St Benedict (480–543), having himself lived the life of a hermit, corrected the balance by encouraging others to share his life, and establishing a rule by which they could live together in common worship with mutual service and obedience. In this way he founded twelve monasteries with twelve monks each and an abbot appointed by himself; and the Benedictine Rule has served the church ever since. In their rightful attempt to establish the kingdom of God on earth, church authorities identified themselves too closely with the temporal powers of the state and were corrupted by the power they attained. 'Reformation', to right the balance, was necessary; and it came about – but not without its own harsh and Christ-denying tendencies. There is much brutal zealotry in the story of the Christian church – to its terrible and lasting shame.

In our own day, when fanatical religious groups have such power at their command and a global network of communication by which to advertise themselves, the news is thick with the corrupt, suicidal, murderous aberrations of sick societies which masquerade as purveyors of religious truth. Their arrogance and disregard for the lives of individual people betray them. If God is not God of the individual as well as the sect, then God is not the God we know through Christ. Neither is God the God we know if divine care only embraces a circle of peculiar people who make exclusive, religious claims for a piece of land, say, or for ultimate salvation. Sometimes in the Old Testament story the Jews seemed to think that this was their privilege, but they were always being disillusioned by the prophets and later by Jesus himself.[1]

However, the balancing act that is the antidote to false emphases and exclusiveness cannot be performed by sleight of hand and feeble compromise: it is only made possible by high-tension pressure which resolves the differences creatively and compels those who are seeking the truth to keep up the momentum of their search; and makes life very difficult for them while they are doing so.

I think of the tension between the piano and orchestra in the slow movement of the Beethoven Fourth Piano Concerto. The orchestra demands. The piano pleads – but not passively: there is strong passion beneath the tenderness. Piano and orchestra listen to one another. The orchestra then repeats its demands, but in gentler tones. The piano responds, giving vent to its seething emotion. Then it comes to terms with itself. Piano and orchestra go forward together into the Finale, reconciled but not compromised.

In his book *Orthodoxy*, G.K. Chesterton has his own typically rumbustious way of describing the balance of truth that constitutes Christian orthodoxy:

There was never anything so perilous or so exciting as ortho-doxy. It was sanity: and to be sane is more dramatic than to be mad. It was the equilibrium of a man behind madly rush-ing horses, seeming to stoop this way and to sway that, yet in every attitude having the grace of statuary and the accuracy of arithmetic. The Church in its early days went fierce and fast with any warhorse ... She swerved to left and right, so as exactly to avoid enormous obstacles. She left on one hand the huge bulk of Arianism, buttressed by all the worldy powers to make Christianity too worldly. The next instant she was swerving to avoid an orientalism, which would have made her too unworldly ... It would have been easier to have accepted the earthly power of the Arians. It would have been easy, in the Calvinistic seventeenth century, to fall into the bottomless pit of predestination ... To have fallen into any of these traps of error and exaggeration which fashion after fashion and sect after sect set along the historic path of Christendom – that would indeed have been simple. But to have avoided them all has been one whirling adventure; and in my vision the heavenly chariot flies thundering through the ages, the dull heresies sprawling and prostrate, the wild truth reeling but erect.[2]

All this is far from Benjamin Britten's criticism of the Beethoven late Quartets. There is indeed a 'going over the top' in music, and maybe in his sorrowful deafness Beethoven was trying to hear and to say more than could be said by four string instruments. My ears can never catch up with what he does say, so profoundly simple are some parts and so wildly complex are others. But I cannot agree with the judgment that he is 'exceeding his art', certainly not in the Grosse Fuge, though this may seem to be so on a first hearing. Nevertheless, music may sometimes be said to go over the top. The unvaried and raucous beat of some pop music; the drawn-out trick of Ravel's *Bolero*; the vast, motionless chords of Messiaen (I love them: they take me with them into something very deep); the sentimentality of some of Chopin's Nocturnes; Rossini's long crescendos; Beethoven playing about before the finale of the Fifth Symphony or the bit in the Seventh Symphony which made someone exclaim, 'Beethoven, are you mad?' Do these matter? Not at all. Nobody expects one musical idea to 'balance' at any one moment with all the other ideas that there are in music. But religion is life; and while one aspect of it is being emphasized to excess it is important to remember that there are other aspects which balance it. St Paul, recognizing human differences born of different religious cultures, said that he tried to be 'all things to all men'.[3] He also said that to a Christian, Christ's fullness fills the whole of creation.[4] In him, as it were, is our unity, our 'balance'.[5]

There is another sense, however, of 'going over the top' which was certainly not in Britten's mind when he disparaged the Beethoven Quartets. It is relevant to faith because in this respect music and faith serve the same object, namely to 'take a person out of himself'. This happens with different kinds of music for different people; and again we are with the personal and subjective 'tingle factor'. Music certainly has this astonishing power. 'Being sent' used to be the expression for it, and this phrase came from the scene of popular music.

Have not most people who love music had their sublime moments, their 'tingle factors', when a particular phrase or a modulation or the unexpected – but inevitable when you know it – entry of an instrument hits you, flattens you, makes you breathless with its beauty? I indulge myself with two examples: the astonishing sweep of the strings into the second subject in some remote key of the first movement of Elgar's First Symphony, after the slow, inexorable march of the first subject; and (secondly) the sad, rhythmical call of the trumpet, in the far distance, behind but penetrating the orchestra, while the violins are playing a despairing, yearning tune, towards the end of the first movement of Beethoven's Choral Symphony.

But the important question is, 'What "sends" you, the reader?' The restrained chanting of plainsong? Or the insistent jangling and open harmonies of Tudor music? Or lively, decorated Baroque? Or a moment of passionate sadness in a Mozart Quintet? The exalted brilliance of a chorus from *Messiah*? The throbbing pain, staccato exclamations, measured choruses and ultimate joy of Bach's *St Matthew Passion*? The still peace of a Beethoven slow movement? Or the youthful arrogance of his early concertos, or the occasional violence of his rage, or the sublimity of his joy? The long melodies and melting modulations of Schubert? The romantic certainties of Brahms? The sunny lyricism of Dvořák? Mahler's Christmas puddings with delicious brandy-butter and hidden threepenny-bits and silver charms and holly leaves which you scrunch by mistake? The unabashed pleading and sobbing, the limping waltz and the deathly foreboding of Tchaikovsky's *Pathétique* Symphony? Or the teasing, tickling fancies of Poulenc and the French 'Six' who prided themselves on still writing tunes? Or the impressionism of Debussy? Or the assertive clamour of twentieth-century composers who rarely give you the same tune twice? Brittle Bartok? Astringent Roussel? Or the turbulence and yearning of Elgar who sought – not in vain – to pluck the 'Spirit of Delight' out of the air? Or the rich, rhapsodic confusion of Vaughan Williams? Or the wistful lyricism of Rubbra? Or the nostalgic, war-laden, rightfully escapist dance music of the 1940s? Warm swing? The cool and frenetic moods of jazz? Or the mellow sonority of a brass band? Or the pounding beat, unsubtle harmonies and electronically contrived top-of-the-charts appeal of todays's pop? Or heartfelt hymns? This is only a list. The reader may have a personal list. *Desert Island Discs*, *The Tingle Factor* and other such personal-choice programmes on radio and television are popular because people recognize that they can be 'taken out of themselves' by music and enjoy identifying or strongly disagreeing with the well-known guests on the programme.

It is right that religious experience should occasionally 'take one out of oneself'. But sometimes people go over the top. I have in mind an American evangelist whom I saw on television when I was staying in New York. He was exposed later as being corrupt, which may or may not be connected with the embarrassing, 'over the top' appeal I heard him make. With much emotion he seemed to be saying that those who put their faith in the Lord Jesus would undoubtedly be successful in their business enterprises and that if they were to send him, the evangelist, a donation, that would make this all the more certain. For its false theology and its patent dishonesty this may be too extreme an example. But what I have in mind is the putting on of an act which makes the 'feeling' come from inside instead of being received as a gift from outside. People sometimes try to create religious feelings for themselves or to impress and persuade others. This sort of enthusiasm can be like the explosion of a firework, all brilliance until it disappears into the night sky. Then there can be enthusiasm for 'togetherness' that has more to do with the cosiness of a group than with the service of God. There can be 'over the top' enthusiasm about some particular facet of Christianity: the Bible, for instance, or the tradition of the church, or the church building, or the popular curate, or the singing of the choir, or incense, or ritual, or one's own importance in the General Synod. There is plenty of room for idolatry ('goods made into gods') in the practice of religion. Indeed, religion itself can be the idol if people are so immersed in it that they forget that it is supposed to glorify *God*. It was too much religion practised for its own sake that made Bonhoeffer in his later days in prison commend 'religion-less Christianity'.

I have been using the word 'enthusiasm' to mean 'keenness'. But in theological usage 'enthusiasm' has a technical meaning, namely, 'being breathed into by the Holy Spirit'. This implies an immediate excitement experienced by individuals or by a group of Christians together when they feel themselves to be moved by the Spirit to speak and act ecstatically. This phenomenon has been common throughout Christendom from the Apostolic Age[6] to our own, and to some Christians it is this alone that authenticates religious experience. Deep in my own prayers – private as well as liturgical – at moments that I can remember, I have felt something – perhaps just a glimpse of something – like this: a moment of stillness, timelessness; of searing, painful love; more, of reaching, yearning after God: enough to align myself firmly against those who scoff or decry 'enthusiasm'. But I have to say that such moments leave me humbled, moved, pentitent, quiet, not excited. Such moments come, I believe, as a gift. They can never be sought or (perish the thought – but I know that it happens) artificially induced in oneself or (worse still – but I have actually seen this being tried) forced on other people. To hanker after religious experience for its own sake is what I mean by 'exceeding the art' of religion. It happens when 'experience' is prised away from 'truth'.

There is a word common to the experience of faith and music which refers to all of this. It is 'ecstasy', from the Greek '*ek-stasis*', 'standing outside (oneself)'. This is very different from self-dramatization. It can be induced by music and drugs and, when it is allowed to happen but is not sought for its own sake, by religious experience. It was common in Old Testament times – witness the prophets of Baal who danced wildly by the altar Elijah had set up in their attempt to bring fire from heaven upon the sacrifice. Elijah jeered and told them to 'call louder ... for maybe he (their god) is deep in thought, or engaged, or on a journey; or he may have gone to sleep and must be woken up'. So they cried still louder and, as was their custom, gashed themselves with swords and spears until the blood flowed. All afternoon they raved and ranted ... but still there was no sign. Elijah (so the story goes) then gathered the people around him, made things more difficult by having water poured on the altar, and prayed to the Lord God for fire to consume the sacrifice.[7] Such ecstasy, however, was not confined to the worship of foreign gods; it was an important phenomenon in the early stages of Judaism, and out of it there developed the prophets who spoke 'the word of God', partly from ecstatic emotion but also from their ability to pray and think and interpret the will of God in terms of the political circumstances of their day. So the 'ecstatic' element in Jewish prophecy survived, but it was subject to the prophets' devotion to the Lord God and their courageous reading of events.

The ecstasy of 'possession' is still practised in religions today. There is a description of a young Buddhist monk making an important ecstatic utterance in Heinrich Harrer's book *Seven Years in Tibet*. Harrer describes the monk being led in to the sound of eerie music, being dressed in enormous headgear which it took several people to carry, and then, trembling violently, beginning to gyrate and fling himself around, his limbs contorted, his eyes staring. Eventually his movements would subside and, still hissing, he would submit himself to the questioning of the 'secretary', who would write down his answers about matters of state. Harrer comments cynically that perhaps the real oracle was the secretary.[8]

Writing to the Corinthians, St Paul speaks of the 'manifestations of the spirit'. He numbers 'prophecy' and 'speaking with tongues' amongst them, but clearly prefers the gift of 'interpreting tongues' as being more helpful to the Christian congregation.[9] Since then, 'ecstatic utterance' has been a rare phenomenon in mainstream Christianity, and many people doubt its authenticity when it does occur. Indeed with regard to ecstasy, music and faith have this in common: that most practitioners, those to whom people look for guidance, tend to disparage such excesses. Britten thought little of composers who wear their heart on the sleeves of their music to induce easy, emotional response, hence the acerbic nature of much of his music; though there are times when he quite fails to prevent me from wanting to weep. Bishop Butler, the English eighteenth-century bishop and theologian, said that 'enthusiasm', that which leads to ecstasy, 'is a very horrid thing'. Indeed the claim to ecstasy and the attitude that regards it as the definitive religious experience, a *sine qua non* in the Christian life, is something that unbalances and corrupts. I once worked closely with a Baptist pastor whose ministry was blighted in his own eyes because he had never 'spoken in tongues'. This was because of the expectation of his people as well as himself, but both were wrong. His ministry was authenticated by the love he had for them and the selfless service he gave to them. There was no need for an ecstatic utterance to prove this to anyone. Much worse is the claim of an individual that through some religious experience he has his own private hot-line to God which puts him beyond the advice and authority of anyone else. This makes a person invincible in his ignorance and sometimes very harmful in the arrogant exercise of power over others.

In Christianity there is a simple test which Jesus spoke about in the Sermon on the Mount.

> Beware of false prophets, who come to you dressed up as sheep while underneath they are savage wolves. You will recognize them by their fruit. Can grapes be picked from briars, or figs from thistles? A good tree always yields sound fruit, and a poor tree bad fruit. A good tree cannot bear bad fruit, nor a poor tree sound fruit. A tree that does not yield sound fruit is cut down and thrown on the fire. That is why I say you will recognize them by their fruit. Not everyone who says to me, 'Lord, Lord' will enter the Kingdom of Heaven, but only those who do the will of my heavenly Father. When the day comes, many will say to me, 'Lord, Lord, did we not prophesy in your name, and in your name perform many miracles?' Then I will tell them plainly, 'I never knew you. Out of my sight; your deeds are evil.'[10]

Stern words for those of us who dare to presume to minister in his name!

In music one can experience 'tingle factor moments' again and again; but this does not happen in prayer or worship, because such moments cannot be had on demand. However, the parallel is true in this respect: they leave one feeling stimulated, yes; zestful, some of them; but not 'excited'. The Christian philosopher and writer, Baron Frederick von Hügel, makes this point about the difference between zest and excitement:

> A wonderful thoughtful friend insisted to me that the soul's health and happiness depended upon a maximum of zest and as little as possible excitement. Zest is the pleasure which comes from thoughts, occupation ... interests of a good kind – duties and joys that steady us and give us balance and centrality. Excitement is the pleasure which comes from breaking loose, from fragmentariness, from losing our balance and centrality. Zest is natural warmth – excitement is fever heat. For zest – to be relished – requires much self-

discipline and recollection – much spaciousness of mind: whereas the more distracted we are, the more racketed and impulse-led, the more we thirst for excitement and the more its sirocco air dries up our spiritual sap and makes us long for more excitement.[11]

Jesus was zestful in his living and teaching. And what kind of 'fruit', one wonders, did he have in mind when he said, 'By their fruit you shall know them'? St Paul helps us out with his famous contrasting lists of human vices and virtues in his letter to the Galatians.

Anyone can see the behaviour that belongs to the unspiritual nature: fornication, indecency, and debauchery; idolatry and sorcery; quarrels, a contentious temper, envy, fits of rage, selfish ambitions, dissensions, party intrigues, and jealousies; drinking bouts, orgies, and the like ... but the harvest of the Spirit is love, joy, peace, patience, kindness, goodness, fidelity, gentleness, and self-control ... If the Spirit is the source of our life, let the Spirit also direct its course.[12]

Finally, an example of religious ecstasy at its best comes from the story of the Transfiguration. Peter, James and John walked up the hillside with Jesus. At the top of the hill they had an extraordinary religious experience. They saw their friend Jesus, who a moment ago had been puffing up the hill with them, 'transfigured' in divine glory. They saw Moses and Elijah with him and they heard the voice of God affirming his pre-eminence. Peter wanted it to stay like that for ever; but his call for 'three tents' was not heeded. The cloud of glory that both hid and revealed the divine presence parted. They were left to themselves again, just Jesus and the three friends, to trudge down the hillside back into ordinary life – in this case a hostile crowd and a boy with epilepsy needing to be healed.[13]

The merit of any ecstatic experience, however induced, lies in what it leads on to. Many have found themselves strengthened, stimulated, taken out of themselves by beautiful music; and many have found themselves refreshed, strengthened, and filled with demanding love, through finding themselves in the presence of the living God of love.

12

Creativity

Let us now praise famous men, and our fathers that begat us ... Such as found out musical tunes, and recited verses in writing; rich men furnished with ability, living peacably in their habitations (Ecclesiasticus 44.1–5).

You will ask me where my ideas come from. I cannot say for certain. They come uncalled, sometimes independently, sometimes in association with other things. It seems to me that I could wrest them from Nature herself with my own hands, as I go walking in the woods. They come to me in the silence of the night or in the early morning, stirred into being by moods which the poet would translate into words, but which I put into sounds; and these go through my head ringing and singing and storming until at last I have them before me as notes (Beethoven, Letter to Louis Schlösser).

Beethoven hurried out into the open air, rambled across the fields shouting and waving his arms, sometimes walking very rapidly, sometimes very slowly and stopping at times to write in a sort of pocket-book (A.W. Thayer, *Life of Beethoven*).

Sibelius described his symphonies as 'confessions of faith from different periods of my life'. For him, even such a seemingly abstract task as 'arrangement of the themes' could come close to mystical experiences. 'It's as if God the Father had thrown down the tiles of a mosaic from Heaven's floor and asked me to determine what kind of picture it was' (Stephen Johnson, *BBC Music Magazine*, November 1995).

Symphonies are a lot of work to write. Too much. One has to have something really appalling to happen to one, that lets loose the fountain of inspiration (William Walton, in Stephen Johnson, *BBC Music Magazine*, November 1995).

I was once present when someone said to Benjamin Britten, 'I am sure that I should be a composer myself. I often feel inspired to write sublime and wonderful music.' These were not his precise words, but the meaning was the musical equivalent to Bertie Stanhope's remark in *Barchester Towers* when he said to the Bishop of Barchester, 'I once thought of being a Bishop myself'. The Bishop of Barchester was not encouraging: nor was Benjamin Britten.

He might have said: 'Composing music is not a matter of having high inspiration in your head as it whirls around in the clouds. It is a matter of responding to some need and focussing any inspiration or ideas you may have into musical terms; then writing them down on paper. To do this you have to translate a general idea into precise musical form. You also have to grasp the grammar of music; seeing to it that what you intend comes across with clarity. In this way what you intend is focussed and expressed through the actual sounds that you indicate and others after you will make.'

These words are too long in explanation, too short in irritation. Composing, whatever the composer's facility, is very hard work. Britten himself learnt this when he was still a boy, through hours of harsh and disciplined study with his friend and tutor, John Ireland. All his life he struggled to create music as he wanted it, writing at his desk throughout the mornings and evenings, and walking by the sea in the afternoons, wrestling with musical ideas in his head.

One of the mysteries of life is that of creativity. We ask ourselves, 'Is our personal existence something that is "created", or is it just a stretch of an ongoing physical process dominated by chance? Whichever of these, are we able ourselves to "create" anything that does not spring from us by the same inevitable process?' To me it seems that the answers to these questions must go together. If I am a 'creature' then I can also be a 'creator'. Conversely, if I can 'create', then I must have been 'created'. The act of creation implies bringing about a 'new beginning', something which would not have come into being inevitably from a previous state. If my own existence is simply a physical inevitability arising from the succession of events that have preceded it, it is hard to think that I can now choose to break this stream of events and create something new: a poem, a symphony, a picture, a cake, a friendship, a home, a Peugeot 306 or a space-machine. All these things do, of course, come from previous states; they are not created out of nothing. But I can speak of 'creating' them because they come about as a result of my (or someone else's) deliberate choice as I make things that respond to my (or other peoples') needs. Indeed, self-awareness (including knowledge of my satisfactions and needs), choice (of how to behave), love (a deliberately created relationship) and creativity all go together. I do not see how any of them are possible in a world that is confined to physical processes alone. If there are supra-physical factors, however, to which one can respond and by which one can express oneself, then the world and everything in it could be 'the creation' of a personal Creator. And if, as Jews and Christians have always believed, the creative powers of the Creator have been limited by being shared with certain 'creatures' (humankind), then creativity is something which human beings can share in and exercise.

This is what is meant by the sentence in Genesis 1 that God 'created man in his own image'. 'Image' does not imply 'imitation' but 'relationship'. The second (but earlier) creation story in Genesis 2 puts it differently and says that God 'breathed his spirit' into man, so that man became a 'living soul'. Both creation stories go on to say that God gives the human race 'stewardship' over the rest of the creation. One account expresses this as 'giving dominion'; the other speaks of the power of 'naming' animal and vegetable life. This means 'having power over them'. All this implies a Creator who is 'personal', as distinct from an impersonal power such as electricity. This is the most daring claim made by these great monotheistic religions; but it is important to remember that to say that the Creator is 'personal' is not to say that the Creator is 'a person'. To say 'a person' is to speak of 'someone' who is limited, as human persons are limited, each to a particular life. But to say that God is 'personal' is to say that in the ultimate Source of existence there is creative choice. Indeed it is arguable that if human beings are personal in this sense, then their Creator is, too; for the Creator God must be greater in capacity, not less, than the creatures that have been created.

An important instance of human creativity, and one from which we can learn, is the composition of music. It would be fascinating to study the different ways in which composers compose: Mozart getting it all into his head before putting pen to paper; Beethoven with his note-books and sketches and much trial and error before he gets what he wanted; César Franck improvising on the organ for hours on end, often beginning with music composed by someone else; Elgar 'plucking music out of the air'; Tippett, who thought that his inspiration had left him after the war, finding that he could 'sing again' on hearing

Gieseking play Beethoven's Fourth Piano Concerto, and composing a tumultuous piano concerto of his own. But we must be content with only a few observations.

In the first place it is safe to say that musicians write both from an inner compulsion and from a necessity to satisfy some external need. J.S. Bach and Joseph Haydn spent most of their professional lives writing at the behest of their employers. Mozart refused to stay in anybody's employ, but wrote much that was commissioned. So did Beethoven. Britten began his career as a composer by writing incidental music for films, and thus taught himself to write what was required for each moment of each occasion.

The notion that creativity is a combination of inner impulse and external stimulation, making an act of creation an inner response to a set of circumstances, is very important in the consideration of human behaviour. A freely willed action is creative in just that sense. It happens when a person, with all that he has come to be, is confronted with a certain state of affairs and behaves by doing what he decides to do. If he merely reacts to circumstances, the weather, for instance, or the gradient or his digestion or popular opinion or what the papers say, and does what they dictate, then he is being uncreative and to that extent less than human. As a human being he can defy the weather and popular opinion and do what he thinks is right or best for himself. Faced with a storm he can go out into it; faced with a glut he can be abstemious; faced with an insult he can be forgiving: with gossip around he can fall in with it, stir it and make things worse; or he can behave with imagination to make things better. At another level of creativity he can (given the ability and the training) write a play or compose a piano concerto or make beer or arrange flowers or build a church.

A person can also 'forgive'; and it is important to understand 'forgiveness' in this way. Forgiveness does not mean 'forgetting all about it', behaving as if nothing had happened, as if the offender had not offended. This would not only be impossible humanly, but immoral as well. When an offence has been committed, a situation has been changed – probably for the worse. 'Forgiveness' is a new creative attitude and/or action that accepts what has happened (however painful it may be) and makes possible a new beginning. It is therefore *forward-*

looking. The 'forward' may include reparation and punishment; it will certainly include the beginning of the mending of relationships that have been broken by the offence. The repair of a relationship may be a long process, because it is difficult and has to be exercised and accepted from both sides. To make our attitudes and actions creative and effective, we have to go on praying urgently, 'Forgive us ... as we (try to) forgive'.[1]

What about social constraints and the laws and guiding principles that one is given to live by? Look again at composers. There is a grammar of music that they have to learn. There are also methods of composition which they learn from the inherited experience of other composers, what Vaughan Williams called the ABC of composition. These are vital to begin with. But it is unlikely that a composer will remain within the bounds of these conventions. Sometimes he will take what comes to him and 'firm it up' into something stronger and more helpful. Sometimes he will break away from it altogether. Thus Bach 'firmed up' the art of fugue; Haydn, sonata form; Mozart created dazzling new possibilities for piano concertos; Beethoven accepted sonata form but then broke out of it in order to give music a larger framework for his new, explosive ideas; later Romantics went further still as they wrote with the intention of giving vent to their feelings. Soon composers were thinking more of the colour of the sound than the form of the piece. In the development of music, composers have assimilated what they have received from the past but, in making it their own, have gone on beyond it into new modes of musical sound and its organization.

Consider John Sebastian Bach. A silly joke that one of my school friends made to me was that Bach wrote his music with the help of logarithm tables. It is of course possible to analyse Bach's music and see the rules of composition which he followed. Read Tovey's introduction to the Forty-Eight Preludes and Fugues and you will learn about the subjects and counter-subjects and their inversions and much else; but you may never dare to try to play them! Bach's rules, however, were for the framing of musical thought, not a prison for its captivity, nor task-masters to bully it into submission. Bach's music has a consistency of pattern; but some of its greatest moments come about when he defies or enlarges the pattern.

The combination of inner inspiration, the call to write music for a particular occasion, and his readiness to follow or break self-given ways of procedure, resulted in music that gives you total confidence with regard to the direction it is taking you, yet sparkles and throbs and delights and soothes and bounces you on your way, making you ache with the pain and the beauty of life.

(I once heard a radio play which presented J. S. B. as a vigorous young man. It helps a lot to think of him like this; just as it helps to think of God as being eternally young rather than everlastingly old.)

And take Beethoven. His note-books really are a mess and must be very difficult to decipher. He used to go on afternoon walks and have musical ideas and work himself into a frenzy as, walking along, he let them take him over and develop into a composition. He would stop and scribble them down and use them later, changing bits, scrapping them, pulling them around, until he got the music as he wanted it. Sometimes the result is so serene that it is hard to believe that it did not arise straight out of a moment of peaceful contemplation. Sometimes (dare I say?) a passage does sound contrived: some of the endings which he seemed reluctant to reach, for instance; or the build-up to the Finale of the Fifth Symphony or even (sacrilege!) the build-up to the Finale of the Choral Symphony when he reviews the previous movements and then dismisses them to proceed to the even greater, choral movement. Sometimes, we are told, he was driven by the irregularity of his own heart-beat; certainly he was driven – by wild temperament, by the dark dungeon of deafness, by financial insecurity, by a defensive awareness of his rightful position in society which he felt should be a matter of talent, not birth; by a sensitive political awareness which made him rage against any threat to freedom; by a longing for personal affection and care, which he covered up by gruffness and a stormy temper. Take one work, the *Grosse Fuge*, originally written to be the last movement of the Quartet No.13 in B Flat, opus 130, but later substituted by a lighter movement and left to stand on its own as opus 133 because he thought it too overpowering even for that gigantic work.[2] The two subjects of this fugue are one of leaping, furious energy, ending with a fierce trill and then a strident dotted rhythm, and another of pleading, caressing tenderness. They vie and clash and cry and scream at one another but neither wins, neither is subdued; they become reconciled, the fierce becoming calmer, the tender stronger. By the end the listener feels uplifted, exhausted, but wonderfully satisfied. What a 'creation' was this, by a man whose inner drive and conviction made him overcome all adverse circumstances to give to the world proof of the depth and the power of human creativity.

In matters of behaviour it is the same. Besides the rules by which people are taught to live sociably, there needs to be passion, love, conviction, sensibility to the feelings of others near and far, the desire to serve and the courage to overcome obstacles, human and circumstantial. Creative living springs from inner strength and desire being applied to outward needs and demands. Creative living benefits from conventions and rules and laws and commandments, received wisdom from the past and the good sense of those around; but it cannot be rule-bound and it must sometimes break the logic of moral consequences in its reaction to evil. Creative living is bringing a new infusion of goodness into a bad situation. It goes with forgiving, offering the other cheek, giving away the extra coat, going the extra mile. The Sermon on the Mount[3] is a lesson in creative living. It comes with the authority of the person whose very life was the supreme creative act of the Creator God. This was Jesus of Nazareth, the incarnate Word of God. His life was the life that focussed the creative love of God upon human affairs. Throughout his life the creative goodness of God was poured into the lives of human-beings to make them 'good' in this creative sense. Am I confusing aesthetic with moral creativity? Beethoven with Mother Teresa? Maybe I am; but it is in the conviction that they both come from the same source, work in the same way, and that they can destroy or reinforce one another, that I am writing this book.

More needs to be said with regard to 'rules'. These are essential. They are there to pass moral wisdom down from generation to generation. They protect society against maverick individuals, and individuals against the power of society. But in order to be helpful they have to be not just learnt and applied but assimilated and 'inwardly digested' so that they guide human choice but are not a substitute for it. Otherwise people become like the student who learns the elementary rules of harmony but does not hear the 'right' and the 'wrong' notes in his head. He is taught not to 'double the third', or write 'consecutive fifths', and 'always to make the leading note rise to the tonic'. He can get full marks for his exercises by keeping them free from these and other enormities. Nevertheless, what he writes comes out dull and unmusical because the rules are being kept for their own sake instead of as a help to musical expression. Rule-bound composers are not likely to be original; rule-bound human beings find it difficult to empathize with others and to forgive.

Another principle that one can see at work in the composition of music is that creativity is a matter of limiting the infinite number of possibilities and *focussing* upon that which is limited and identifiable. The word 'focus' is the key to this, as it is the key to the technical Christian word 'sacrament'. 'Sacrament' is defined in the catechism in the Book of Common Prayer as 'an outward and visible sign of an inward and spritual grace'. But most Christians take it to be more than that, for a sacrament is not only a 'sign', as it were, a 'statement' of what is taking place; it is also a creative *act* by which something is brought about. This is like saying that a piece of music not only expresses what the composer is feeling; it is also a means of creating that feeling, that mood, in the listener. So music and sacraments convey a truth as well as stating it. All people perform quasi-sacramental actions when they communicate with one another through bodily signs. Thus shaking hands, kissing, hugging, smiling, frowning, dressing up for an occasion, acts of conventional etiquette, indeed, all forms of 'body language': these are 'creative signs' being used all the time in human relationships. People use the same kind of 'creative signs' in their worship: sometimes at the level of individual devotion, such as making the sign of the cross; sometimes acting corporately as in matters of ritual. The 'offertory procession' in the eucharist, for instance, seen in the context of Christ's all-sufficient sacrifice, is a corporate sign on behalf of the congregation of their responsive offering of human-made bread and wine, ready for consecration. But sacraments are best thought of as the creative signs (because they tell the story and make it work) of God's gifts to humankind. The supreme sacrament is the life of Christ himself: the human being who focusses the love of God upon the world. From this life – and by his expressed command – the church has its sacraments: seven, if you count the Roman Catholic list of baptism, confirmation, holy communion (mass or eucharist), penance (for forgiveness), marriage, unction (for healing or for last rites) and orders (consecration of bishops, ordination of priests and deacons); or two, if you only count the two 'dominical' sacraments mentioned in the catechism in The Book of Common Prayer (baptism and holy communion); or an infinite number, if you count all the ways in which people find 'signs' of God's presence in the course of life. Some people find that God is creatively alive in all the experiences of living. Through the power of this creative presence they try to be creative themselves in the way they live and in the things they make and do.

I will earth this chapter and end as I began it, with Benjamin Britten. At the Aldeburgh Festival, Britten used to busy himself putting out the music and making sure that the piano was in the right position and that there was enough light for the players to see by. This is the behaviour of a man who despite his genius did not live with his head in the clouds, 'above' such things as music-stands and piano-stools. His desire to communicate with others was focussed, earthed, on the music paper on which he wrote, and through the kind, humble acts that he performed for the good of other people.

13

Journeys of Faith

'One jazzer's jazz is another jazzer's junk' (Ian Whitcomb, *After the Ball*).

A wave of vulgar, filthy and suggestive music has inundated the land. The pabulum of theatre and summer hotel orchestra is coon music. Nothing but ragtime prevails and the cake-walk with its obscene posturings, its lewd gestures. It is artistically and morally depressing and should be suppressed by press and pulpit (*The Musical Courier*, 1899).

If you stray from the path, whether to right or to left, you will hear a voice from behind you sounding in your ears saying, 'This is the way; follow it' (Isaiah 30.21).

'Mercy and truth are met together' (Psalm 85.10).

I find an ambivalence in my attitude to 'good' and 'not so good' music, detecting that whereas I feel strongly about what is good and what is not so good to me, I am nevertheless loath to pass judgment on the differing tastes of other people. Both intellectually and morally it seems wrong to say of music that I do not like (other peoples' music), 'This is bad'; yet that is what I sometimes feel. Even more strongly I often want to say of music that other people do not like, 'This is very good'; and I have to be content with saying that it is very good *to me*. 'Because it is so good to me,' I would add, 'I naturally want to share it with you; not to persuade, let alone force, but *share*; so that I do not keep it to myself. You can have it too. Listen! and I will listen to yours; and we may each of us enrich the other's enjoyment.'

But what gives me my particular tastes? It is not a matter of moral virtue; nor is it intellectual prowess; nor is it even musical ability, because mine, judged by performance, is only slight. The answer must come from the story of my life, upbringing, education, experiences. It happened, for instance, at my school that I fell in with a number of others whose hobby was listening to music (amongst many other things; cricket, for instance, and cycling and keeping up-to-date maps of the ebb and flow of the war). We had a Gramophone Society which met weekly in the Housemaster's study and drank his Lapsang. Each programme chosen was a matter of hot debate, and I can remember the first time that we heard an Elgar Symphony the secretary wrote in the minute book, 'Rarely, rarely comest thou, Spirit of delight'.[1] I remember too the Vaughan Williams Fourth Symphony which we called 'The Bloody'; and the Shostakovitch Leningrad Symphony which, despite the importance of the place on the map at that time, we thought very long and dreary. Chamber music came slowly to us; opera never. We were divided between lovers of the 'classics' and the 'romantics'. 'Baroque' was a poor third. Tudor music did not exist; nor did Mahler. We could most of us sing (or rather, in a most peculiar way, imitate) any theme from any of the symphonies and concertos of Beethoven and Brahms, a great deal of Mozart (but, oddly, only one piano concerto – the 'Little' B Flat, K450), most of the Schubert, Tchaikovsky and Dvořák symphonies. This is no boast: it was just our enthusiasm, as others know their *Wisden* or their film stars or (today) their pop groups.

After that there was a lean period, as far as music was concerned, except that I once went to a Promenade concert in the old Queen's Hall, conducted by Sir Henry Wood. There was an air raid and we had to wait until it was over: meanwhile members of the audience got up and performed. I can also remember the lunchtime concerts in the National Gallery, hearing Britten and Pears perform Schubert and Britten's *Michelangelo Sonnets*; and Dame Myra Hess herself playing Schumann's *Carnaval*. When I was doing my naval training near Warrington I used to hitch-hike to Manchester on Saturday afternoons to hear the Hallé under Sir John Barbirolli and then hitch back to Liverpool for the Liverpool Philharmonic under Sir Malcolm Sargent in the evenings, and back to camp – just in time. Like everyone else, I fell for Vera Lynn; and *Lilli Marlene* takes me straight back to the mess-deck. Also I joined an élite music circle that used to meet in the house of a rich Egyptian in Alexandria. My presence surprised the other English members, because I was not an officer. It was there that I first heard *Les Illuminations* by Britten and the Classical Symphony by Prokofiev. All through my professional life my tastes have broadened, mostly through the acquisition of

gramophone records, now CDs; also through chamber-music
societies; and in the cathedral at Ripon there have been not only
the daily offering of sung services, but also a great variety of
concerts and recitals from professional orchestras and amateur
groups from all over the world. All this is not important to anyone else; but it is reminding me to make the point that my enjoyment of all the music that has enriched my life has not been
because of my deserts but because of particular good fortune.

Then I look across at other people with their good fortune.
Many live lives which are enriched by music that is very
different from that which I love so much. Far back in human
history people were extolling the power and the beauty of
music. What would we think today of the music they enjoyed?
And how surprised they would be at hearing a Brandenburg
Concerto or The *Nutcracker* Suite or the programme at yesterday's Promenade Concert: *The Flight of Icarus* by John Pickard,
Shostakovich's Cello Concerto No.1 and Rachmaninov's
Second Symphony, all of which would be new, and some
perhaps strange, to my ears. Today indigenous music from all
over the world, sometimes of great rhythmical complexity, is
readily available. Indeed, tonight's Promenade Concert (10 p.m.
to midnight) is Indian music, played by the Calcutta Drum
Orchestra with Pandit Shivkunar Sharma (santoor) and Pandit
Anindo Chatterjee (tabla). I gather that part of this is modern
Indian music, which has sprung from the traditional, but has
developed, as today's modern music has developed from
Western classical music. Making such music available to us
today is in the spirit of what I am writing in this chapter – and
I wish I could be there to hear it. There is also the Western 'top
of the charts' music, which gives more people more enjoyment
than has ever been known. To all this I am a complete outsider,
finding it difficult, but ready to share – both ways.

But one is not a victim of circumstances, drawn inevitably
along certain lines of development into particular areas of taste.
Temperament and choice come into it. Does one go along with
one's peer-group, or not? Is a boy chorister certain to rebel,
when his voice is broken, and turn to heavy rock? Is this person
prepared to enlarge her experience? Is that person capable of
listening? And is it not true that there is a difference in the
quality of music? And a difference in the degree of concentra-

tion needed to listen to it? And a difference in the moods that
music can induce? And are not some moods more pleasurable
and some less so to different people? Taste in music depends on
a mixture of circumstances, temperament, the influence of other
people, innate musicality, readiness to learn; and, in particular,
hovering at every level, individual choice.

I find the same problem, the same ambivalence, and the same
pattern of answers, in matters of faith. More importantly so; for
faith is not a matter of rich enjoyment, as music is, but a
commitment to a way of life involving belief, worship and
behaviour. Again, it comes from the combination of personal
circumstances and the deliberate picking of one's way through
them by acts of choice. It involves risk and hope, choice and
intellectual integrity; much which shakes the confidence, but the
determination to persevere. As in music, the influence of other
people is of great importance; but in matters of faith, too, one
has to make one's own decisions. Faith – like music – comes to
a person in particular ways; but unlike music, it is something
which commits and affects the whole of life.

Having said that about one's own faith, one looks across and
sees many other faiths in the world: many religions; many
branches of one's own religion; and even within one's own
branch, much variation of emphasis and practice. In the sight of
all this, who am I to say, 'My faith is right'? And who am I to
say to everyone else (Baptists, Quakers, Roman Catholics,
Muslims, Hindus, very low church – or very high church –
Anglicans), 'Your faith is wrong'?

It helps to remember that listening to music is not something
that merely happens within oneself; it is the process of relating
to the music that is being played outside oneself, so that it can
'speak' in whatever way it does. This is like faith. Faith is the
experience of relating to God. It therefore depends on what a
person does to be open to what God does. Faith is a personal
relationship; so of course the faith of each person is unique, as
people themselves are unique.

Nevertheless, though we are unique, we are not alone. Indeed
we find that the faith by which we relate to God is a faith
that relates us to one another. We are in a group, and we see
other groups. We can categorize and compare. Amongst the
categories of those who claim to relate to God is the one that we

broadly call Christian. This goes with the claim that God has uniquely revealed himself through the human life of Jesus Christ; and that what once happened in and through this human life is true and effective for ever more through the Spirit of God. We find the Spirit at large in all creation, but also focussed day by day in the lives of Christian people, individually and corporately. The Christian church, to its shame, is divided; and I happen to have been born into that branch of it known as the Anglican Communion. The characteristic of this particular Christian 'denomination' is that it contains within itself in tension many of the aspects of Christianity which other denominations tend to have one at a time. So the Anglican way is one to which one can apply those adjectives which sometimes people use as nouns in an exclusive sense, such as 'catholic', 'reformed', 'evangelical', 'rational', 'traditional', 'charismatic', 'orthodox'. Different Anglicans stress these in different degrees – and disagree with one another as they do so. But they are still part of the one church, whose unity is not the subjective unity of people who agree, but the given, objective unity of those who through Baptism and Holy Communion are members of the same church. Into this church I was born. In it I have been brought up, and through it I have practised my life's ministry. I find myself admiring the robust enthusiasm, the deep spirituality, the practical good sense of other denominations. I try to keep these qualities in balance in the practice of my own Anglican-style faith in God. That is where I am. I have a long way still to go on my journey of faith. As I try to advance in the knowledge and love of God, I find myself strengthened by other people who are making their journeys. We all start from different positions, and therefore have to go by different routes; but *en route* we sometimes join up so that we can help one another along the way. We can also call, across the barriers that seem to divide us, to those who are making their own different journeys.

A confusion is creeping in. Faith is said to be a *relationship* with God. Now it is also being described as a *journey* to God. It is both. God is the End, the Object, the Goal of all living. In our lifetime we are called to go to him: beginning at birth, strengthened on the way by baptism, constantly redirected; strengthened again by confirmation, holy communion, prayer, forgiveness; helped by human encouragement and advice; grow-ing, changing, developing; coming ultimately by Christ's promise to be with God in heaven. But faith is also an ever-growing relationship with God whose love we experience day by day as we go forward. God is in every situation. We learn to find that this is so by prayer. St Teresa put it nicely when she said, 'All the way to Heaven is Heaven; for He has said, I am the Way.'

I look across and think of millions and millions of people on their own journeys of faith, starting from different positions, guided and helped through other means: a small child in the Australian Bush; an old lady in an Indian village; a boy living rough in the outskirts of Los Angeles; as Eskimo girl; a family in Peru; one of the crowd of Muslims demonstrating in the street; a Buddhist monk in his cell; a courting couple in Kazakhstan; an English child of twelve being prepared for confirmation.

If God exists, they come from and go to the same God. If faith in God is possible through the ubiquitous Holy Spirit of God, people can cultivate their faith and make their journey of faith from where they are to where God is calling them through the scenery of their own particular lives. If God has truly been revealed through Christ, then knowledge of that revelation will help anyone and enhance anyone's life: if they know about it. If not (by whoever's fault), they can respond in whatever way they learn personally to find God: through their conscience; in the beauty of people and things; through sacred books; through the prophets and wise men and women of all religions that have come to know God and interpret God for the guidance of others.

That which is common to all these 'ways to God' is 'con-science'. 'Conscience' is a person's inner call to respond to what is true, what is good, and what is beautiful. I have heard Christian people argue that they would continue to be Christians even if Christianity were found not to be true, so enriching is it in this life and so promising for eternal life. This view would seem to be held by those who speak of 'faith' as if it were in contrast to 'reason' and as if the intellect had no part in it. I have heard the phrase 'man-made reason' used in scorn of scholars who study biblical texts and those who believe in the validity of scientific discoveries. I cannot believe that this view accords with the exercise of conscience, for conscience is *response* to the truth, not a denial of it. Such an obscurantist attitude leads to a harsh and narrow religiosity which denies the most important principle of Christianity, namely, that God is universal, creative Love. The worst thing about it is that this attitude has led millions of people away from the faith because, naturally and rightly, they consider the pursuit of truth to be of the utmost importance. If God is, then the truth will lead people, now or later, to what God is. To obscure the truth is to obfusticate knowledge of God.

But a *caveat* is necessary. Sometimes people think arrogantly that their little bit of 'knowledge' is the whole truth, arguing that whatever does not fit into a particular branch of knowledge must be false. This cannot be so. I have been told that by the exploration of physics alone, you will not find the laws of chemistry; and by the study of chemistry alone, you will not find biology; and by none of these will you find the so-called 'human' sciences. The whole truth must embrace and be greater than any particular 'compartment' of knowledge. The search for truth is a necessary function of a person's conscience, but it must be open-ended, not closed upon a particular system.

It hardly needs saying that a person's conscience is also the guide to 'goodness' in matters of moral attitude and behaviour. Some such matters are relative, of course, to the ethos and customs and laws and *mores* of a particular society. But there are also 'universal principles' which are to do with the value of life and concern for other people. Sometimes a person's perception of 'goodness' has been warped by cruel treatment and moral and spiritual starvation. Everyone, therefore, has to make her or his own 'journey' towards what is right, some starting from a position of great disadvantage. This person may have learnt by bitter experience that the only wrong thing is to be caught. That child is being taught to shop-lift. Here is a man who has been brought up to assume a natural right to be obeyed by everyone else. Here is someone who has never known sexuality except as a means of making money. There are 'absolute' standards of right and wrong – ultimately. But people have to thread their way through the circumstances that confront them towards the attainment of these standards. Sometimes there is no simple choice between 'right' and 'wrong'. The response of conscience to goodness, therefore, is a matter of progress and direction; not a complete experience in the present.

Another *caveat* is needed at this point. Sometimes people abuse the word 'conscience' by allowing it to validate their own moral attitudes and behaviour even when these seem to other people to be anti-social and wrong. Strong racial prejudice, for instance, will drive people ('according to their lights') to monstrous behaviour; so will a narrow, cruel moralism such as is sometimes displayed by religious sects and perverted individuals. Sometimes enthusiasm for a cause which is good in itself can get out of proportion and lead people into obsessive and dangerous behaviour. Equally, there are those of us whose conscience is debilitated by a cosy attitude to the *status quo* of our particular society. We are capable of remaining wilfully ignorant or feebly ineffective with regard to the subhuman conditions being endured by masses of the world's population. Conscience influences what one sees and learns. It prompts our choice in the matter of the newspapers we read, the programmes we watch, the friends we allow to influence us – indeed every influence that we allow into our lives. What we let in becomes the source of our reponses and our moral attitudes. To be defective in listening and looking is to become defective in doing. Indeed, with the complexity of experiences that come our way, the bewildering hierarchy of loyalties that we have to put into place, and all the possibilities around us of doing evil or good, it can be safely said that 'conscience' must be more than a glib endorsement of our habitual attitudes. It is a faculty that has continually to be stimulated, informed, reminded, fed, refreshed, poked.

It is possible to speak of the 'journey' to truth and the 'journey' to goodness. I am not so sure about a 'journey' to beauty. Beauty, to me, is more like the disciples' experience of the Transfiguration:[2] that is, a sudden glimpse of truth, of harmony, of goodness, evoking wonder and delight, seen in the immaculate form of a flower, or in the exquisite colours of the sky at dawn, or the grandeur of the Dolomites, or the supple grace of a human body, or the generous profusion of colours in a picture by Matthew Smith, or one of Messiaen's chords, or Mozart's inevitable surprises, or Schubert's modulations, or the slow movement of Ravel's Piano Concerto, or the restless sea of dancers in *Swan Lake*. These to me (and many more to many other people) are not 'journeys to'; they are 'glimpses of' heaven; and response to them is not a response of the intellect or the will but a joyful leap of feeling.

In the Prologue of the Fourth Gospel, St John writes of 'the light that lighteth every man that comes into the world'. He later identifies this 'light' with Jesus Christ, the incarnate Word of God; and, according to this Gospel, Christ himself claims to be 'the Light of the world'. Jesus giving sight to the 'man born blind' is described as a 'sign' of the truth of this claim.[3] What is being said is that everyone is born with this inner light by which it is possible to respond to the light of truth and goodness and beauty; ultimately to God. If this is true, then whatever name or none we give to God, whatever route we are given to follow, whatever knowledge of truth we are given to grasp, whatever opportunities of love (received and given) we have to exercise, whatever glimpses of beauty – by sight, ear or touch – we are given to delight us, the most important thing in life is our chosen response to these things; for these, whether we begin to realize it now or will find it to our surprise later, bring us ultimately (if there is an ultimate) to the vision of God.

I will end this chapter with better words than I can find in myself, from St Paul's letter to the Christians of Philippi:

Finally, brethren, whatsoever things are true, whatsoever things are honest, whatsoever things are just, whatsoever things are pure, whatsoever things are lovely, whatsoever things are of good report; if there be any virtue, and if there be any praise, think on these things.[4]

14

Words, Opera, Involvement

Opera to me comes before everything else (Mozart, Letter, 1782).

An opera must draw tears, cause horror, bring death, by means of song (Bellini, Letter to his librettist, 1834).

Certainly religion was all too often the opium of the people, and music too ... can befog, bewitch and mislead. Many Christians are in danger of using musical solemnity to ward off the 'outside world', of lulling themselves into a world of religious feeling which can also be produced by music, and thus failing to take note of the practical problems of the time. Hence religion and music as the opium of the people. Who can overlook the fact that the church hierarchy, too, is often enough in danger of celebrating only itself with solemn masses, and confusing the triumph of the grace of God with its own triumph? (Hans Küng, *Mozart: Traces of Transcendence*).

I discovered later ... that it is only by living completely in this world that one learns to have faith (Dietrich Bonhoeffer, *Letters and Papers from Prison*, 21 July 1944).

The German theologian and martyr, Dietrich Bonhoeffer, could be said to be one of the saints of our century. On 14 July 1934, at the age of twenty-eight, he was appointed by Pastor Martin Niemöller[1] to be Director of the Berlin-Brandenburg Preachers' Seminary which became established at Finkenwalde in Pomerania. Here he led a community of 'brethren' in a *Life Together* (the title of one of his books) in which prayer and meditation, open personal confession, mutual admonition, theological study and a commitment to obey any call from the church were part of the rule. At this time Bonheoffer wrote *The Cost of Discipleship*, which shows Christ at the centre of the living church's life, a life that must therefore be lived strictly by the teaching of the Sermon on the Mount. There was a public side of this life, and Bonhoeffer found himself being drawn into the stormy waters of church and state politics. Hitler wanted a church which would back the state in all respects, but

Bonhoeffer knew that that was not possible. The church was deeply split, and Bonhoeffer became known as one who stood for a pure Christianity that would resist the evil doings of the state, with particular reference to its treatment of the Jews. As early as 1935 he had said, 'Only those who cry out for the Jews may also sing Gregorian chant.' In August 1937 the Gestapo closed Finkenwalde, but the community life continued in Lower Pomerania. In January 1939 Bonhoeffer was prohibited from staying in Berlin on church business. In April, what was now called 'the collective pastorate' moved to Sigurdshof, where Bonhoeffer taught theology for the last time with the clergy living together.

On 23 January 1939 he became liable for conscription to military service, but he managed to obtain a passport to go to England. He wrote to Bishop Bell, 'I am planning to leave Germany at some point. The main reason for this is the conscription which has been introduced this year for all men of my year of birth (1906). I cannot reconcile it with my conscience to take part in a war in these circumstances.' In June he went to America to give lectures in Chicago. He was then invited to stay in New York and look after the German emigrants there, thus postponing, even avoiding, his return to Germany. But in July he wrote to his friend Reinhold Niebuhr, 'I have come to the conclusion that I made a mistake in coming to America. I must live through this difficult period of our national history with the Christians of Germany. I shall have no right to take part in the restoration of Christian life in Germany after the war unless I share the trials of this time with my people.' So when he could have stayed in the remote comfort of America, Dietrich Bonhoeffer decided to go back home, knowing that he would have to dirty his hands in the affairs of his country if he were truly to serve God. Five weeks after leaving Germany he returned, to be embroiled in the affairs of a country wickedly at war.

Reading about his pre-war years, one gains the impression of someone who was sadly aware that he was missing the mark. Striving for perfection by keeping himself clean from sin did not seem to work. He was never self-righteous; yet there was something slightly awry, a lack of joy, a failure to find the 'blessedness' which Christ promised in the Sermon on the Mount. From the high moral stance that he had taken up as a result of his Christian principles, he found himself desperately opposed to Hitler and the cruel regime that governed Germany. Having personal contacts with men who had equally high scruples and a position of greater power, Bonhoeffer became involved in the catastrophic plot to kill Hitler, first in 1943, then in July 1944. He was arrested on 5 April 1943 and sent to the military interrogation prison at Tegel.

To the fastidious Bonhoeffer who had sought 'perfection' by blameless living, to be imprisoned on a charge of high treason was a most humiliating and appalling 'dirtying of hands', worse than anything he could imagine; and being forced to do menial duties in the course of the harsh prison regime was almost more than he could bear. But there were other prisoners there, too, people who had needs which to some extent he could meet. Also he found, in his profound spiritual struggle, that physical hardship affected him less than he thought it would. Maybe it was in this situation that he 'found his soul', experiencing a new closeness to 'Christ Crucified' and a new vein of 'blessed reality' in his Christian profession. This set him against much that had passed for 'religion' in the old pre-war days and made him write in his letters to his friends about the 'religionless Christianity' for which he is remembered.

'Religion' is 'relationship with God'. Bonhoeffer saw that this relationship was to be found in 'this-worldly' living. Also he believed that in the practice and development of religion as he had inherited it in his church (and this would be equally true of all other branches of the church), 'religious rites' were often being treated as a substitute for, instead of an aid towards, 'knowing God'. Meanwhile, in his dreadful prison, Bonhoeffer was finding God, and finding other people, and finding them in God and God in them. And slowly, painfully, he was finding himself, as one can see from his letters which he was able to write and smuggle out of prison. He was also able to read, and through the books that he read he sent messages in cypher to his friends.

Bonhoeffer was at Tegel until the failure of the July plot, after which the friends who had been supporting him were arrested and executed. In February 1945 he was taken secretly to the concentration camp at Flossenburg. On Low Sunday, 8 April, he presided at a service held with his fellow prisoners. On 9 April he was taken out and hanged.[2]

The strong lesson of Bonhoeffer's 'saintliness' is that for Christianity to be 'real' it must be 'involved'. Yes, it must 'lift us up to Heaven'; but yes, too, it must be 'earthed', as God's love was earthed through the 'humanization' of the Spirit of God in the life of Jesus Christ.

In music there is no equivalent so painful and so 'dirty'. Nevertheless, music moves into the mode of human experiences and moral issues when it is set to words. What the music 'lifts up to heaven', the words 'bring down to earth'. Sometimes singers ignore the importance of the words they are singing, maybe in laziness or incompetence, or even because they feel that the beautiful liquidity of the sound they are making is spoilt by the intrusion of consonants and difficult-to-sing vowels. But this makes the music insipid. It loses its colour and spring. True, the words themselves are sometimes clumsy and ill-fitting, especially when they have been translated from their original language. But there is more at stake than the sound of the musical line, or even the poetic quality of the words. When music is set to words, it is involved with *meaning*. To lose the meaning of the words is to lose half of what is being performed. It is like watching a game of football for its patterns and not caring about who wins, or looking at a picture for its colour and not noticing its shapes. Music and word are part of a single artistic statement. They need and enhance one another.

Musicians are sometimes tempted to ignore the spoken word in services of worship. Some organists go off for coffee; choirmen have been known to read books; boys to play 'sermon-cricket'. I am sure they can be forgiven, pleading that their part in the liturgy is exacting: they have done their bit and now they need some relaxation. But if they succumb, they not only weaken the liturgical act which the rest of the congregation are trying to perform faithfully, but they miss a lot themselves. Christian worship is not confined to soaring up to heaven on musical ladders; it is also Christ, the Word of God, challenging, judging, stimulating worshippers to work for the Kingdom of God on earth. Music lifts. The Word earths. What is earthed needs to be lifted; but what is lifted needs to be earthed.

There is, of course, music which does take hold of earth-bound situations, lifts them and reveals their universal nature. Sometimes it pokes fun; sometimes it spells out human dilemmas and moral problems. It can expose the ever-recurring entanglements of love, the contrasting quirks of human character, the struggles of the individual against the collective, mankind against nature, human beings against their destiny. This is opera. Opera does not set out to moralize; nor does it inspire people to a virtuous way of life. But it illuminates the human siuation in all its tragedy, glory and fun.

The Marriage of Figaro, for instance, treats with joyful irreverence the absurdity of an aristocracy which is based on the privilege of birth rather than merit. The worldly-wise servant gets the better of the amorous count – but all continue to live happily together. *Carmen* affirms human sexuality as something glorious and irresistible, but tragic, too, when it overrules duty and loyalty. *Peter Grimes* is the lonely, unhappy man driven to despair by the gossip and cruel judgments of the village fishing community, with its pub and its parson, its church services and its scandal-mongers; all amidst the sunshine and the storms of the North Sea. The moment when Grimes' friend speaks to him quietly and tells him to go out in his boat and sink it is to me one of the 'moments in opera'. In *The Ace Of Spades* Tchaikovsky's big tunes and thick score draw us into the tragedy of a soldier who is obsessed by gambling and physical love. For the public who do not go to other operas, there is Gilbert and Sullivan. To my ears Sullivan's music is delightful; and if Gilbert's plots are somewhat dated and his humour rather arch, nevertheless here again is music and drama about people, however peculiar and however odd their situations. Much fun is poked at the British establishments: military, legal, ecclesiastical and hereditary. Silly artistic aestheticism is lampooned; the cruelty of the Orient exposed. Some Gilbert and Sullivan operas are too sexist and ageist for our generation, but the finest of all, *The Yeomen of the Guard*, is a tragic study of the essential sadness of the professional clown.

The impact of opera comes from the parts as well as the whole, and the music helps at every point to emphasize the intricacies of the plot, the clashes of temperament, and the movement of the story towards tragedy or glory. Think of Tarquin's ride to Rome in *The Rape of Lucretia*; the way the orchestra makes the storm blow in every time the door opens in the pub scene in *Peter Grimes*; the delicious truth-revealing mix-up in *Cosi Fan Tutti*; the desperately slow, grief-bound sea journey at the beginning of *Tristan and Isolde*; Albert's defiance (in *Albert Herring*) of the class-ridden rules and taboos of Edwardian England, once he has been liberated by innocent intoxication; the delicious caricatures in Gilbert and Sullivan 'patter songs'; the problems a possessive husband can have with his wife in *Don Pasquale*.

In opera human lives are exposed. Sometimes we see the external qualities of heaven resounding through the lives of unexpected people. We also see nasty wickedness in those who are supposed to be good. There is much distress; self-righteousness; heroes and saints. And the music illumines, characterizes, caricatures, weaves together all that is most tragic, most splendid and most ridiculous in the drama of human living.

I turn to Beethoven, who wrote what could be said to be the greatest opera of all, *Fidelio*. For public and for personal reasons, Beethoven had to write an opera. The public wanted operas more than anything else in music, so Beethoven felt the need to give them one. But he also felt the need to write a work in which he could sum up his attitude to life, death, society, politics, despotism, heroism; above all, what he longed and strove for, *freedom*. Emerging from an age in which professional musicians were regarded as servants, Beethoven regarded himself as definitely not a servant, but a master, a genius. Yet he was poor; and despite his mastery as pianist and composer, he had to depend on those who would commission and pay him. Meanwhile society everywhere was being shaken by revolution, with the rise of Napoleon and his astonishing conquests, which delighted but later outraged Beethoven. He hated political tyranny; and he hated the petty tyrannies to which he was subjected through his drunken father, his negligent nephew, and aristocratic people who kept making demands on him. Above all, there was the growing tyranny of his deafness – a terrible affliction for a musician. Yet he loved God and life and music. There was delight and beauty as well as ugly injustice in the world around him. All this comes out in his only opera, *Fidelio*, 'The Faithful One'.

It is a 'salvation' story: of ruthless power, corruption, heroic resistance, and selfless love. Florestan is in prison for daring to speak the truth against the district governor, Pizarro. But Leonora his wife is determined to save him. She is the 'perfect woman', perhaps reminding Beethoven of his mother, who had suffered so grievously at the hands of his father. Leonora disguises herself as a young man (Fidelio) and manages to get the job of gaoler's assistant in the prison. The opera begins with the sort of domestic scene which was typical of operas, but which gives one a false security in face of the tragedy of the situation and the drama that is to follow. The gaoler's daughter, Marzelline, is doing the ironing and quarrelling with her fiancé, Jaquino, her father's assistant. Jaquino loves her more than she is prepared to love him, for she has lost her heart to the handsome 'Fidelio'. There is a delightful quartet, with Marzelline cooing her love for Fidelio, Rocco, her gaoler father, expressing his obvious satisfaction, Jaquino being distinctly annoyed, and 'Fidelio' very upset at this unexpected and embarrassing complication to her plans for rescuing her husband. Meanwhile, however, the orchestra is growling away in its pit with music which more than accompanies this domestic mix-up. There are dark sounds. Listen, and you know that all is not well. Soon the governor appears amidst much empty pomp and give orders for Florestan to be murdered. Rocco refuses to do the deed, but is persuaded (having just sung a song in praise of money) to help; yet the act ends with the prisoners coming out of the darkness below for a glimpse of the light and air of freedom. They sing a restrained chorus during which the orchestra plays and develops a haunting tune which rises a little, and tries again and again to rise more, but never succeeds.

Act Two begins in the dreadful darkness of the dungeon, with Florestan's body sprawling across the floor. One thinks of Bonhoeffer. One thinks of all prisoners: of hostages like Terry Waite, John McCarthy and Brian Keenan; of 'death row' cells in America. The condemned man stirs, and then sings softly and very high an agonizing but uncomplaining lament. O God! this darkness! this emptiness! this silence (Beethoven's silence?)! these chains for the truth he had spoken! The clarinet plays the calm, sad tune that comes in the Leonora overtures,[3] and the voice joins in. There is pain, but no bitterness. God's will be done. The prisoner accepts the price he is paying for telling the truth.

The music then quickens. Florestan feels a draught of cool air and a glimmer of light as the gaoler, with Fidelio in attendance, comes in to make grisly preparations for the prisoner's death. They manage to be kind by giving him wine and bread, and Fidelio begins to steel herself for the task of rescuing him. But Pizarro enters, intent on confronting Florestan and killing him – to another of those musical quartets in which all the characters sing their own thoughts, contrasting, yet blending with one another. Pizarro then raises his dagger to strike. But Fidelio intervenes and acclaims herself as Leonora. We expect a struggle, a fight, a murder, or two. But a distant trumpet calls, heralding the arrival of the just and progressive minister of state. Salvation is at hand. The music surges – and the climax is almost unbearable. There is such love in the duet between the saviour and the saved; the noble, 'faithful' wife and her husband; surprise and satisfaction for the good-at-heart gaoler; disgust in the voice of Pizarro. The scene changes to the court-yard. Everyone is there: the minister of state, the confounded governor, all the prisoners, the crowd who have been clamour-ing at the gates, the gaoler and guards, Marzelline and Jaquino (now, it seems, reconciled), and Leonora with her husband. Love has defeated the odds against it. Freedom has won the day.

So has Beethoven. Beethoven was a 'man of God', but not a 'man of religion'. His sense of morality was not so much private as public. It was on the world scene that he saw and took his part in the struggle: to the end that merit should be recognized; people should be judged for what they do, rather than for the circumstances they are born into; that tyranny should be opposed and freedom established: here on earth.

15

Affirmations of Faith I: J. S. Bach –
Mass in B Minor

Bach opens a vista to the universe. After experiencing him, people feel
there is meaning to life after all (Helmut Walcha).

Bach is the supreme exemplification of the thesis that the greatest artists do
not so much originate as fulfil; the supreme confutation of the notion that
an artist's greatness reveals itself in the extent to which he 'expresses the
spirit of his age' ... He was the only composer in his own day, before him,
or after him, who was able to use to the full, in practice, the theoretical
possibilities of his art (Ernest Newman, in *International Cyclopaedia of
Music and Musicians*).

> For the glory of the most high God alone,
> And for my neighbour to learn from
> (J.S. Bach; *Epigraph to the Little Organ Book*).

Christians are a blissful people who can rejoice at heart and sing praises,
stamp and dance and leap for joy (Martin Luther).

The writer of the Epistle to the Hebrews began by saying that
whereas in former days God had 'spoken' to the human race
through 'the prophets', now, at last, God had 'spoken' through
the human life of Jesus, the 'Son of God'.[1] Now it has been
cynically said that ever since then, theologians have been busy
turning that 'life' back into 'words' again. This is more than a
jibe; it is uncomfortable truth. The source of Christianity is not
a book,[2] nor a vision, nor a manifesto, but a human life: one
that we know little about except that the last two years were
vastly effective. So there had to be 'words' to explain the truth
of this 'life'. There was the Bible itself, a library of books which
relate to the life of Jesus. It was painfully put together from
multitudes of ancient and contemporary sources in the course of
the first two centuries of Christendom. As well as the Bible,
millions more words have been used by men and women who

have wrestled with the truth of Christianity and have tried to express, account for, defend it, spell it out, define it. Word-users go to the historical origins of the faith, to their own and other peoples' experience, to knowledge and opinions gleaned from religious, literary and scientific sources. They have sought, too, to describe its philosophical, sociological and ethical implications. To do any of this they have had to speak or write in *words*. So the pouring forth of words has gone on in every decade of every generation – and will go on doing so as long as people are alive and communicating with one another. Indeed, as regards the mystery of God, no words can encapsulate the truth; so no one can ever say 'the last word' on the subject.

There are, however, other ways in which religious truth can be expressed: the visual arts, obviously, drama and dance. Pre-eminently there is music. This is not because a composer sets out to 'compose' what he believes. It is more that in the process of writing music, the composer is expressing innermost feelings and attitudes which are more 'religious' to him than any verbal statement of them can be. There is a difference between music and words. Music is less defining but more expressive. Music does not 'pin down', it 'opens up'. It speaks not so much to the intellect as to the heart. It does not explain, spell out, define. It affects one's feelings. It casts down and lifts up. It aches and exhilarates, soothes and challenges, gives and demands, cries and glorifies. Is this why so many musicians pay little regard to the 'words' of faith in creeds, the Bible, sermons, but nevertheless have a deep, if sometimes unstructured, grasp of religious truth which they express searingly in music of their own creation?

Is this why John Sebastian Bach wrote the B Minor Mass? Not that he disregarded the 'words' of faith. He himself was a committed Christian with an intellectual grasp of what Christianity was about. But he wished to re-express the meaning of the words in music. In doing so he used all the technical devices which as a master musician he had at his disposal. So he knit together Christian doctrines and stories and feelings and symbolisms and the musical language of keys and counterpoint, harmony and rhythm, into patterns of great complexity that are truly astonishing. Bach was not a Roman Catholic, and it may seem strange that such a staunch Lutheran should have used

Latin words, even if they are not precisely from the Roman Mass, and were not intended to be used liturgically. Could it not simply be that Bach wished to gather together the best of his musical life, add to it, and put it all into one mighty work which in its entirety comes as near as he could make it to expressing the truth as he understood it? The Latin words of the Mass suited him well because of their immediate and their eternal meaning. They gave him scope to express the passion and the glory, the bathos and the splendour of Christianity as he could never have expressed it in words. Indeed, in the whole of literature and art is there any statement of Christianity which comes so near to the sublime truth as the B Minor Mass?

When I was at school I was taught axiomatically that the B Minor Mass was the finest music ever written. I accepted this from Jasper Rooper my teacher without any idea that he was repeating what the Swiss critic, Hans Georg Nägeli, had written in 1817, when the work was hardly known. 'The B Minor Mass is the greatest work of music of all ages and of all peoples.' Nor did I doubt him as I listened to the B Minor and tried to sing my part first as a second treble, then as an alto and twice since as a bass. To question such a statement is to succumb to its pre-supposition that one piece of music is in competition with another, like athletes or football teams or aspirants for Young Musician of the Year. Competition between musical works is not necessary; but anyone who loves music and loves Christianity can love them both together – to a high degree – in the B Minor Mass.

Faith is about promise, not certainty. It requires response, not gullibility. The opening chords of the B Minor Mass give assurance; but as the sopranos soar upwards and then upwards again, they challenge us to venture, and beckon us with a glimpse of the glory to come. Immediately the fugue starts and we are swept into the middle of it. It has an assured theme which begins with a dotted rhythm and gives us the confidence to go forward and upwards, a step at a time. At each step there is a pause for confirmation before the theme takes us on to new sets of possibilities, for it ends differently every time it comes round: sometimes to question, sometimes to agonize, sometimes to affirm. Then the voices start beckoning us one by one to go with them and to engage ourselves with the music. This chorus is an 'opening', not a 'closing', experience. Uncertainty, mystery, glory lie ahead: a mystery that puzzles; a glory that dazzles the eyes, but hides the ultimate truth and the way towards it, like the burning brightness of the sun.

The *Kyrie* is about asking for God's mercy – not in breast-beating self-pity as our prayers of confession so often imply, but in the recognition of a beautiful but flawed world in which we offer our best but flawed selves to God. So there is sadness to come but great joy, too, as our hearts are wrung by the love of God and the pain of the sullied world. Surely the Good God will show his mercy on it and us. Then the two sopranos, against a background of a poignant tune played by two violins, continue to plead to Christ, more personally, more insistently, with a view perhaps to particular troubles. The chorus then returns with a chromatic cry that is even more urgently demanding than the first *Kyrie*: '*Kyrie eleison*, Lord, have mercy; *Christe eleison*, Christ have mercy; ***kyrie eleison, Lord have mercy***.'

There is no one so woebegone as a person who suffers tragedy and cannot call upon God to blame or curse, let alone ask for mercy. There is only blank void, impersonal chance, bad luck: no God; certainly not a God who understands and empathizes with human suffering. By contrast, Christian belief in the God whom we call on to have mercy is belief in the God of all creation, infinitely glorious, infinitely loving. The first religious duty, therefore, is to acclaim God joyfully and to give thanks for all his goodness.

So we are bounced into the *Gloria* and our hearts are made to dance in quick three-in-a-bar rhythm as the orchestra proclaims sensational news with uninhibited joy, and the trumpets join in like angels from on high, ringing out the truth of the Glorious God in the Highest. Human voices join the melée in whirling chaos. All is ecstasy and delight: no darkness; no discord; nothing hurtful in this wild confusion of radiant colour and sound. But then the rhythm squares up and order is reclaimed as the noble human prayer for peace is proclaimed: '*et in terra pax hominibus bonae voluntatis*', 'and on earth peace to men of goodwill'. Out of that, as if to show with total clarity and undiminished ecstasy what are the implications of this 'goodwill', the voices, led by the sopranos, sing a long, twisty extension of this prayer in swiftly running semi-quavers. (How

can human voices sing so fast? It is a nice example of the effec-
tiveness of collective action that people find they can sing much
faster together than they ever can by themselves in the bath.)
The orchestra continues to pound out the rhythm of the prayer
for peace. The music grows in volume and energy. 'Peace'
becomes less a longing, more a shout of triumph. Trumpets
scream their agreement. Kettledrums rattle their applause. The
whole universe seems to be acclaiming in sound the inextrica-
bility of the glory of God and the peace of humankind; and the
wild joy of the two put together.

So to the Creed. The Latin word *credo* from which we derive
our word 'creed' does not imply an intellectual stance alone: 'I
believe that this is so'. It implies 'moral belief', for which we use
the word 'trust'. Intellectual belief and trust do, of course, overlap, and it is unlikely that a person can profess one without a
measure of the other. Indeed, they feed on one another. So the
Credo which we say when mind and heart are in growing
alliance is a commitment to the truth more than an arid
certainty about it. It becomes a way of life. 'Yes,' we say, 'on
balance, I think that this is true; therefore (with a necessary
degree of boldness) I commit myself to it. This is now my
chosen way of life.' In the Nicene Creed (the one used in the
eucharist, originally written in Greek) the word used for '*credo*'
is in the plural: *pisteuomen*, '*We* believe. This is *our* commitment; *our* way of life.'

For this statement of collective, intellectual and moral belief
(the *Credo*), Bach composed music which is emphatic and
uncompromising. But the theme, announced immediately by the
basses, is undergirded by a succession of moving crotchets on
the 'cellos which give the music flexibility and a readiness to
advance. That which is stiff is brittle and easily breaks. The
affirmation of belief is all the stronger when it allows for movement and growth. We are, after all, growing into the truth, not
standing on it.

When the Creed reaches the '*Incarnatus est*' ('He was incarnate', 'made a human being') the violins weep and the voices
sing the words in descending minor intervals, the sopranos very
softly from a great height, as if to stress the costliness of this
incredible (but we believe it) act of divine love. We had already
prayed in the *Gloria* (for that exalted music had to come to

earth) that the God who 'takes away the sins of the world' would 'have mercy on us'. Now in very similar music we hear the shattering answer to this prayer. '*Incarnatus est*': 'He was incarnate'. Bach sees the incarnation, as it were, from God's point of view, that is, as an act of supreme self-abasement. Here is the price that God paid for Christmas; not the joy that human-beings receive from it. We remember St Paul's words to the Philippians:

> Take to heart among yourselves what you find in Christ Jesus: He was in the form of God; yet he laid no claim to equality with God, but made himself nothing, assuming the form of a slave. Bearing the human likeness, sharing the human lot, he humbled himself, and was obedient, even to the point of death, death on a cross![3]

The sadness is compounded as incarnation ends in crucifixion. There is no break in the music, but instead of the painful interval at the end of the incarnation arpeggio, we now have an even more painful semitone which is stressed again and again in the phrase 'crucifixus': 'he was crucified'. That chorus ends calmly, however, with one of those arresting key-shuffles that Bach uses, to end on a note of peace; resignation; (dare we say?) hope.

From the peaceful chord in G major, chorus and orchestra spring to life in a full-throated, vigorous roar in D major: '*Et resurrexit*': 'And he rose again.' The music dances with joy as voice after voice takes up the message in long, breathless runs that intermingle almost to the point of chaos. Then the men take over with a rumbustious, confident (but tricky) assertion which allows no space for contradiction or qualification. This is sung, maybe roughly because of its difficulty, by 'us men together'. 'We *do* believe: "*et iterum venturus*": "that he will come again in glory to judge the living and the dead."'

There is more to come in the Creed: a lyrical '*Et cum spiritu sancto*' ('and in the Holy Spirit') sung by the bass soloist with two oboi d'amore playing tenderly together in thirds and sixths, in lilting six-eight time, in loving accord with one another and the bass and the Spirit of God and the world. As the soprano soloists did after the *Kyrie* with their '*Christe eleison*', making personal what the chorus had made universal, so here the bass seems to be saying that because of the Holy Spirit the universal truth of resurrection is also an individual person's most precious gift.

When Thomas the Twin met Jesus after the resurrection, having said the week before that he would never believe unless he received positive proof by touch and by sight, he worshipped Jesus, saying, 'My Lord and my God'. The supreme religious activity is to worship. One can think of it in the broadest sense of bringing the whole of life and offering it to God, so that worship governs the direction of all activities. But one can also think of worship as the 'point of focus' at which people open their hearts and mouths to praise God. This is what Christians do in the eucharist. Having been bidden to lift up their hearts, and having agreed that 'It is meet and right so to do', they sing the *Sanctus*: 'Holy, Holy, Holy is the Lord God of Hosts'. So we come to the awe-ful climax of the B Minor Mass. Wave after wave of sound sweep the music and the musicians and the audience up to heaven and to God in huge moving chords that climb and hover and change and strengthen as the sopranos soar and the basses mark out the pace in descending octaves. Then the tenors cry out 'Heaven and earth are full of thy glory', and all the voices and all the instrumentalists join to acclaim this gospel truth.

After those heights it is as if we were with Peter, James and John as they came down the Mountain of Transfiguration with Jesus, back into ordinary life. Jesus talked of the passion to come and gave a hint of the resurrection.[4] They were then plunged into a difficult situation with an angry crowd and a man pleading for his epileptic son. Jesus healed the boy and then began to instruct his disciples on the nature of prayer.

After the '*Agnus Dei*', 'O Lamb of God', in which the alto and flute remind us poignantly of our need for mercy, the B Minor Mass ends with the chorus '*Dona Nobis Pacem*': 'Give us Peace'. Peace? The peace that we ask for musically reflects the thanks we have given to God, for this is the same music as the *Gratias agimus* in the *Gloria*. It is the peace that comes from God in and through and regardless of circumstances: for when we respond, God comes to us in all circumstances. 'Peace', therefore, does not require the absence of crisis or anger or

sorrow or joy; it is God's love for us *within* the crises and
sorrows and joy. It is not a balm to soothe our feelings: it is
strength to do what we are given to do. The measured pace of
this music is assuring and challenging. It is literally 'comforting',
for 'com-fort' means 'strength together'. The quaver runs, given
to all the voices in turn, raise the tension. They seem to penetrate all the corners and recesses of life, but remain within the
bounds of the four steady, unrelenting, comforting, upward-
moving, stride-on-into-life minims which rule each bar. The
Mass ends on the life-giving chord of D major.

I have written less than I feel about the religious and musical
impact that the B Minor Mass has made upon me, and I have
left much of it unmentioned.[5] What I love is its clarity and
unalloyed truthfulness; the coherence of its contrapuntal complexity; and the way it opens me up to more and more instead
of closing me down to something neat and confined. There is no
hint of 'religiosity' in this work. 'Religiosity' means false
gestures, pretence, words that have lost the cutting edge of
truth, ritual actions that no longer mean anything, reality
greased over with sentimentality, piety that stifles love, the
stuffy much-breathed air of traditional shibboleths[6] which resist
the Spirit of God, the dreary closing of the mind and heart upon
a private, petty 'God-in-my-pocket'. Bach's music with its
moments of crunching crisis and unrestrained joyfulness blazes
with real glory, throbs with real pain – and is always beyond my
comprehension.

16

Affirmations of Faith II:
G.F. Handel – *Messiah*

The Christian message, with its deeply mystical and symbolic doctrine of the Incarnation, has been traditionally a message of the unity of the worlds of spirit and matter, and of God's manifestation in this world and in mankind (The Prince of Wales, addressing a private meeting at Wilton Park, Sussex; as reported in *The Times*, 14 December 1996).

I did think I did see all heaven before me, and the great God Himself (G.F. Handel: words to his servant, who found him alone and weeping, after completing Part Two of *Messiah* with the Hallelujah Chorus).

Listening to the immortal masterworks performed by the enormous musical body in one of the loveliest churches in the world (Westminster Abbey), feeling the veneration with which Handel's music was received 'in a silence almost devotional' ... by an audience taught by their king to see in the music the most sublime achievement, Haydn was so deeply moved that at the 'Hallelujah' chorus he burst into tears, exclaiming: 'He is the master of us all' (Karl Geiringer, *Haydn: A Creative Life in Music*).

George Frederick Handel was born in Saxony in 1685 and came to live in London in the autumn of 1710 with a glowing reputation as one of Europe's finest composers of opera. Despite the snobbish, xenophobic opposition to Italian opera displayed by some of the critics and foremost wits of the day (and there was plenty to be scathing about), Londoners flocked to the Drury Lane Theatre for this new-fashioned entertainment. On arrival Handel was presented with the script of *Rinaldo*, a verse translation of an Italian drama, which he made into an opera (using some music from his previous works) in two weeks. Despite the absurdities of thunder, lightning and fireworks and sparrows and chaffinches which flew out of the 'delightful grove' into the auditorium, to the inconvenience of the audience, London fell for it and Handel was soon a central figure in the royal, aristocratic and cultural life of the city.

So he remained for many years: an adopted Englishman who was never really accepted as English (he always spoke with a strong German accent); a bachelor living in a large house in Barnes; definitely a 'character', not 'one of us'. But England was proud of him all the same. He quarrelled, of course, with his fellow professionals, singers and librettists; but he was much sought after as an organist and as a superb improviser on the harpsichord. Above all, wonderful operas continued to flow from his pen. London was pleased to find itself a strong centre of musical culture, rivalling the longer-established capitals of Europe.

But in 1741 Handel suddenly and unexpectedly turned from opera to oratorio. Although some have ascribed it as such, this does not seem to have been a matter of 'conversion'. Handel was a man of strong faith. He was a Lutheran, and a communicant in the Church of England. The practice of his faith meant much to him, as is shown by the fact that when he received communion three weeks before his death he made sure first that he was reconciled with those with whom he had quarrelled. It may be that far from turning to oratorio for religious reasons, he turned away from opera for artistic and financial reasons. Weary of operatic conventions and fossilized traditions, he found in the stories and incarnate truths of the Bible subjects which could engage to the full his powers of musicianship. Certainly when Jennens produced a libretto called *Messiah*, Handel found a statement of faith into which he could pour his inspired, fiery but fully matured powers of creation.

That is what Jennens hoped he would do. 'Handel says he will do nothing next winter,' he wrote to Edward Holdsworth in July 1741, 'but I hope I shall perswade (*sic*) him to set another Scripture Collection I have made for him, and perform it for his own benefit in Passion Week. I hope he will lay out his whole Genius and Skill upon it, and that the Composition may excell all his former Compositions, as the Subject excells every other Subject. The Subject is Messiah.' Later, in 1745, he was not so sure. It seems that he regarded the Messiah with (in W.S. Gilbert's phrase) 'modified rapture'. 'I shall show you a collection I gave Handel, called *Messiah*, which I value highly, and he has made a fine Entertainment of it, tho' not near so good as he might and ought to have done.'[1]

The first performance of Mr Handel's new *Grand Oratorio call'd Messiah* took place in the Musick Hall in Fishamble Street in Dublin on Monday, 12 April 1742. It was to be given 'For Relief of the Prisoners in the several Gaols, and for the Support of Mercer's Hospital in Stephen's Street, and of the Charitable Infirmary on the Inns Quay'. The performers were 'Gentlemen of the Choirs of both cathedrals' and some 'Concertos on the Organ, by Mr Handel' were to be included. The *Dublin Journal* that contained this advertisement also reported the rehearsal on the 9th, 'to a most Grand, Polite and crouded Audience' with a request for ladies to come for the first night 'without Hoops, as it will greatly increase the Charity, by making room for more company'. Gentlemen were also asked to appear without swords.[2]

The first-night performance which took place on 13 April 1742 was rapturously received. 'Words are wanting to express the exquisite Delight it afforded to the admiring, crouded Audience.' So wrote a critic in a local paper. 'The Sublime, the Grand, and the Tender, adapted to the most elevated, majestic and moving Words, conspired to transport and charm the ravished Heart and Ear.' An audience of about 700 paid £400. Handel gave his share of the proceeds and the performers gave theirs: all to be divided between the Society for the benefit and enlargement of poor distressed prisoners for debt in the several Marshalseas of the City of Dublin, the Charitable Infirmary and Mercer's Hospital.[3]

The libretto of *Messiah* was prefaced by Jennens with a text from St Paul's First Epistle to Timothy:[4] 'And without controversy great is the mystery of godliness: God was manifest in the flesh, justified in the Spirit, seen of Angels, preached unto the Gentiles, believed on in the World, received up into glory.'

There are two obvious differences between *Messiah* and Bach's B Minor Mass. The first is that the words of *Messiah* are drawn from the Bible itself rather than the mass. Thus *Messiah* is not a statement of the broad truths of Christianity as formulated in the Creed; nor is it a setting of the acts of worship that are at the centre of the Christian eucharist. *Messiah* is about prophetic statements from the Old Testament, the good news of the birth of Jesus as told to the shepherds, the sorrowful poems about the Suffering Servant of God composed by Isaiah of the

Exile,⁵ the confident assertion from the Book of Job that 'My Redeemer liveth', and the biblical hope of eternal life with God.

The second difference is that whereas the B Minor Mass is in Latin, *Messiah* is written in English. Does it matter (except to the lungs of the singers) that in the B Minor Mass Bach writes instrumental music for his human voices? The Latin words do have meaning, of course; and it is their meaning that moved Bach to write as he did. But the *sound* of the words was less important, and the stress and emphasis of particular syllables did not matter to Bach in the same way as they mattered to Handel writing *Messiah*; for although English was not his native tongue, Handel's music is right for the words, not only their meaning, but also their sound. Indeed it is hard for us to hear the words without inwardly hearing the music that immortalizes them. In *Messiah*, words and sound, meaning and music, are gloriously tuned together into one resounding affirmation of faith.

So, after the arresting 'Grave' opening in dotted rhythm in E Minor and the scene-setting fugue of the Overture, we have three bars in the 'comforting' key of E Major dominated by the repetition of four pounding staccato quavers. Then 'Com-fort ye' in a musical phrase which exactly fits the words. 'Comfort ye': that is, 'Have strength together.' Isaiah of the Exile was proclaiming hope to his fellow-countrymen in the miserable refugee camp in Babylon, by whose waters they had 'sat down and wept', quite unable to sing to their captors 'one of the songs of Zion'.⁶ 'Your warfare is ceased, your iniquity is pardon'd', says the Lord through the prophet; and the universal nature of this prophecy, which lifts it out of Babylon and gives it to all of us, is immediately obvious to the Christian reader. The next verses from Isaiah 40 are the ones which Mark's Gospel refers to and St Luke spells out when they introduce John the Baptist, the immediate forerunner of Jesus.⁷ John is identified with the 'voice of him that crieth in the wilderness, "Prepare ye the way of the Lord, make straight in the desert a highway for our God."' So, 'Comfort ye', sings Handel's tenor: 'Prepare the way for the Lord. Every valley shall be exalted, every mountain and hill laid low, the crooked straight and the rough places plain.' A riven, crooked, imperfect world is being prepared for the Messiah who will come to restore it. 'And,' sings the chorus, 'the Glory of the

Lord shall be revealed.' 'All flesh shall see it together; for the mouth of the Lord hath spoken it.'[8]

Then comes a thunderous warning from the bass in words from Haggai and Malachi and music of sharp dots and long, trembling runs. 'I will sha-a-a-a-ake all nations, the heavens, the earth, the sea, the dry land'; and will 'suddenly come to the Temple'; in judgment, no doubt, as Jesus did, to cleanse it and make it fit for the Gentiles to worship in.[9] If goodness is to triumph, evil must be shaken out; so with the fulfilment of hope there is bound to be judgment. 'Who may abide the day of his coming?' asks the alto, to notes which fit this very straight question. The chorus takes up the implication of the question as it continues with more words from Malachi.[10] The 'He' who will come is the 'He' who will 'purify'. The music is clean and clear and swift, like the cleansing waters of a mountain stream; but in the last words of the chorus the stream becomes a river, confident and assured, with strong chords: 'that they may offer unto the Lord an offering in righteousness.'

Then – the statement of statements – 'Behold, a Virgin shall conceive, and bear a Son, and shall call his name Emman-u-el: *God with us*.'[11] The alto and the chorus exult: 'O thou that tellest good tidings to Zion ... Lift up thy voice with strength ... saying, "Behold your God ... arise, shine; for thy light is come: the Glory of the *Lord* (on a low sustained note, the orchestra seething with excitement) is risen upon thee."'[12]

The bass then reminds us of the gross darkness of the earth and the people who dwell in it. Darkness is universally the symbol of evil and ignorance. But (we remember from the Prologue of St John's Gospel),[13] 'The light shines in the darkness and the darkness has never mastered it.' So now (the bass continues), 'The people that walked in darkness ... upon them hath the light shined.'[14] Indeed, as Simeon saw, when he took the infant Jesus into his arms in the Temple in Jerusalem, Jesus was destined to be 'the light to lighten the Gentiles' as well as 'the glory of his people, Israel'.[15] How so? 'For unto us a Child is born ... and the government shall be upon his shoulders ... and his name shall be called "Wonderful, Counsellor, the mighty God, the Prince of Peace".' No Hebrew scholar or modern translation will persuade those who know *Messiah* to take away the comma between 'Wonderful' and 'Counsellor'.[16] These telling titles come clear and lucid, sometimes gentle, sometimes fortissimo, always with joyful emphasis. And we note, with the coming of the 'Person', there must come also that sort of government which is implied by the nature of the Person, who will be called 'Prince of Peace'.

The Pastoral Symphony follows to give us time to ponder the news we have heard, to fear it and to glow with it.

The birth of Jesus was announced as prophecy. Now we assume that this is fulfilled, because the scene is the fields with the shepherds and their sheep.[17] Enter an angel – and then a host of angels, singing 'Glory to God in the Highest' and, what goes with it, 'Peace on earth and good will towards men'. Handel makes the words 'good will' resound throughout the chorus, the voices interrupting each other as they compete to give them emphasis. So we are bidden to 'rejoice greatly' with Zechariah[18] and the soprano and all who welcomed Jesus into Jerusalem on the first Palm Sunday. On his way to Jerusalem Jesus healed blind Bartimaeus, according to Mark, or two blind men according to Matthew:[19] so the alto takes us back to Isaiah's prophecy, to which Jesus himself drew attention when John the Baptist's disciples came and asked him if he really was 'the one who is to come'. 'The eyes of the blind shall be open'd and the ears of the deaf unstopped. Then shall the lame man leap as an hart, and the tongue of the dumb shall sing.'[20] More: the ministrations of the Messiah will be moral and spiritual as well as physical, so we have a quotation from Isaiah 40.11 seen as fulfilled by Matthew 11.28–29: 'He shall feed his flock like a shepherd'; and the soprano to the same tune but soaring downwards from a greater height, a tune that has made the words unforgettable, sings, 'Come unto him, all ye that labour. Come unto him, (ye) that are heavy laden, and he will give you rest. Take his yoke upon you, and learn of him; for he is meek and lowly of heart: and ye shall find rest ... unto your souls.'

The gospel of the impact that God has made upon the world through the life, death and resurrection of Jesus Christ was indeed 'good news' to the world, and Part 1 of the Messiah ends with the chorus happily singing that the yoke and the burden of Christ are easy and light – called so by Jesus himself because he came to make it so.[21] But he did also say that we were to follow him bearing his cross. The principle (in St Paul's words) that

'I have been crucified with Christ: the life I now live is not my life, but the life which Christ lives in me'[22] does not seem to make Christ's yoke all that easy. What is certain is that the same impact that God made upon the world through Jesus Christ, however much it was 'good news' to the world, was very painful news indeed to the human Jesus.

Now we are into Part 2 of *Messiah* and are being bidden by the alto to 'Behold the Lamb of God'. By saying 'O Lamb of God' so often in our eucharists, are we in danger of forgetting what a poignant metaphor 'lamb' is for the incarnate Son of God? A commentator has written that one of the themes of the Book of Revelation can be summed up in the phrase 'For "lion" read "lamb"'. One would naturally expect the Son of God, the anointed king to come as a lion to earth, proudly regal, savagely effective, a figure of divine power, bringing judgment and justice to disobedient people: but it was not so. At the very beginning of his ministry, according to the Fourth Gospel,[23] John the Baptist pointed to his cousin Jesus and said, 'Behold the Lamb of God' – a phrase which resonated with the appalling fate that Jesus was to undergo. Innocent lambs were taken for slaughter to be offered in sacrifice for the salvation of the people. The point of sacrifice was not to destroy life but to take it and offer it, even to the point of death. It was in this sense that Christ's whole life was to be a sacrifice for the sins of the world; not as a bloodthirsty act to appease a vengeful God, but as a life lived out in service, and offered through death, to make the love of God available for all humankind. It was in this sense too that Jesus 'loved his own' 'even to the end';[24] that is, to the very ultimate limit. It was in this sense that he allowed himself to be the 'lamb' whose life was 'given' for the sake of others.

So: in terrible, rugged solemnity, with more feeling for the guilt of the world than for the innocence of the lamb, the chorus, led by the altos, sings, 'Behold the Lamb of God, that taketh away the sin of the world'; and the alto soloist goes on to describe this human lamb as one who was 'despised and rejected ... a man of sorrows, acquainted with grief'. Again the quotation is from the suffering servant poems of the Isaiah of the Exile.[25] No one knows precisely to whom the prophet referred, but from St Matthew onwards the church has always seen the poems as prefiguring Christ. Handel matches the truth of the poetry with music that trembles and shakes with sorrow. 'Surely,' sings the chorus, 'it is our grief and our sorrow that he has borne. He was wounded for our transgressions; bruised for our iniquities: the chastisement of our peace was upon him'; and then 'With his stripes we are healed'. Why? Because 'All we like sheep have gone astray'.[26] The mood seems to change here, and the light touch of this chorus suggests a kind of silly happiness which makes the sheep in their long semiquaver runs go prancing about all over the place, straying and turning 'ev'ry one to his own way', until they are arrested by the crushing adagio: 'And the Lord hath laid upon him the iniquity of us all.'

We are then taken to Psalm 22, from which Jesus was quoting when he made the aweful cry, 'My God, My God, why hast thou forsaken me?'[27] Death by crucifixion was, according to Jewish belief, something that made a person accursed, that is, separated from God. Jesus was thus experiencing in his human consciousness this 'separation from God' which we – because of our sins – deserve but from which we can now be saved. In St Paul's words, 'Christ was innocent of sin, and yet for our sake God made him one with human sinfulness, so that in him we might be made one with the righteousness of God.'[28] The Psalm goes on to express the foul jeering that people indulge in as they taunt an innocent man; and the Gospel accounts reflect this when they describe the scene at the cross.[29] Handel gets the mood with the jagged, dotted semiquavers on strings as the tenor describes the laughter and the head-shaking, and the chorus comes in with the confident but jeering fugue: 'He trusted in God that he would deliver him: let him deliver him, if he delight in him.'[30] What terrible irony when we remember the words, 'You are my beloved Son; in you I take delight',[31] and Jesus' own words in the Garden of Gethsemane to the effect that he had only to ask for it and legions of angels could be called to his rescue.[32] The tenor sings again of the broken heart and the sorrow and the loneliness of Christ, quoting from Psalm 69.21 and then Lamentations 1.12; and the ultimate statement of degradation from Isaiah 53.8: 'he was cut off out of the land of the living: for the transgression of thy people was he stricken.'

But you cannot kill God. Whatever the truth of the incarnation as a historical event lasting the length of Jesus' life, God, the Creator, who holds all things together in love, exists in eternity that covers all time: that is, before, during and after the human life of Jesus. So as the Spirit of Christ is the Spirit of God, it is right to understand that 'the soul of Christ' (irrespective of resurrection on earth) continues to exist in the eternal existence of God. The Epistle of Peter speaks of Jesus' soul in 'Hades' to release the imprisoned spirits.[33] This means that what Jesus did through his incarnate life and death, he did for all eternity, past and present. This is Good News to the people who lived before Christ. So at this point in Messiah the librettist takes us back to Psalm 16.10 to affirm that Christ's soul is not left in hell: 'Nor didst thou suffer thy holy one to see corruption.' We go on to address Heaven itself, or rather its gates, quoting Psalm 24.7–10. They are to be lifted up, shouts the chorus, for the King of Glory to come in. 'Who is the King of Glory?' 'The Lord of Hosts: he is the king of Glory.' We seem to be back into early Old Testament thought about the Lion God, the God of battles. Rightly so, because we are singing about *victory*, the victory of goodness over evil, of love over hatred, of life over death. This victor – this Lion King – deserves the glory.

Part 2 continues with the exaltation of the Messiah and the good news about him spreading through the great company of preachers, praised for their beautiful feet(!) as they bring the gospel of peace.[34] But not everyone likes the gospel. The nations rage furiously and would 'break their bonds asunder' and 'cast away their yokes' – but to no avail. In Heaven they will be derided and broken and dashed to pieces, like a potter's vessel.[35]

So – Hallelujah. We are now in heaven sharing the vision described in the Book of the Revelation of St John.[36] Unfettered exaltation: no wonder King George III wanted to stand up and associate himself more closely with this release of spiritual and emotional energy. The Hallelujah Chorus has made a greater impact upon the music-listening world than any other single piece. It is a joyful shout of triumph. It soars to glory as it proclaims the truth that the kingdom of this world is become the 'Kingdom of our Lord and of his Christ'. It challenges the world with the claim that 'he shall reign for ever and ever': *King of Kings* 'Hallelujah! Hallelujah!' and *Lord of Lords* 'for ever! for ever'.

Part Three begins with the burning conviction that joy in

Heaven affects us personally on earth. The performance of
'I know that my Redeemer liveth'[37] depends very much on the
soprano's ability to sing the word 'know' with sufficient weight
(because it must carry conviction) and sufficient brightness on
that high E, and sufficient beauty in the vowel sound 'O';
because this is the most beautiful thing one can say. Job, in his
misery, was in fact saying that he really was innocent and that
the just God would surely vindicate him. But the Christian,
applying the word 'Redeemer' to Christ, is saying that whatever
we are guilty of, Jesus Christ has restored us with his healing
love, and he has the last word because he is risen and alive.

'And though worms destroy this body.' Poor Job was thinking of the worms that were already destroying his living body.
The Christian is saying that worms can do what they like after
death because the physical body will be transformed into a
spiritual body and in this body 'I shall see God'. St Paul spoke
of this when he tried to explain the mystery of human resurrection which Christ gives us through his resurrection. We will be
'bodies', that is, 'personal entities', but without the physical
limitations that confine us here on earth. His analogy is that
of the seed which grows into wheat. The seed is already
potentially wheat; but it has to die as a seed in order to pass into
its new, transformed life.[38] The 'vision of God' is what Jesus
promised to the 'pure in heart' as part of the blessedness which
would be theirs.[39] St Augustine once wrote: 'We shall rest and
we shall see: we shall see and we shall love: we shall love and
we shall praise.' I find something of the resting and the seeing
and the loving and the praising in this most beautiful of all
arias.

These thoughts are carried on in all the music that follows.
The chorus sings St Paul's words to the Corinthians, softly,
radiantly, unaccompanied: 'Since by man came death.' Then the
outburst: 'By man came also the resurrection of the dead.'[40]
Then again (unaccompanied, sad and with hushed expectancy),
'For as in Adam all die'; then (an explosion of joy), 'Even so in
Christ shall all be made alive'. The bass, who often sings
furiously, now allies himself to the ringing notes of the trumpet
to proclaim more words from the same passage of St Paul to the
Corinthians that 'the trumpet shall sound and the dead shall be
raised incorruptible'. There is little more to be said, but the

oratorio goes on, exulting over death, giving thanks and praise to Christ, and giving the chorus a final fling with words from the Book of the Revelation of St John, as they gather round the throne of God and join with 'the living creatures and the elders, the voices of many angels, thousands on thousands, myriads on myriads; proclaiming with loud voices': 'Worthy is the Lamb that was slain, and hath redeemed us to God by his blood, to receive power: and riches: and wisdom: and strength: and honour: and glory: and blessing.'[41] What a cheerful and light-hearted blessing it is to be, led by the men, echoed by the women, with a solo accompaniment to give extra edge to the words 'Blessing, and honour, glory and power, be unto him that sitteth upon the throne (leaping up an octave), and to the Lamb.'

You would think that all has been said that could be said. But no: we still have the final Amen fugue which gives not only to this chorus but to the whole work a huge seriousness and strength. The voices not only follow one another as you expect them to do in a fugue; they shout their agreement with one another, the basses proclaiming 'Amen', 'it must be so'; the rest following in turn, commenting on the musical phrase, lengthening it, giving it new twists and turns. At last the sopranos, instead of building the tune up from the bottom of the scale, come conclusively down from top A, only to be matched by the tenors doing the same thing a bar later with thrilling effect. We come to the final close. You would expect a penultimate chord on the dominant, A: and you get it, except that the basses are singing G. This disturbed chord[42] seems to be asking, 'Can it really be so?' A bar's pause; then the perfect cadence to the tonic, D Major. Yes, Amen, it is so.

17

Affirmations of Faith III:
Joseph Haydn – *The Creation*

Then the Lord answered Job out of the tempest:
Who is this that darkens counsel
with words devoid of knowledge ...?
Where were you when I laid the earth's foundations ...?
Who fixed its dimensions ...?
Who stretched a measuring line over it?
On what do its supporting pillars rest?
Who set its corner-stone in place,
while the morning stars sang in chorus
and the sons of God all shouted for joy ...?
Who supported the sea at its birth,
when it burst in flood from the womb –
when I wrapped it in a blanket of cloud
and swaddled it in dense fog ...?
In all your life have you ever called up the dawn
or assigned the morning its place?
Have you taught it to grasp the fringes of the earth
and shake the Dog-star from the sky ...?
Can you bind the cluster of the Pleiades
or loose Orion's belt ...?
Do you give the horse his strength?
Have you clothed his neck with a mane?
Do you make him quiver like a locust's wings,
when his shrill neighing strikes terror ...?
Did your skill teach the hawk to use its pinions
and spread its wings towards the south?
Do you instruct the eagle to soar aloft
and build its nest on high ...?
Did you proclaim the rules that govern the Heavens
or determine the laws of nature on the earth ...?
Job answered the Lord:
I know that you can do all things
and that no purpose is beyond you ...
Therefore I yield,
repenting in dust and ashes
(Job, from chapters 38–42).

The audience was in an unusually receptive state of mind. When thunderous applause followed the words 'Let there be light – and there was light,' Haydn lifted his hands upward and exclaimed, 'Not from me, from thence comes everything' (Karl Geiringer, *Haydn: A Creative Life in Music*).

The master of music, Mr Haydn, is reminded to apply himself more assiduously to composition than he has done so far ... and, to show his zeal, he will hand in the first piece of every composition in a clean, tidy copy (Prince Nicholas Esterhazy, from Gal, *The Musician's World*).

Often when I was wrestling with obstacles of every kind, when my physical and my mental strength alike were running low and it was hard for me to persevere in the path on which I had set my feet, a secret feeling within me whispered: 'There are so few happy and contented people here below, sorrow and anxiety pursue them everywhere; perhaps your work may, some day, become a spring from which the careworn may draw a few moments' rest and refreshment.' And that was a powerful motive for pressing onward (Joseph Haydn, Letter to a group of music-lovers in Bergen).

Different people come to the realization of Christian faith in different ways. Some are brought up within it so that religious beliefs are held, albeit childishly, as part of the intellectual framework of everyday actions (such as saying prayers at night or grace at meals). Religious practices (such as going to church on Sundays and joining appropriately in the festivals of Christmas and Easter) are then part of the weekly, monthly and annual rhythm of life. Others have no such religious consciousness fed into their minds and pattern of life. If they come to Christianity at all, they come through some experience or encounter later in their lives. For both kinds of people there has to be a time when suddenly, like the sun coming out on a cloudy day, or gradually, like the dawn when the light begins to be there before the sun can be seen, the truth shines and they begin to see life clearly in terms of religious belief. This may happen through an intellectual or a felt, religious experience. These may not come at the same time, but both are ultimately necessary. Feelings will have no sway over the will unless the mind is engaged; and intellectual grasp by itself is ineffective unless there is some inner sense of God's creative and redeeming love.

God's love is paramount for the sense of creation and redemption. But which of these two comes first? There are some whose primary experience is of being redeemed. They become aware of themselves as being incomplete, flawed, unfulfilled, unworthy, tyrannized by greed or power or lust; selfish, sinful; or restless, empty. They may then come to faith through a sense of need. But there are others who become aware of being alive in a beautiful world in which they have a significant part to play: a world and a personal part which are flawed, yes, but a world in which the beauty and glory and variety and splendour of things is the dominant factor of life and in which a person's first and considered response is to give thanks and praise to the Creator God.

What is certain is that however a person comes to the realization of Christianity, the two sides – creation and redemption – must complement one another both in theory and in practice. There is little point in saying 'Jesus forgives me my sins' unless one is identifying Jesus with the Word of God of whom St John wrote in the Prologue of his Gospel:

The Word was in God's presence, and what God was, the Word was. He was with God at the beginning, and through him all things came to be; without him no created thing came into being. In him was life.[1]

Nor is it Christianity to believe in God the Creator without also believing that God's creative Word has become human in order to be amongst us and to give his life for the salvation of the world.[2] Creation and redemption; goodness given and restored; life endowed, marred and renewed: these flowing, discordant combinations are at the heart of Christian faith and practice, and cannot be untangled.

Joseph Haydn was one who grew up with the Christian faith from childhood, and in spite of the harsh experiences of it that he encountered through the unkind discipline and meanness of the establishment which served the Cathedral Church of St Stephen's in Vienna, his faith remained the strongest influence upon his life and music. He prayed constantly for inspiration and skill, and gave thanks for it when it came, insisting on giving all the glory for the results to his 'Heavenly Father'. Indeed the grafting and growing of religious experience seems to have been shared with the grafting and growing of musical experience. He was given no formal musical education in the cathedral 'school'; but he grew up performing and loving the best church music of his day. Only when he was thrown out on a matter of high-sprited indiscipline (but really because his voice had broken and the choir had no more use for him) did he take himself off to live with a kindly friend, scratch a living and get himself taught the rudiments of musical theory. But he remained cheerful and hopeful. Eventually his talent was spotted. He was invited to join the court of the Bohemian, Count Ferdinand Maximilian von Morzin, as musical director and composer; and then (the decisive moment of his life) he was appointed by Prince Paul Anton Esterhazy to be the Vice-Capellmeister at his court. Here he remained virtually in charge of the music from 1 May 1761 to 1790. And here, by the grace of God, inwardly enriched with the music with which he had grown up, and able to apply his newly-found theoretical knowledge, he found himself with a team of professional musicians at hand to play whatever he asked them to play. Thus Haydn was able to develop his creative powers to the full. For nearly thirty years he performed and composed every kind of music for every situation as requested. In particular he developed 'sonata' form to a flexible perfection, for instrumental sonatas, orchestral symphonies and string quartets. This form dominated the writing of music for the next one hundred and fifty years.

Haydn's married life was not a happy one, but he made many friends, women and men, including the much younger Mozart. Between these two there was a strong bond of mutual admiration and affection. Mozart used to call Haydn 'Papa' and asked his advice on many matters. But Haydn thought that Mozart was really 'the Master'.

On a visit to London in 1791, Haydn heard a performance in Westminster Abbey of *Messiah*. This, it seems, bowled him over and he determined that like Handel he, too, would compose an oratorio, praying that God would give him grace to make this his masterpiece for which he would always be remembered. When he was looking for a libretto, one of his friends pointed to the Bible and said, 'There! Take that and begin at the beginning.'[3] This is what he did, being determined to start with the first principle of all: that 'In the beginning God created everything – and saw that it was good.' Both of the creation myths in Genesis 1 and 2, coming from widely different periods in Jewish

history, written in different styles and giving a different order of
events, stress not only 'the beginning' (our Big Bang?) but also
the subsequent stages of creation.[4] So, as Haydn had learnt his
own creative skills in the exercise of them, he was able to see
God (as Christians do) ordering the creation not in one moment
alone but in a gradual evolutionary process.

The Christian doctrine of creation is not belief in an event,
nor is it a theory about the physical nature of matter. It is belief
in the Creator God whose existence is self-sufficient and outside
space and time, on the one hand; and in the physical universe
which exists within space and time and is dependent at every
point upon God, on the other. It is belief about the relationship
between God and the universe, a belief that seeks to answer the
question, 'Why?', not the question, 'How?' It is therefore a
philosophical, religious belief about purpose and value, not a
scientific, space-and-time account of precisely what happened.
In the chapter 'God's Utility Function' of his book *River Out of
Eden*, Professor Dawkins argues that there is no reason to ask
the question 'Why?'; in fact it is not sensible to do so. Things
just are. He writes:

> The Universe we observe has precisely the properties we
> should expect if there is, at bottom, no design, no purpose, no
> evil and no good, nothing but blind, pitiless indifference. As
> that unhappy poet A. E. Housman put it:
> 'For Nature, heartless, witless Nature, will neither care nor
> know.'
> DNA neither cares nor knows. DNA just is. And we dance to
> its music.[5]

But whether or not it is 'legitimate or sensible to do so',
people continue to ask the question, 'Why?' and believers of
many faiths continue to affirm that it is God who 'just is': the
universe 'is' because God makes it to be so. God and the universe are different, but at every point related. In this relationship
we find a meaning to the word 'good'. In the wilful breaking of
it we find a meaning to the word 'evil'. Christians also believe
that through the incarnation of the creative Word of God the
relationship is potentially restored, and that in their relationship
with the timeless God, individual beings have a purpose, which

can develop, according to God's will, along the line of time. Professor Dawkins identifies many oddities, quirks and destructive self-contradictions in his 'heartless Nature', but one wonders whether he takes sufficiently into account the consciousness of goodness and beauty and humour and glory that human beings experience when they dance to the music of – DNA? or God! Such 'consciousness' is not just an explanation put forward by ignorant religious people: it is a factor that needs to be taken into account when people consider the possibility of the existence of God.

Haydn in the confidence of his faith believed in people dancing and singing and laughing to the music of God, and he prayed fervently to be helped to realize this in the greatest of all his compositions, *The Creation*. He cannot 'be' God and create 'out of nothing'. He is a human being and he creates out of what he has to hand; and the first thing he has, singing in his head, is the musical note C: the very basic note of all notes; the affirmative note; the note in the middle, from which all notes rise and fall. Out of this strong note C, played loudly yet emptily by the full orchestra, arises the introduction, called 'The Representation of Chaos'. This is not the chaos of an angry sea or tempestuous winds; it is vast tranquillity as in very slow time harmonies appear and shift: C Minor, then an A flat, then a high F on the strings which sharpens, rises and falls to a strident and unexpected chord, E flat with an A flat underneath and a C at the bottom; then soft again for the bassoon and then the 'cellos to rise up in stately triplets: through G major to the full chord of E flat (53 seconds).[6] All goes quiet: a flute calls out, and strings; a clarinet pleads; the sound fades, rises, swells – till four pounding quavers on D flat (2 minutes) repeated again and again bring new focussed urgency in *a fortissimo* climax. The music keeps surging upwards in a dotted quaver phrase accompanied by golden notes on the clarinet. The tension rises until (2 minutes, 43 seconds) the clarinet runs up the scale to bring us more pounding quavers and more upward surging, until the whole orchestra in seven urgent semiquavers affirms the note C again (3 minutes 45 seconds). The gentle sequence flows on with moments of alarm: a startled exclamation on the bassoon; pleading, upward rising, calls on oboe, clarinet and flute; and slowly we come back to the very soft chord of C minor. This

chord seems incomplete rather than sad; and we find ourselves
ready for Raphael to sing, 'In the beginning God created the
heaven and the earth ...'

Belief in the doctrine of creation comes from the experience
of life lived with perceived purpose in dependence upon the will
and the love of God. But this truth (believed in long before the
story of Genesis 1 was written) needs a story to tell it. So some
Jewish writers – fresh from the nation's experience in Babylon
where they encountered idolatrous, dualistic religion at its
worst – told the story of the God of heaven and earth who
spoke his creative word to bring about (in stages, as God
thought fit) the creation of the universe, with humankind
(Adam and Eve together) as its crowning glory. Haydn uses this
story as the basis of his oratorio. The story is told in solo recitative, arias and choruses. The simple biblical statements are
embellished with words adapted from Milton's *Paradise Lost*,
and the chorus represents the hosts of heaven responding with
excitement and joy to the goodness of God and the beauty of
the universe.

So from the huge, quiet space of the Introduction with its
pregnant calm and moments of movement and colour, the
narrative proceeds peacefully to the creation of heaven and
earth, formless, void, with darkness upon the face of the deep.
Still in C minor, the chorus tells us *sotto voce* of the Spirit of
God moving on the face of the waters, and of God speaking his
'word': 'Let there be light'. Suddenly, dramatically, with the
tremendous chord of C major sfortzando on the orchestra, there
was *light*: light indeed, the light that throws into the realm of
human experience the perceivable beauties of the world; the
light which (according to St John) God is; the light that lightens
every living person, making people aware of goodness and
truth; the light that Jesus told his followers to 'let shine before
men', 'that they may see your good works and glorify your
Father which is in heaven'.[7] This light deserves all that Haydn's
orchestra can give it. So his C major quaver chord pounds, not
with foreboding now, but with triumph.

(Christian congregations give themselves a taste of this
explosion of sound and light very early, at about the time of
dawn, on Easter morning. In silent, dimly lit churches, at a given
moment, all the lights go on, bells are clanged and the organ

and any other instruments available blaze forth with as much noise as they can make: all this to mark Christ's resurrection, the event which vindicates God's creation.)

After all this excitement in C minor and C major, Haydn refreshes us with the sparkling key of A major to tell us of the vanishing gloom and the ordered appearance of the first day. Chaos is over; and the affrighted spirits of hell sink with cursing rage into endless night. Then – in music of startling simplicity and happiness – we are told that a 'new created world springs up at God's command'. Haydn has been criticized for the childishness of the music at this point; but Jesus told his disciples to be 'like children' in their response to the gospel, or they would not be able to enter the kingdom of God. Certainly the truth of Christianity is not childish, but it can be expressed with profound simplicity; and a childlike response which is open and generous may be a better guide than narrow sophistication. It is better not to sneer at this passage, but to enjoy it, especially the violins' cheeky flourish at the end of each phrase. Professor Tovey allies himself with Beethoven in his appreciation of the melody which he describes as 'the quintessence of Haydn in his most dangerous innocence'.[8]

Then comes the second day. God makes the firmament and divides the waters. Raphael (the bass) tells us of furious tempestuous rage, clouds driven like chaff, fire in the sky and awful thunder, rain, hail and the 'light and flaky snow'. Without trying to imitate them, Haydn prepares us for each one of these with appropriate orchestral sounds. The archangel Gabriel (soprano) then makes a first appearance along with the 'the glorious hierarchy of heav'n' (the chorus); and they make the 'ethereal vaults resound' with the praise of God.

Professor Tovey writes:

In plausibility the case for canonizing Haydn ranks midway between the cases of canonizing Pepys and Dr Johnson. But the critic who can frown at the glorious cheerfulness of this choric song has not the remotest conception of real saintliness; he is in the state of Bunyan's Talkative whose notion of the first workings of Grace is that it begins by producing 'a great outcry against sin'; and he can know nothing of Christian's or Bunyan's feelings when his burden fell off or of

Haydn's when, as he tells us, 'Never was I so pious as when composing *The Creation*; I knelt down every day and prayed God to strengthen me for my work.'[9]

Part 1 ends with the chorus, 'The heavens are telling the glory of God', which is sung boisterously with more or less musicality by every church choir at Harvest Festival. Clergy have been known to grumble at the number of Harvest Festivals they are asked to attend, and there is certainly a limit to the number of times one can sing 'We Plough the Fields and Scatter' in one season with any degree of devotion. But peoples' instinct for the importance of this festival is right, even if it does not find a place in the Book of Common Prayer.[10] Affirmation of religious truth must begin with the affirmation of creation. We can give thanks for this – and then begin to look forward to Christmas, and Easter beyond.

Haydn's *Creation* is really one long Harvest Festival, the Harvest including a motley array of trees, flowers, sea-creatures, birds (in 'cheerful host' as they 'hover in the air' and 'whirl their glittering plumes', 'dyed as rainbows in the sun'); every kind of animal, from the tawny lion who makes you jump as he roars on the trombone, to the flexible tiger, the nimble stag, cattle who seek their food on fields and meadows green, the fleecy, meek and bleating flocks; down to swarms of insects and the sinuous worm. The music sparkles with Haydn's delightful humour as these and many more of God's creatures parade before us. At last, to bring the work of creation to completion, and to release its potential for development, come Adam and Eve, humankind: beautiful, courageous, upright, King of Nature, wise in appearance, eyes bright in the image of God; man with woman, in love and joy and bliss.

There is more narrative and more praise to be offered, better heard than described. We might grow weary of *The Creation* (words and music) if that were the only disc we had on our desert island. But Haydn's music along with his religious faith went far beyond that. In *The Seven Last Words of Our Saviour on the Cross* he shows distressingly the reverse side of 'creation truth'; and in all his masses he presents, in sublime music, a comprehensive ark of the rainbow of light which is Christianity.

I see in *The Creation* by Haydn, *Messiah* by Handel and the

B Minor Mass by J. S. Bach a fine human response to the all-shaping truth of the Holy Trinity of God: the Father who creates all things good; the Son, the Messiah, who by life amongst us and life-giving death for us restores us to God; and the Holy Spirit, the unifying love, who makes the truth of the Father and the truth of the Son available to us; and who, through the gift and offering of 'the mass', makes human life vibrant with the music of the love of God.

18

The Music of Eternal Life

Sing again, with your dear voice revealing
A Tone
Of some world far from ours,
Where music and moonlight and feeling
Are one
(P. B. Shelley; 'To Jane: The Keen Stars were Twinkling').

He is dead, the sweet musician!
He the sweetest of all singers!
He has gone from us for ever,
He has moved a little nearer
To the Master of all music,
To the Master of all singing!
O my brother, Chibabos!
(H. W. Longfellow, *Hiawatha's Lamentation*).

It may be that when the angels go about their task of praising God, they
play only Bach. I am sure, however, that when they are together *en famille*,
they play Mozart and then too our dear Lord listens with special pleasure
(Karl Barth, in the *Luzerner Neuesten Nachrichten*, 21 January 1956).

What I thank you for is simply this: Whenever I listen to you, I am transported to the threshold of a world which in sunlight and storm, by day and
by night, is a good and ordered world. Then, as a human being of the
twentieth century, I always find myself blessed with courage (not arrogance), with tempo (not an exaggerated tempo), with purity (not a weari-
some purity), with peace (not a slothful peace). With an ear open to your
musical dialectic, one can be young and become old, can work and rest, be
content and sad: in short, one can live (Barth, 'Letter of Thanks to
Wolfgang Amadeus Mozart').

A problem that everyone has to face sooner or later is the
problem of death. What follows? Anything? Nothing?
Judgment? A new life on earth, in better circumstances or
worse, depending on how one has behaved? 'Everlasting life',
going on and on and on, through purgatory, into heaven or
hell? A timeless existence in which a soul is absorbed into the

infinite glory of God and the universe? 'Eternal life', related to mortal life, in which a person retains identity but is no longer subject to physical limitations? An everlasting blank? Or the self-forgetful, self-fulfilling vision of God?

All these ideas and many more are held in theory. There is also a common feeling that this is a subject which is better not discussed: it should be put off till it has to be confronted at the end of life, even if by then no amount of conviction or lack of it will make any difference.

When they come to die, however, people often seem to belie their lifelong convictions. The sternest atheist can panic, the most convinced churchman can be fearful. Sometimes a deep calm comes over a person; sometimes radiant joy. There are those who go to their death in heroic self-giving; and there are those who cling frantically to life. As a priest one is called to stay with people who are very close to death. This privileged moment is not one (I believe) for speculation or certainties about the future. I prefer to read the psalms, especially Psalm 23 with its emphasis on the present tense. 'The Lord is my Shepherd ... yea, though I walk through the valley of the shadow of death, I will fear no evil; *for thou art with me. Thy rod and thy staff comfort me.*'

Jewish/Christian belief in the 'after-life' came late in Jewish religious development. For centuries the Jews had a shadowy belief in the 'underworld'. In Hebrew the word for it is 'Sheol', from which we get our words 'hollow', 'hill', 'hole', and 'hell'. This is where departed spirits go, to a formless, lifeless existence. Immortality was a matter of the survival of one's name. The name stood for the self; and the best that one could hope for was that one's name would continue to resound and be praised by future generations. Until the second century BC there was no general belief in personal survival; and, until the promises made to the national heroes of the rebellion against Antiochus Epiphanes,[1] no suggestion of punishment or reward.[2]

That was Job's problem, and it is reflected again and again in the Psalms. Job was innocent; yet he was being hurt. Many ungodly people were wicked indeed; but they seemed to get away with it and prosper. Surely God would vindicate the righteous; but he did not seem to be doing so – anyway in this life. And yet, 'I know,' said Job in a moment of despairing and faithful courage (for faith is often at its strongest when things seem to be going against it), 'I know that my Redeemer (i.e. "vindicator") liveth: and though worms destroy my body,' (which they were doing: this was a present state he was speaking about) 'yet in my flesh I shall see God.'[3] It is the hope of this ultimate vision of God that sustained him and began to open up the possibility of continued consciousness: consciousness at least of the glory of God, that may be faintly felt now but would come to fulfilment after death. It has to be said that in the prose story of Job,[4] this does not come about. Job in the midst of all his doubts and questionings is suddenly confronted – most awfully – by God in all his glory. With this sight of the mighty Creator God, who asks him scornfully what he knows about anything at all, Job's pitiful complaints vanish into nothing and he simply adores God 'in dust and ashes'.[5] There is no theory of immortality here. But the reader may begin to see that the 'answer' to life's problems is 'relationship with God'. In so far as a person experiences this here and now, he is experiencing the eternal dimension of life – as a 'depth of the present moment'.

Nevertheless in the first century BC Jewish thinkers began to be influenced by the Greek idea – as propounded by Plato – of the 'immortal soul'. So the author of the Book of Wisdom writes:

But the souls of the righteous are in the hands of God, and there shall no torment touch them; they are in peace. For though they be punished in the sight of men, yet is their hope full of immortality.[6]

Most Christians find this idea helpful, but also find it hard to get away from the dualism of body and soul that it implies. Even St Paul seems to suggest this dualism at times;[7] but in his most extended writing on the theme of immortality[8] he speaks clearly of the seed 'growing into' the flower which it already potentially is.

There is no one doctrine of the after-life in the New Testament. Nevertheless there is the consistent conviction that Christ has conquered sin and death, and that through his teaching and his resurrection he has given us the certainty of life after death. Two of Jesus' sayings are straightforward on this matter.

Set your troubled hearts at rest. Trust in God always; trust also in me. There are many dwelling-places in my Father's house; if it were not so, I should have told you; for I am going to prepare a place for you … so that where I am you may be also,

and words spoken to the thief who was dying at his side and asked to be 'remembered' 'when you come to your throne':

Truly I tell you: today you will be with me in Paradise.[9]

Jesus was once asked a teasing question which seemed to make nonsense of the concept of 'after-life'.[10] In reply he made it clear, first, that the after-life could not be understood if its terms were reduced to the limitations of mortal life; and secondly, that belief in eternal life springs from belief in the living God. God is the God of the living: therefore, if he is the God of Abraham and other honoured patriarchs, they too must be living, not dead. God is God in the present tense. The present tense contains the past; so people of the past are with God in eternity – alive.

Words, of course, continue to fail: partly because the subject is too deep for words, there are no words to describe it; but also because words are too sharp and clear for something which we can feel deeply but cannot understand enough to define clearly.

So, once more, we turn to music. Musicians can take words and, by setting them to music, give them a depth of meaning which transcends their literary limitations and transforms their philosophical and religious uncertainties. You do not have to understand German to feel transported by the joy that Beethoven was expressing when he set Schiller's 'Ode to Joy' to the choral music of the Ninth Symphony. People say that some of Schubert's songs are poor poetry. But the music puts them right. The words still count for something, and they do their best to describe, say, the lot of a girl to whom her lover's kisses are the pearl of great price. But the crudity of the words is forgotten in the melting beauty of the music which Schubert wrote to them. Some of the silliest words I have ever sung come in Elgar's *Caractacus*; but the heroism which the story is about is rousingly expressed by the music.

Now composers have no better understanding of the after-life than anyone else. But like everyone else they are mightily concerned with this universal problem, and we hear of their concern, their fear, their confusion and conviction through their music. This is not always in a religious context or through the setting of religious words. For instance it is generally supposed that Schubert had an intense awareness of impending death when he wrote the String Quintet in C Major, which was published posthumously. Perhaps this quintet would have to be the 'one disc I must have' on my desert island. The beauty of the sound of the five string instruments together; the themes they play and embellish; the questions and answers, the searchings and uncertainties, the pleading and the profound faith, in the first movement; the long, peaceful calm of the slow movement as the instruments sing to one another and one of the 'cellos makes its gentle comments pizzicato; the outbreak of troubled passion, and the return of the calm which prevails to the end of the movement. Is this not enough? No, for there follows a most extraordinary movement: a boisterous, urgent, assertive scherzo, as you might expect; but for the middle section, no elegant 'Trio', but a despairing cry for help. Assurance is given, but it is not enough. The demand is repeated, deeper, and deeper still. The assurance is given again; but it is still not enough. The music takes us further down the steps to – what? Despair? Oblivion? No – for assurance is given more strongly than ever; and then the scherzo knocks and calls the music back to its former spirit of affirmation. The grim descent of the 'Trio' is quite forgotten in the last movement, which is skittish and a return back to Schubert's confident self, as if the assurance has been accepted. But has it? The movement ends on a jagged question mark. If Schubert was aware that he was soon going to die, did his natural optimism give way to fear as he peered into the blackness ahead of him? Or was he reassured and led back into his buoyant, but in the last resort questioning, self? Most people will feel at one with him both in his hopes and in his doubts.

Many composers have used the words of the Latin Mass as a vehicle for their feelings about death and judgment and eternal life, for the Mass presupposes an eternal present affected by the past and affecting the future. Consider the Byrd Mass in Three Voices, which I choose because I have intimate knowledge of it.

William Byrd was a Roman Catholic at a time when to be so openly in England required great courage. Byrd did have great courage and was determined to write settings for the Latin Mass which would enable the Recusants (however illegally) to have the best possible music for their worship. He wrote Masses for five, four and three voices; and all three are consummate examples of English counterpoint at its most expressive, mystical best. Counterpoint is essentially 'horizontal' music in which the interest is in the forward movement of the parts, even while the vertical moments are harmonious. It is the combination of the vertical and the horizontal that is so important.[11]

Indeed it was his Mass for Three Voices that first made me realize that 'time' is not like a 'line', with 'length, but no breadth, depth or thickness'. The 'line of time' has indefinite (horizontal) length, certainly; but it also has *breadth*. The time-line in the Byrd in Three Voices is as broad as the three voices together. They go by different ways in the same direction at the same time. Indeed the time experience in the Mass could be said to be broader still; for in addition to the three voices there are the experiences, musical and religious, of those of us who are listening and worshipping alongside them. The three voices go forward and we go with them. We cannot follow one voice alone – at least I cannot, except the one in the middle which I know from having sung it; but we can follow them 'three thick', with sometimes one voice, sometimes another, prevailing. What they sing, they share, passing the themes from one to another. Thus in the *Agnus Dei* one voice sings the words to a long, lilting, lifting, falling tune which never dies because it is taken up and carried forward by another voice, then another. I believe that the 'breadth' dimension of the music ('three thick') is made possible because there is also the 'depth' dimension, the music itself, which goes on broadly and deeply, each moment having its precious depth of harmony and counter-point.

I have emphasized what I feel to be true, the sense of three dimensions in every given moment, as I find it in music. I find it also in life. If one thinks of one's life as being strung out along a thin line of time whose only dimension is length, then every present moment is confined to what rises inevitably from the past and leads on to the equally inevitable future. Inevitable or not, there is a narrowness and a blinkeredness about this way of thinking which diminishes the quality of living. Life becomes like the kind of journey you make when your only concern is to go forward 'in order to get there', with no interest at all in whatever it is that is being passed on the way. Long journeys by aeroplane are very much like that. A sense of the 'breadth' of the moment, however, invites one to look sideways at all the people and things which are going forward in company at the same time: the Alps down there out of the window, their snowy peaks sticking out of the cloud; people with their lives to live, with their opinions and cultural differences; fascinating sights; so much that is beautiful; so much that needs attention and restoration. One discovers that there are other voices besides one's own in the music! I believe that there is also the 'depth' dimension of every present moment, in which all things cohere: things in heaven and earth, all people alive now with God, the 'Glorious Company of Heaven', including those whom I have loved and still love, for 'The Lord is my Shepherd'. God is with us. In God is the fullness of all things, earthly and heavenly.[12]

It is important, however, that, alongside this mystical notion of 'God in the present moment' harmonizing all things in his love, we retain a sense of the drama of 'change'. Change is necessary because we live in a time-long, dynamic, ever-developing universe. It is also necessary because we are imperfect and need to be made perfect. If we die in separation, isolation, non-fulfilment (or 'malfunction' as an American commentator euphemistically put it when a space-rocket swooped upwards and crashed back to earth), then we need a process of change after death in order to be restored to our true, God-given selves: hence the traditional Catholic speculation about the process called 'purgatory' and the route through judgment to heaven. The prospect of wrath, of change, of ultimate judgment is one that has gripped composers and moved them to write some of their best music.

One way of doing this has been to write a Requiem Mass, in which the words of the Latin Mass are supplemented by special prayers for the dead and reflections on the prospect of judgment. The *Dies Irae*, for instance, 'The Day of Wrath', was written by a Franciscan in the thirteenth century and was first used in a Requiem Mass in 1492. It is still used on All Souls Day and at Mass for a person's death or memorial. Here are four of its eighteen verses, in the rather flaccid translation, lacking the bite of the Latin, of *English Hymnal*, No.351:

Day of wrath and doom impending,
David's word with Sybil blending!
Heaven and earth in ashes ending!
Wondrous sound the trumpet flingeth,
Through earth's sepulchres it ringeth,
All before the throne it bringeth.
Low I kneel, with heart submission;
See, like ashes my contrition!
Help me in my last condition!
Spare, O God, in mercy spare him!
Lord, all-pitying, Jesus blest,
Grant them thine eternal rest.

These words make one feel glad for Latin – and music!

Mozart's *Requiem Mass* (K 626) was written literally on his death-bed. A 'mysterious stranger' came to Mozart's house and asked for a Requiem Mass to be written, and was prepared to pay well for it. He probably came from Count Franz von Walsegg, who wanted a Requiem composed in memory of his beautiful young wife. He also wanted to persuade people to believe that he had written the Requiem himself. Mozart, already very ill, was much troubled by this visitation and thought of it as an omen to do with his impending death. He worked desperately to finish the mass before he died, as if it were his own Requiem that he was writing. Mozart was not a churchgoer. He had quarrelled earlier in his life with the church authorities and had defied the church by becoming a freemason. Nevertheless he had confidence in the ultimate goodness of God and said that he was ready to trust his soul to him. On 4 April 1787 he wrote to his father from Vienna:

As death, when we come to consider it close, is the true goal of our existence, I have formed during the last few years such close relations with the best and truest friend of mankind, that his image is not only no longer terrifying to me, but it is very soothing and consoling. And I thank my God for graciously granting me the opportunity (you know what I

mean) of learning that death is the key which unlocks the
door to our true happiness.[13]

In his book *Mozart: Traces of Transcendence*, Hans Küng illus-
trates the profound understanding of Christianity that Mozart
showed when he composed his masses. He writes particularly
about the *Missa Brevis* (K 258), and the *Coronation Mass* in C
major (K 317). Again and again Mozart's music speaks the
truth; so much so that in Hans Küng's opinion a mass is not so
much 'a musical setting for the liturgy': rather, 'the music is the
liturgy'.[14] Yes, and those who listen to it find themselves caught
up in the movement between God and God, and God and
human beings, and human beings and God that the mass effects.

So it was with the *Requiem Mass*. Amidst the daily turbulence
of his life, brilliant in performance, assiduous in the demanding
task of composition, rebuffed in fashionable circles, scorned by
jealous fellow-professionals, always on the edge of bankruptcy,
his mind awash with physical love and uninhibited affection for
his wife, distressed by his illness, overcome by the bitter sense of
having to leave her and their children destitute, his life's work
unfinished, Mozart, with no trace of self-righteousness in his
nature, knew himself to be quite a sinner. So the *Dies Irae* and
all the other death-laden words of the *Requiem* were carved
deeply into the trunk of his being. 'Day of reckoning', judgment
to come, his personal need for forgiveness, the change that was
necessary to prepare him for the peace of heaven which he
longed for and believed in: all of this goes urgently, with painful
pleading, into the music of the *Requiem*.[15]

The *Requiem* begins darkly with the 'cellos and violins
stepping forward in the minor key and the bassoon sounding
the note, D. Soon the choir is pleading for eternal rest and for
the Lord to have mercy. The mood is calm, as if no one disputes
the need; but when the Day of Wrath is mentioned the music
breaks into terrible urgency, the notes trembling on a semi-tone
at the prospect of the descent of the terrible Judge. The trumpet
('*tuba mirum*') 'flinging its wondrous sound' ('*spargens sonum*')
is a trombone, its awful significance described by the four
soloists, as it summons all to the throne of God. Then in crash-
ing descent and leaping chords the orchestra prepares us for the
Rex Tremendae Majestatis, the King of Awful Majesty; but with

equal emphasis (because this is what we have been taught to expect: is it not God's nature to forgive?) the chorus pleads for mercy from the Merciful One. The four soloists dare to remind Christ of the mercy he had shown in his incarnate life, and the chorus begs vociferously for salvation from the flames of hell. This will indeed be a 'day of weeping', *Lacrymosa Dies*; and the music at this point rends the heart – certainly of us who listen, but surely of God too. And will not the merciful Jesus spare and give peace – as the music describes? The Offertory is addressed to Jesus and begins for two bars with quite an ordinary, musical phrase; but then it leaps passionately at the words '*Rex Gloriae*', 'King of Glory', and begs for deliverance for faithful, departed souls. The chorus ends with a harsh, insistent cry, emphasized in an unrelenting fugue, '*Quam olim Abrahae*', 'as you once promised to Abraham and his seed'. This is the demand that God's word be proved trustworthy. We humans claim this. We wish to appropriate the work of Christ and apply it to those for whom we are praying. Then comes the *Sanctus*. In the strength of all we have asked for, and in amazed confidence, we worship the Holy One, as we always do in the Christian eucharist, and remind ourselves that the wonderful thing about God is not the pomp and glory but the self-empty-ing service and the humility that Christ showed when he came amongst us in the divine name. Christ is the 'Lamb of God', the one who lives his life and gives it in the perfect sacrifice of death. The *Agnus Dei* is sung to music of deep simplicity; but while the words are being sung, the violins weave a tune of ecstasy and agony around them. Let no one suppose that the Cross of Christ is anything but appalling grief in the heart of God. With that understood, the music returns to the mood of strong assurance with which it began.

Thus Mozart died, bequeathing to mankind music which makes the heart ache with its loveliness, its sadness and its serene confidence.

I wish to reflect at this point on Mozart's music in general in order to try to understand something of the way in which he meets us and lifts our hearts to pleasure, happiness, joy, bliss. I use these words advisedly and reflect upon them.

'Pleasure' describes the stimulation and satisfaction of the physical senses. Thus there is pleasure in the scent of roses, the feel of silk, the splashing sound of a fountain, the taste of vintage port. Pleasure delights, as good, external things penetrate consciousness through bodily sensations. The reverse of pleasure is pain. In pain, the physical senses are assaulted by something wrong within, or something external and alien. In pleasure everything 'feels' right.

'Happiness' can be born of pleasure, but embraces more than that which is giving the pleasure. It is a conscious satisfaction with life as a whole as we accept what is happening and are pleased with all that surrounds us. But happiness depends on circumstances. It can be hindered by such things as pain, bereavement, a bad conscience or distress on behalf of a friend. Happiness cannot be compelled – by oneself or other people; but it can be induced as circumstances are made right.

'Joy' is a more inward quality. It goes with a conscious response to all the circumstances of living, including the pleasures, despite the pain, irrespective of happiness; as a person glows inwardly with a sense of harmony and fulfilment. Joy goes with inner integrity. It can harmonize outward circumstances as long as there is inner freedom to be oneself and to be at peace within oneself. Joy is timeless and comes with that deep sense of the present moment in which all things cohere. Joy is an intensely human quality. Animals can feel pleasure and can be happy, but they cannot experience joy, which is a quality of the human soul.

'Blessedness' I take as a religious word. It is the consciousness of joy that comes from God. The Greek *'makarios'* means 'the blessedness of the gods'. It is a key word in the Bible. Men and women in their worship ascribe 'blessedness' to God and pray to be allowed to share in it. Blessedness comes from relating to God in all things, finding God present in all the circumstances of life and offering all enjoyments and all activities to God in thanksgiving and service. This is one way of prayer; and it is the Christian way of finding the blessedness promised by Jesus in the list of people whom he described as 'blessed' in the beginning of the Sermon on the Mount.[16] 'Blessed are the pure in heart ... the merciful ... the peacemakers ...' 'Theirs is the kingdom of heaven'; 'they shall be called the "sons of God"'. *'They shall see God.'*

Even beyond 'blessedness', there is 'bliss'. This comes when conscious response becomes less an activity and more a state of being. This is what the saints find at rare moments of contemplation. Bliss is an eternal quality because it is timeless and untouched by physical circumstances. It is the quality of the presence of God *whether we know God or not*. It is a gift that comes independent of ourselves, our efforts, our deserts, our opinions. It is the ultimate joy.

In Mozart's music I derive much *pleasure* from the very sensation of the sounds that Mozart has devised from musical instruments and human voices. There is often ebullient *happiness*, tinged with humour and a delicious response to human situations in all their goodness and absurdity. We find this throughout the operas and in such works as the Haffner Symphony (K 385), which was written from music composed for a wedding; and the *Alla Turca* rondo at the end of the A Major Piano Sonata (K 331) with its rumbustious ending. Mozart also wrote music which is *joyful*, even though much of this was rooted in sadness. It is well known that he tended to use the key of G Minor for such dark but radiant music as, for instance, the G Minor Quintet (K 516), the Piano Quartet (K 478) and the Symphony No.40 (K 550). There is nothing light-hearted in this symphony, written nearly at the end of his life, but there is strong joy as the sad elements are accepted and unified. I think of the sublimely sad slow movement which pushes forward relentlessly with occasional pauses for moments of quiet reflection. After the development section of the urgent, leaping Finale, the second subject returns in the *minor* key. This is indeed a bitter-sweet moment and it speaks to me of something even deeper than joy. *Blessedness?* No – because, unlike Bach, Mozart never consciously directs our hearts to God or invites us to give God thanks and praise. But *'bliss'*, yes. This is the highest quality of all, because it is not tied – even to awareness of God. It is just itself. And if some of us are right about God, bliss is God's very presence in a mode that is far beyond the refusal or grasp or aspiration of the human mind.

It is bliss that we can find in Mozart's music, not least in the *Requiem Mass*. This music contains fierce judgment and infinite love. It is, for me, the music of eternal life.

19

The Music of Resurrection: 'My God and King'

The trumpet shall be heard on high,
The dead shall live, the living die,
And Music shall untune the sky.
(John Dryden, 'A Song for St Cecilia's Day').

There is an old Jewish legend about the origin of praise.
'After God created mankind,' says the legend,
'He asked the angels what they thought of the world he had made.
"Only one thing is lacking," they said.
"It is the sound of praise to the Creator." '
'So,' the story continues,
'God created music,
the voice of birds, the whispering wind, the murmuring ocean,
and planted melody in people's hearts.'

Mozart was not the only composer to write music to words about death and eternal life. Verdi, for instance, wrote a *Requiem Mass*, although he too did not profess Christianity. The death of his friend Rossini shook him so much that he tried to get eleven other composers to co-operate in the writing of a requiem in his honour. This did not come off; but when the Italian novelist Alessandro Manzoni died, Verdi, greatly stricken, wrote the *Requiem Mass* for the anniversary of his death. 'With him,' he wrote of Manzoni, 'ends the most pure, the most sacred, the highest of our glories.' He set out to write music for a Requiem to match.

This ravishing music says what Mozart had said but in romantic, operatic language. 'Operatic', because Verdi was supremely a composer of opera. Indeed, some have praised and some have disparaged the *Requiem* as being his 'finest opera'. The criticism comes from those who wish their religion to be something 'apart' and expect religious music therefore to be 'different'.[1] As regards liturgical use, to which we shall return in the next paragraph, there is sense in this – for reasons to do with length, musical resources and the acoustical nature of the building. Nevertheless, the desire for religion to be 'apart' is both right and wrong. God is apart, 'wholly other', as the theologians say. Those who are 'with God' beyond this life are also 'apart'. But in Christ, God comes to be 'with us'. Belief in the incarnation accepts, transforms and glorifies time-and-space life, so that the beauty and the ordinariness and the pain of life become transfigured by 'God who is involved with us'. For this reason artists and musicians can seek to express ultimate truths in the terms of their own art. This, to me, justifies the dramatic, operatic, searingly beautiful music by which Verdi poured out his heart on the subject of death (the very word – *'mors'* – is given poignant emphasis in the *Mass*) and judgment and the loving mercy of God.

The music, however, was definitely not written for use in the liturgical performance of the eucharist. It is too long, and would be out of proportion with the rest of the service. But can we not rejoice when we find some of the profound truths of the faith expressed outside the context of the church? All the wonders of nature do that; and so do a billion billion selfless acts of love; and so do a billion billion expressions of truth in the art and literature of the world. The Christian church may have its own reasons to believe in its faith, draw attention to it, reinforce, spread, and consciously rejoice in it. But the church does not create the truth; nor can it monopolize or in any way limit the goodness of God. We are free to find this everywhere – including a concert hall in the performance of Verdi's *Requiem*.

Not everyone wants to savour the truths of Christian redemption in terms of dramatic confrontation and splendour, and Gabriel Fauré, choirmaster at the Madeleine in Paris from 1887, wrote a *Requiem* 'just because he wanted to'. His aim was to speak gently and lovingly of human pleading and divine mercy. The *Pie Jesu* soars to heaven on the voice of a soprano (or, indeed, a boy treble, whose impersonal, 'innocent' voice can make it all the more poignant) in blissful adoration of Christ; and the whole mass resonates with a quiet, confident rapture.

This particular religious mood is characteristic of the late nineteenth/early twentieth-century French organist/composers: for instance, Duruflé, Vierne, Widor, Messiaen. Here is a rich seam of music written for the religious 'insider': pious but never lugubrious, restrained but zestful and deeply joyful.

Pre-eminent in this school was Olivier Messiaen (1908–92), who was that rare phenomenon, a modern composer with a strong Christian faith (John Tavener is another). To Messiaen the resurrection of Christ, and with this, the resurrection of all life, was a very strong conviction. His best-known work on the resurrection theme is *Et Expecto Resurrectionem Mortuorum*, written in 1964. This is scored for an orchestra which includes bells, gongs, cencerros, tam-tams and brass and woodwind choirs. In the preface, Messiaen speaks of Grünewald's risen Christ 'who seems to be flying in a rainbow generated by his own light'. The second movement is inscribed with St Paul's words, 'Christ, being risen from the dead, dies no more'; and the fourth movement refers to the time when 'the morning stars sang together and all the sons of God shouted for joy'. This is a work of colour and sound, birdsong and plainchant, ethereal space and light.

Benjamin Britten also wrote a Requiem, indeed, a *War Requiem*. But he gives very little space. He compels the listener to go along with him and experience the bathos and the brittle beauty of what he is writing. One must concentrate, for there will be no repetition![2] Hummable tunes turn unexpected corners, arpeggios stretch themselves, strange harmonies give special colour and meaning to particular moments, catchy rhythms captivate but then jolt one's complacency, orchestration never ceases to astonish and delight. In his music there is an economy; a stark earthiness; a playfulness that keeps poking its head. But tragic beauty dominates; and sometimes there is and sometimes there is not 'peace at the last'.

Britten has an intellectual concept of what he is doing even before he finds the music with which to do it. In the *War Requiem*, his aim was not simply to glorify God or to call for mercy, but to inveigh against the cruelty and waste of war. So he weaves into the religious affirmations of the mass the bitter anguish of death as men inflict it upon one another in warfare. The work was commissioned for the dedication of the new

Coventry Cathedral, built in the shadow of the ruins of the old one, which had been destroyed by the Germans in the war. Britten's twin object was to comment bitterly upon the madness of war and to affirm the message of reconciliation to which the cathedral had been built to bear witness. Recognizing their heroism as well as the sadness of their loss, Britten dedicated the *War Requiem* to four friends who had been killed at sea in the war: Roger Burney, Piers Dunkerley, David Gill, Michael Halliday; and wrote as a text words from Wilfrid Owen: 'My subject is War, and the pity of War. The Poetry is in the pity ... All a poet can do today is warn.'

Britten uses mighty musical resources to express the rage and the sorrow and the muffled hope inside him. There is a large orchestra with brass that barks and snarles and weeps. Distant trumpets call and echo and re-echo; drums mutter like far-away guns and then burst into shattering cacophany like exploding shells. A large chorus responds and augments the changing moods of the *Requiem*. Two male soloists (a German and an Englishman in the first performance), accompanied by a chamber orchestra, go on their way singing the poems of Wilfrid Owen about war, its futile waste, its cynical cruelty, and its strangely impersonal hatred, as enemies meet as friends on the other side of death. Meanwhile, high and detached, a choir of boys' voices, accompanied by an organ, sings as if from Heaven. A soprano (meant to be a Russian singer in the first performance) swoops and soars through wide intervals in ecstatic praise of God whose greatness must be great enough to contain all this – and redeem it? Certainly, for the *Agnus Dei* ('O Lamb of God') in its serene simplicity is the spiritual climax of the work. Benjamin Britten was a pacifist, but in the *War Requiem* he tells of hope as well as terror, reconciliation as well as strife; and he leaves us praying with him that God through his 'Lamb' will have mercy, and that, in the end, those who have been killed may 'rest in peace'.

For a musical account of a soul's journey through Purgatory into the presence of God we go to *The Dream of Gerontius* by Sir Edward Elgar. Elgar was a practising Roman Catholic, and he was irritated that much of the early criticism of his major work came from those who resented the Catholic doctrine contained in the libretto. But he was not ashamed of this and knew within himself that the music, coming from the deepest marrow of his being, was good. 'I do not know what fate has in store for this work, but this much I can tell you, it is *GOOD*', he said to his friend and mentor, Augustus Jaeger, the 'Nimrod' of the *Enigma Variations*.[3]

For a libretto Elgar used Cardinal Newman's poem, *The Dream of Gerontius*. Maybe he saw something of himself in Gerontius. 'Look here,' he wrote to Jaeger, 'I imagined Gerontius to be a man like us and not a priest or a saint, but a sinner, a repentant one of course but still no end of a worldly man in his life, and now brought to book ...'[4]

Certainly, after dying, Gerontius is made aware of his many sins and gets by only on his readiness to confess the faith ('Firmly I believe and truly ...') and through the prayers of his Christian friends, also by means of the good work of his guardian angel, who leads him through into the presence of God, running the gauntlet of the cursing demons. These know themselves (through a menacing fugue) to be 'dispossessed, aside thrust, chuck'd down, by the sheer might of a despot's will ...' The devils taunt him and try to snare him into their company; but the angel succeeds in bringing him into the presence of God. This to me is one of the 'moments in music'. Chorus and orchestra have been singing 'Praise to the Holiest in the Height' with a restrained, spacious rapture. 'It gives me the impression of great doors opening and shutting,' Dora Powell ('Dorabella') replied when Elgar asked her what she thought of it. 'Does it?' Elgar said, 'That's exactly what I mean.'[5] Then the 'great blaze'. The music swells and heaves in wonderment as brass crashes and clamours and calls with reverberating intensity; and Gerontius cries, 'Take me away'. Elgar had a lot of difficulty with his friend Jaeger about this terrified cry and what should follow it, Jaeger wanting something very dramatic. But after meeting him part of the way, Elgar stuck to what he had written. 'I won't alter p. 159,' he wrote, '& be darned to you ... for one semi-quaver value (my "moment"!) fffffzzzz is the one glimpse into the Unexpressible – then it (the Music) dies down into the sort of blissful Heaven theme which of course fades away into nothing.'[6]

It is like Job when he was confronted by God. All human complaints and doubts and remembered sins crumble away into nothing in the presence of the all-powerful, all-embracing, all-loving God.

Gustav Mahler believed in that love, and in the way of the Romantics he wrote music to express what he believed. The difficulty comes when you accept that a piece of music has 'meaning' and then try to put the meaning into words; for the words never succeed in meaning what the music means. Mahler realized this when he told a journalist that the meaning of his Second Symphony – 'The Resurrection' – was expressed clearly enough in the music itself. 'I was in no way concerned with a detailed programme of events,' he wrote; 'but at most with an emotion.' Later on, however, when pressed, he did give this symphony a programme; and even though later still he rejected this, the programme he wrote is so explicit that it is worth quoting from.

'I have named the first movement "Totenfeier" ("Funeral Rites"),' he wrote, '... it is the hero of my D major symphony whom I bear to the grave there, and whose life I catch up, from a higher standpoint, in a pure mirror. At the same time there is the great question: "Why did you live? Why did you suffer? Is it all nothing but a huge, frightful joke?" We must answer these questions in some way, if we want to go on living – indeed, if we are to go on dying! He into whose life this call has once sounded must give an answer; and this answer I give in the final movement.'

There follows a detailed description – in metaphor, not notation – of the second and third movements. Five years later, for a performance at Dresden, he wrote:

Fourth Movement: the morning voice of ingenuous faith strikes on our ears.

For the Fifth Movement he described a procession of people ('kings and beggars, righteous and godless') at the Last Judgment. The trumpets of the Apocalypse ring out, followed by an eerie silence in which we just catch the distant song of a nightingale. Then a chorus of saints softly sings: 'Thou shalt arise, surely thou shalt arise.'

Then appears the glory of God, a wondrous soft light pene-
trates us to the heart – all is calm ... And behold, it is no
judgment; there are no sinners, no just. None is great, none
small. There is no punishment and no reward. An overwhelming love illuminates our being. We know and are.

Mahler confessed the inadequacy of his description when on
the day of the performance he wrote to his wife: 'I only drew up
the programme as a crutch for a cripple ...'[7]

Throwing away my own 'crutches', I recall my first hearing of
the Resurrection Symphony. It was at the Festival Hall on the
eve of an important debate in the General Synod at which I
hoped to speak and the outcome of which was very, very important to the church. I went full of pessimism and foreboding; and
the first movement of the symphony picked up my mood precisely. The opening bars are aggressive and demand attention.
Soon the music involves you as life involves you – with lots of
bits and pieces, some of them delightful, some quite unpleasant.
There is one moment of bullying assertion, the whole orchestra
in discord hammering at you. But beauty flows, and love, and
then a cynical, ugly ending, deep down in a groan of brass and
a rumble of drums: the death of Mahler's 'hero', presumably;
but to me it seemed like the death of all that I was longing for
in the church.

The next movement starts in pure delight; like walking in the
Yorkshire dales on a beautiful day. Perhaps things are not so
bad. There are pleasant people about. Beauty and good sense
have not been ousted. But clouds appear and race across the
sky: the mood of happiness does not seem to be substantial.
Nevertheless, after a fearful storm, the soft sweetness of the
strings returns pizzicato and the walk continues in golden,
melodious sunshine.

A violent drum-roll wakens us out of our dreams for the third
movement, which is a restless scherzo. There is so much to be
done. Work and pleasure and troubles and awkward people and
light entertainment jostle for attention, sometimes in frantic
clamour. Perhaps I am a workaholic and too fussed. The work
and the pleasure are hindering one another. Then good sense
tries to prevail, but it is quickly shattered by noisy elements –
and the movement ends with a growl.

'What follows is clear to you,' wrote Mahler. Indeed, it is made so by the words. The contralto begins the fourth movement with the poem *Urlicht* ('Primeval Light'), which contains the words: 'I am from God and will return to God. The dear God ... will light me to eternal blessed life!' This is the voice of faith which takes up all that has happened so far and shows the way forward.

The last movement begins by rocking you back to all that is worst. This must surely be the music of terrifying judgment, a frightful reminder of harshness and strife and self-assertiveness. But at that moment a remote trumpet sounds the clear open interval of the fifth, an interval that has been at the heart of nearly all the themes in the symphony; and the trumpet-call is subsumed by the delicious sounds of birds calling on flute and piccolo. Then there is silence – the 'silence of heaven'? From this the chorus breathes the solemn command:

> Rise again, yea, thou shalt rise again ... To bloom again art thou sown! ... O believe nothing is lost with thee ... What has come into being must perish, what perished must rise again ... Prepare thyself to live! ... What thou hast fought for shall lead thee to God!

In the last analysis human concern about what happens after death is a question about God. If God is, we may continue to be: if God loves, we may be spared to live eternally in the realm of that love. Whatever our intellectual stance, the question is ultimately decided for us. The longing for it, the hope and, for some, the belief, has been expressed – and experienced – most profoundly, in music.

Christian belief in eternal life, however, is not only the conviction that God creates and restores and loves us for all eternity; it is also the conviction that Jesus Christ, the incarnate Word of God, who was crucified to death by the Romans, is alive.[8] 'On the third day he rose again', we say, every time we say the Creed. The greatest Christian festival is Easter; and the special day of the Christian week is Sunday, the festival and day of the Lord's resurrection.

The historical occasion of the resurrection is shrouded in mystery. There is no agreement amongst the Gospels on precisely what happened on that 'first day of the week' when, at crack of dawn (a detail common to all the accounts), a woman? some women? – later, two men – went to the tomb and found: a young man in a white robe? two men in dazzling garments? an angel, his garments as white as snow? two angels in white? The important thing, common to all the accounts, is that the body of Jesus was not there.

Nor is there agreement about the resurrection appearances of Jesus. Mark makes no mention of them, but records the promise that Jesus will meet his disciples in Galilee;[9] Matthew, on the other hand, has Jesus appearing to the women as they left the garden and then, following the promise recorded in Mark, appearing to the disciples on the mountain in Galilee; Luke describes appearances taking place in and around Jerusalem; John has stories of Jesus appearing first to Mary Magdalene in the garden, then to the disciples in Jerusalem on two occasions a week apart, and then by the lake of Galilee. St Paul in I Corinthians 15 gives a list of people who saw Jesus alive after his death, including 'over five hundred of our brothers at once, most of whom are still alive ...'; and including himself.[10]

Certain facts do emerge. The tomb was evidently empty of the body of Jesus, something one has either to accept or explain. Certain people from the circle of those who knew him best and had best reason to grieve for his absence were convinced that they 'saw' Jesus alive. But there is no suggestion anywhere that Jesus went on living as before, his body resuscitated as if he had never been killed. The 'live' Jesus that people 'saw' was the 'spiritual body' of Jesus, recognizable to the touch and to the ears and eyes, but no longer subject to physical limitations. The third certainty is that the group of people who were most shattered by Jesus' death were the people who, in the words of their detractors,[11] 'turned the world upside down' with the speeches they made about the effect of Jesus' life, death and res- urrection. Were they hoaxing? You could think that. But do people 'turn the world upside down' for a hoax? And do they die for it, as many of the early Christians – and most of the apostles – did?

The next indisputable fact is that none of the objectors at the time (the Roman and Jewish authorities) could put a stop to the spreading of the story. Why did they not just produce the body?

Most important of all, the Christian church has lived on the strength of this belief from the first century onwards, and still does. To us, belief in the resurrection is belief about something immediate, that we experience. We do not know precisely what happened. But we do go on saying, 'Christ is alive: his Spirit (the Spirit of God) is with us.'

Christian composers cannot describe the event any more than the rest of us can. But they can say more about the conviction that arises from the event than we are able to do with words alone. The '*Et resurrexit*' in the Creed in choral settings of the eucharist comes in many modes ranging from ecstatic shout to awed hush. But I will end this book by referring to the *Five Mystical Songs* by Ralph Vaughan Williams. Vaughan Williams chose to use the profoundly joyful poems of the priest and poet, George Herbert. Words and music seem to come from a single overwhelming inspiration.

This set of songs for baritone and orchestra and (optional) chorus starts with Herbert's poem, 'Easter Day': 'Rise heart, thy Lord is risen ...' The voice thrills with the news of the risen Christ and sees in this a blessedness even for the wood on which he had been crucified. Lute and heart are summoned to 'twist a song pleasant and long'; and the Holy Spirit is bidden to make good what is lacking in the harmony. The second song is 'I Got Me Flowers'. We are now in the garden of the resurrection, where the flowers and the rising sun and the scent of early morning cannot vie with the glory of this day of days in which Jesus – very early – had risen from the dead. In 'Love bade me welcome', 'Love' is the risen Jesus, the generous host at the eucharist. He bids us welcome and insists on honouring, forgiving, feeding us despite our natural reluctance. Vaughan Williams' music is a gentle dialogue between the softly pleading strings and the amazed, longing, penitent, in the end yielding voice who, after much desperation, does 'sit down and eat'. Then comes 'The Call': 'Come, my Way, my Truth, my Life, such a Way, as gives us breath; such a Truth, as ends all strife; such a Life, as killeth death.'[12] All this is because Jesus is alive. And there is more. 'My Light ... my Feast ... my Strength ... Come my Joy, my Love, my Heart ... Such a heart as joys in love.' In a strong, lilting tune which rises and swells and falls again in hushed devotion, the voice calls on these names for

Jesus because they express the glorious truth of the ever-living Christ.

Finally, there is 'The Antiphon', not a reasoned argument, not a historical proof, but a burst of praise. The orchestra lets rip, and the chorus sings:

> Let all the world in every corner sing,
> My God and King.
> The heav'ns are not too high,
> His praise may thither fly;
> The earth is not too low,
> His praises there may grow.
> The church with psalms must shout,
> No door can keep them out:
> But above all, the heart
> Must bear the longest part.
> Let all the world in ev'ry corner sing,
> My God and King.

Notes

Preface

1. I have had published Christopher Campling, *The Order of Holy Communion: A Setting of Rite A from the Alternative Service Book* for unison voices and/or choir (SATB) with organ accompaniment, realized by Neil Richardson: published 1988 by Scalewise, 29 Inwood Rd, Hounslow, Middx, TW3 1UX. Part of it was performed on Radio Three 'The Great Thanksgiving'.
2. The Reverend Canon William Charles Campling, 1887–1991.
3. The extra H is for 'Hellenic'.
4. John Taylor, *The Go-Between God*, SCM Press 1972.
5. 'Central Advisory Council for the Training of the Ministry'. I never heard the result!
6. When I went back to see it three years ago, the hotel staff did not understand my story and did not believe it!
7. The Reverend Canon John Hayter was also educated at Lancing College and St Edmund Hall, Oxford. He became Vicar of Boldre in 1955 and stayed there until his retirement in 1982.

1. Music and Faith

1. Glenn Hoddle, the manager of the English football team, has engaged a band to support the English supporters at Wembley, and in New Zealand for the 1997 one-day international cricket matches, batsmen went in to music of their own choosing.
2. Genesis 4.21.
3. I Samuel 16.14–23.
4. Uzzah died as a punishment for touching the sacred ark when the oxen stumbled and it was likely to fall. When 'holiness' still meant 'awfulness' and 'awfulness' implied fear, to touch what was holy was indeed an 'impudent action' – even though King David allowed it to be known that he was angry with the Lord for such a fierce reminder of his holiness. See II Samuel 6.6–8.
5. II Samuel 6.5.
6. I Chronicles 15.28; 16.42; II Chronicles 7.6; 29.25.

7. Amos 6.3–7.
8. Isaiah 5.11–13.
9. Daniel 3.5.
10. Luke 15.11–32
11. Matthew 11.17.
12. Mark 14.26.
13. I Corinthians 14.8.
14. Revelation 5.8–9; 8.1.
15. Julian of Norwich, *Revelations of Divine Love*. Julian of Norwich (c. 1342 – after 1413) was an English mystic who lived outside the walls of St Julian's Church at Norwich and received a series of 'Revelations' which she later recorded as the 'Sixteen Revelations of Divine Love'. To her, 'divine love' was the key to all life and evil was an aberration which serves to reveal the extent of God's merciful love.
16. For a book on this important subject I recommend Leslie Bunt, *Music Therapy – The Art Beyond Words*, Routledge 1994.

2. *Casting Doubts on God and the Second Symphony of Sir William Walton*

1. John 11.

3. *Time and Eternity: The Big Bang, Oratorio, and* The Marriage of Figaro

1. C.R. Campling, *The Way, the Truth and The Life, 3, The Word of God in Action*, Edward Arnold 1965, 27.
2. Genesis 1.1–2.3; 2.4–24.
3. There are passages in First Isaiah about Babylon, but the enemy in his day (late 8th century BC) was the Assyrian nation, which had already destroyed the Northern Kingdom of Israel. The prophet who warned the people of Jerusalem so sternly and painfully against the Babylonians and King Nebuchadnezzar was Jeremiah. (But 'Thus spake Jeremiah' would not have scanned!) For a prophecy of what happened, see Jeremiah 25.8–14. For exultation over the Fall of Babylon, seen as the epitome of 'the wicked city' (and probably a pseudonym for Rome in the first and second centuries AD), see Revelation 14.8 and chapters 17 and 18.

4. *Individuality and Harmony*

1. Vertical and horizontal. Any reader who does not understand what I mean by the 'vertical' and horizontal' in music should think of the music as it is written on paper. The 'vertical' is seen by looking up and down the score; the 'horizontal' is seen by looking left and right along

the score. So the 'vertical' is what sounds all at once; the horizontal is the music as it spreads out along the 'line of time'.

5. *Harmony and the Love of God*

1. John 17.22–23.
2. Ephesians 3.18–19.
3. Ephesians 4.15–16.

6. *Interpretation*

1. Frances Young, *The Art of Performance – Towards a Theology of Holy Scripture*, Darton, Longman and Todd 1990.
2. John 1.14.
3. Anglicans base their understanding on the Bible, tradition and reason, seeing these as being complementary and not contradictory, because they all come from God. The Bible is always the 'basis', the 'starting point'. It is indispensable; and it is the 'test' of Christian truth
4. Luke 10.25–37
5. Mark 4.13-20. Some scholars doubt whether the allegorical explanation of this parable of the Sower comes from the mouth of Jesus himself. But the allegorical interpretretation is certainly part of the 'biblical tradition'. I used to put the parable to intelligent students. They always understood it to be about the different sorts of soil, rather than about the growth of the seed.
6. Matthew 1.23 and Isaiah 7.14.
7. Isaiah 7.10–17.
8. The Book of Deuteronomy is traditionally associated with Josiah's reform in the seventh century BC. It may even have been connected (as a source or a later commentary) with the Book of the Covenant which was discovered in the Temple in Josiah's reign and which, according to II Kings 22 and the following chapters, was the basis of the reform.
9. Frances Young, *The Art of Performance* (n.1), 1. I am grateful to Professor Young for her ideas – but not her words – in some of what follows in this chapter.
10. Luke 4.23.

7. *The Unmusical and the Non-Believer*

1. Bertrand Russell, *Why I am Not a Christian*, Allen & Unwin 1957.
2. Matthew 7.20; 7.15–19. See also Galatians 5.21—23.
3. 1 John 4.20.
4. 1 John 4.7.
5. Matthew 7.1.

8. *Faithful Listening*

1. Mark 5.25–34.
2. Luke 7.36–50.

9. *Music for Worship*

1. *In Tune with Heaven – The Report of the Archbishops' Commission on Church Music*, Church House Publishing and Hodder & Stoughton 1992.
2. I Corinthians 14.8.
3. *BBC Music Magazine*, October 1996.
4. Charles Dickens, *A Tale of Two Cities*, Oxford Illustrated Dickens, Oxford University Press, 264.
5. Revelation 8.1.
6. Genesis 28.17.
7. St Paul's word 'fellowship' (Greek, '*koinonia*') as in 'the fellowship of the Holy Spirit' (II Corinthians 13.14) refers to that 'interlocking' of persons which is brought about by the indwelling Spirit of Christ.

10. *Playing and Living*

1. Luke 10.37; John 13.34; Matthew 10.7; John 21.22.
2. Humphrey Carpenter, *Benjamin Britten. A Biography*, Faber and Faber 1992, 31f.
3. Romans 7.21–25.
4. Exodus 21.2–11.
5. Leviticus 20.10.
6. E.g. Leviticus 18.22; Romans 1.27.
7. Exodus 22.25.
8. Exodus 31.14; Numbers 15.32–36.
9. E.g. Mark 2.23–3.6.
10. John 8.11.
11. Exodus 20.1–17.
12. 'All things are become new', II Corinthians 5.17.
13. Leviticus 17–26.
14. Leviticus 19.18; Deuteronomy 6.4; Mark 12.29–31.
15. Matthew 5.1–13.
16. See for instance Isaiah 1.21; Jeremiah 3; Ezekiel 16.8–43; Hosea 2; Psalm 106.38.

11. *Over the Top*

1. The Old Testament book most directly concerned to teach a non-exclusive, missionary attitude is the Book of Jonah, whose reluctant

hero is sent to the men and women of Nineveh. Jesus himself commended the faith of Gentiles, for example the Roman centurion in Matthew 8.5–13 whose faith exceeded anything he had found in Israel itself. The action of clearing the Temple was to restore to the Gentiles their rights of worship, and according to Mark 11.15–18 this was the immediate cause of Jesus' arrest and execution. The rending (Mark 15.38) of the 'veil of the Temple', that is, the veil which separated the 'Holy of Holies' from the rest of the Temple, is generally interpreted as a sign that with the death of Jesus the separation between God and man has been potentially destroyed.

2. G.K.Chesterton, *Orthodoxy*, John Lane, The Bodley Head 1915, 183–5.
3. I Cor.9.19–23.
4. Ephesians 1.23.
5. Ephesians 2.14.
6. Speaking with tongues. See Acts 2.4–11; 10.46; I Corinthians 12.10, 28; 14.2–9.
7. I Kings 18.21–40.
8. Heinrich Harrer, *Seven Years in Tibet*, Rupert Hart-Davis 1953, 206–8.
9. I Cor.12–14 (esp.14.13).
10. Matt.7.15–23.
11. Gwendolen Greene, *Letters from Baron von Hügel to a Niece*, Dent 1928, 96.
12. Gal.5.19–23.
13. Mark 9.2–14.

12. *Creativity*

1. See Matthew 6.14.
2. For a full account of the relationship of the *Grosse Fuge* with the Quartet in B Flat op. 130 see Barry Cooper, *Beethoven and the Creative Process*, Oxford University Press 1992, 209ff.
3. Matthew 5–7.

13. *Journeys of Faith*

1. Shelley, 'Song': the motto of Elgar's Second Symphony.
2. Mark 9.2–8.
3. John 1.9; 9.5; and the whole of Chapter 9, in which the Pharisees who think they 'see' end up in spiritual blindness, and the man who had been blind from birth ends up believing, on his knees before Jesus.
4. Philippians 4.8.

14. Words, Opera, Involvement

1. Pastor Martin Niemöller was arrested and sent to a concentration camp in 1937 for his resistance to Hitler.
2. For a biography of Bonhoeffer, see Eberhard Bethge, *Dietrich Bonhoeffer. Theologian. Christian. Contemporary*, Collins 1977, or Eberhard Bethge/Renate Bethge/Christian Gremmels, *Dietrich Bonhoeffer, A Life in Pictures*, SCM Press 1986.
3. For an account of Beethoven's need to write four overtures for Fidelio, three Leonora overtures and Fidelio, see William Kinderman, *Beethoven*, Oxford University Press 1995, 102.

15. Affirmations of Faith I: J.S.Bach – Mass in B Minor

1. Hebrews 1.1–4.
2. The Bible did not receive its final form until nearly two hundred years after the death of Christ.
3. Philippians 2.5–8.
4. Mark 9.9–10.
5. Lest readers should think that I am being fancIful about Bach's intentions, I refer them to Wilfrid Mellers' book, *Bach and the Dance of God*, Faber and Faber 1980. There is a chapter of eighty-four pages on the B Minor Mass containing a detailed analysis of Bach's religious and musical thinking. The book is technical and deeply felt, and I would recommend anyone to read it who wishes to explore the heights and the depths of Bach's expression, through music and the words of the Mass, of the heavenly and earthly glory of God.
6. The word 'shibboleth' has its origin in the story in Judges 12.1–6.

16. Affirmations of Faith II: G.F. Handel – Messiah

1. Jonathan Keates, *Handel: The Man and His Music*, Victor Gollancz 1985, 243.
2. Ibid., 242.
3. Ibid.
4. I Timothy 3.16.
5. There are at least three 'Isaiahs' whose widely separated writings appear in our 'Book of the Prophet Isaiah'. One (chapters 1 to 39) was the Isaiah of Jerusalem who lived in the Southern Kingdom of Judaea in the second half of the Eighth Century BC. He witnessed the fall of the Northern Kingdom (Israel) and warned his own countrymen and stood by them when the Assyrians came and besieged Jerusalem. 'Second' or 'Deutero' Isaiah (chapters 40–55) was in Babylon with the Jews for the later part of their seventy years of exile following the capture of Jerusalem by Nebuchadnezzar in 597 BC. In this book I

refer to him as 'Isaiah of the Exile'. Chapters 56–66 were also concerned (very joyfully) with the Return, but were written later in Palestine itself. The writer of these chapters (though there may have been more than one) is often referred to as Trito (Third) Isaiah.

6. See Psalm 137.1–4.
7. Mark 1.2–3 and Luke 3.4–6.
8. Isaiah 40. 1 and 5.
9. Mark 11.15–19.
10. Malachi 3.1–3.
11. Isaiah 7.14 (Matthew 1.23).
12. Isaiah 40.9; 60.1.
13. John 1.15.
14. Isaiah 9.2.
15. Luke 2.32.
16. Isaiah 9.6.
17. Luke 2.10–13.
18. Zechariah 9.9–10.
19. Mark 10.46–52; Matthew 20.29–34.
20. Matthew 11.2–6; Isaiah 35.5–6.
21. Matthew 11.30.
22. Galatians 2.20.
23. John 1.29.
24. John 13.1.
25. Isaiah 53.3.
26. Isaiah 53.4–6.
27. Mark 15.34.
28. II Corinthlans 5. 21.
29. See Mark 15.29–36.
30. Psalm 22.
31. Mark 1.10.
32. Matthew 26.53.
33. I Peter 3.1–19.
34. Romans 10.15.
35. Psalm 2.1–3.9.
36. Revelation 19.
37. Job 19.25–26.
38. I Corinthians 15.35–49.
39. Matthew 5.8.
40. I Corinthians 15.21–22.
41. Revelation 5.11–13.
42. It is the chord of the inverted dominant seventh.

17. *Affirmations of Faith III: Joseph Haydn* – The Creation

1. John 1.1–14.
2. See John 1.14 and 3.16.
3. See Karl Geiringer, *Haydn. A Creative Life in Music*, George Allen & Unwin 1947, 142. Another story is that Haydn was presented with a libretto by an otherwise unknown person, Lidley, whom Professor Tovey suggests might in fact have been the violinist, Linley. See Donald Francis Tovey, *Essays in Musical Analysis 5*, Oxford University Press 1937, 119. The libretto consists of the Creation Story from Genesis 1 and words from Milton's *Paradise Lost*, Book VII. It seems that Van Swieten, the librettist, translated Lidley's English into German and then back into what Tovey calls 'English as She is Spoke'. Haydn set to music both the German and the English versions.
4. The two creation stories are Genesis 1.1–2.4a and Genesis 2.4a–25. The second and earlier story may have been put together by a member of the prophetic movement in the seventh century BC from sources from the Northern and Southern Kingdoms dating from the tenth century BC. The first account would have been written by the 'Priestly' school of writers after the return from exile in Babylon; possible to be chanted at a New Year Festival at which the victory of Yahweh (The Lord) over evil and disorder was being celebrated. See Professor J.H. Hooke's essay in *Peake's Commentary on the Bible*, Nelson 1962, 109.
5. Richard Dawkins, *River Out of Eden*, Phoenix 1995.
6. I cannot give a 'note by note' account, but have tried to describe the atmosphere of 'chaos' unfolding into 'created order'. The timings are roughly from the performance of *The Creation* at a Promenade Concert in August 1996.
7. See I John 1.5; John 1.9 and Matthew 5.16.
8. Tovey, *Essays in Musical Analysis 5* (n.5), 127.
9. Ibid., 128.
10. The Harvest Festival is supposed to have been started by my wife's great-great-great uncle, the nineteenth-century poet-parson, Vicar of Morwenstow in Devon, The Reverend Robert Stephen Hawker.

18. *The Music of Eternal Life*

1. Antiochus Epiphanes was king of Syria from 175 BC. He tried to unify his empire through the propagation of Greek culture, and was therefore determined to stamp out Judaism, first using persuasion, but later resorting to force. He was resisted bitterly and violently by the faithful Jews in the Maccabean Rebellion. See the Books of the Maccabees in the Apocrypha.
2. Early Jewish belief was in the Lord, the God of the Hebrew nation; so concern with an individual's personal survival did not occur. But as

awareness of the importance of the individual grew (it was stressed, for instance, during the Exile by the Prophet Ezekiel), so did the question of 'after-life'. So, in some of the late Psalms (16, 49, 73) we find the belief that God must be concerned with people after their death. Also, through the influence of Greek philosophy, there came the notion of the 'immortal soul' that would be for ever 'in the hand of God' (see Wisdom of Solomon 3). In New Testament times there were the Sadducees who believed in no after-life (see Mark 12. 18–27); the Pharisees who expected a bodily resurrection at the Last Day; the Essenes who believed in the immortality of the soul; and the Covenanters of Qumran who did not believe that the body would rise, but believed instead in an eternal, heavenly existence. See Paul Badham's article on 'Death' in *A New Dictionary of Christian Theology*, ed. Alan Richardson and John Bowden, SCM Press 1983, 145.

3. Job 19.25.
4. The Book of Job consists of a story told in prose (chapters 1,2 and 42), and a series of commentaries on the story (chapters 3–41) written in verse. The prose story asks the question 'Is disinterested goodness possible?' and answers that it is, and that it is rewarded. The verse section is a dialogue between Job, who is suffering unjustly, and his 'Comforters', who tend to believe that he must be guilty of something. The question is, 'Why should the innocent suffer?' There are also the chapters in which God appears and answers Job 'out of the whirlwind' and shows him the superhuman wonders of creation (38–41).
5. Job 42.6.
6. Wisdom 3.1, 3,4; and the rest of the chapter.
7. For example, Romans 7.7–25.
8. I Corinthians 15.
9. John 14.1–3; Luke 23.43.
10. Mark 12.18–27.
11. See Chapter 4, note 1.
12. See Ephesians 1.23; 3.19; 4.13: Colossians 1.19 and 2.9.
13. Mozart letters, 907: quoted from Hans Küng, *Mozart. Traces of Transcendence*, SCM Press 1992, 27.
14. Hans Küng, *Mozart* (n. 14), especially 54.
15. For a full discussion of how much Mozart did and did not write of his *Requiem* see H.C. Robbins Landon, *1791: Mozart's Last Year*, Thames & Hudson 1988. From the sources he quotes and from one's instinctive response, it does seem that Mozart himself was responsible for most of it even if his pupil Sussmayr put much of it on paper for him after his death.
16. Matthew 5.1–12.

19. *The Music of Resurrection: 'My God and King'*

1. For the trouncing of this point of view see again Hans Küng, *Mozart. Traces of Transcendence*, SCM Press 1992, 48–50. He concludes by saying, 'There is no one style in church music. A division between sacred and secular music is unhistorical.'

2. I am reminded (irrelevantly) of the story of General Montgomery, who is said to have told his assembled officers after a briefing, 'I have made myself perfectly clear. There will be no questions.'

3. Michael Kennedy, *Portrait of Elgar*, Oxford University Press 1987, 114.

4. Ibid.

5. Ibid, 1.

6. Ibid., 111, 113.

7. Deryck Cooke, *Gustav Mahler. An Introduction to His Music*, Faber Music 1980, 53–60.

8. I Corinthians 15.12–14. St Paul makes it clear that 'eternal life' for human beings and the resurrection of Christ are inseparable.

9. I am taking the generally accepted view that Mark's Gospel ends at chapter 16 verse 8a. Verses 16b–20 are a later addition, written in a different style.

10. I Corinthians 15.5–8.

11. See Acts 17.6.

12. The allusion is to Jesus' words to Thomas in John 14.6: 'I am the way, the truth and the life'.

Index

Cello Concerto No. 1, 128
Second Symphony, 89
Leningrad Symphony, 127
Sibelius, Jean, 117
Sitwell, Osbert, 33
Six, Les, 111
Smetana, Bedrich, 36
Smith, Matthew, 133
Sonata form, 165
Speaking with tongues, 112–14
Spirit, *see* Holy Spirit
Stalin, Joseph, 89
Stanford, C. V., 12
  Magnificat in G Major, 88
Stravinsky, Igor, 19, 32
Sullivan, Arthur, *see* Gilbert and Sullivan
Swing, 111

Taizé, 31, 91
Tavener, John, 9, 12, 186
Taverner, John, 9
Taylor, Bishop John
  The Go-Between God, 5
Tchaikovsky, Piotr, 26, 78
  Nutcracker Suite, 128
  'Pathetique' Symphony, 111, 127
  Swan Lake, 134
  The Ace of Spaces, 139
Ten Commandments, 102f.
Teresa, Mother, 123
Teresa of Avila, St, 130
Thibaud, Jacques, 39
Three Choirs Festival, 40, 54
Tippett, Michael, 52, 119
Tortelier, Paul, 55, 64
Tovey, Donald, 121, 169, 202
Trollope, Anthony
  Barchester Towers, 117
Tudor music, 111, 127

Unity (and disunity), 36–54

Vaughan Williams, Ralph, 87,

111, 121
Five Mystical Songs, 193f.
Fourth Symphony, 127
Verdi, Giuseppe
  Requiem Mass, 184f.
Vierne, Louis, 41, 186

Wagner, Richard
  Tristan und Isolde, 88, 140
Waite, Terry, 97, 102, 141
Walker, Vice-Admiral H. C. T., 6
Walton, William, 40, 52, 87, 117
  Belshazzar's Feast, 32f.
  First Symphony, 41
  Second Symphony, 21–5
  Viola Concerto, 19, 78
War, 50, 186
Warsaw Symphony Orchestra, 75
Westminster Abbey, 99, 151, 165
Whitcomb, Ian
  After the Ball, 126
Widor, Charles, 186
Wilde, Oscar
  The Importance of Being Earnest, 96
Wilson, Bishop Leonard, 7
Wills, Arthur
  Concerto for Guitar, Organ and Orchestra, 40
Wood, Sir Henry, 127
Word(s), 138, 143f., 175
Word of God, 57f., 123, 134, 138, 163–4, 166
Wordsworth, William
  The Prelude, 44
  The Solitary Reaper, 11
Worship, 77, 83, 84–95, 106, 129, 138, 149

Young, Frances
  The Art of Performance, 56
Youth orchestras, 100

Zipper, Operation, 6